*Fifty Seasons at*
# STRATFORD

ROBERT CUSHMAN
Foreword by
TIMOTHY FINDLEY

*Fifty Seasons at*

# FORD

A McCLELLAND & STEWART / MADISON PRESS BOOK

*for Arlene*

*(Left) Believed to be a portrait of William Shakespeare, this painting by John Sanders came to light in Ontario as the Stratford Festival prepared to celebrate its fiftieth season. (Opposite) Michael Therriault (top), William Hutt, and Peter Hutt in the Tempest (1999).*

Foreword © 2002 Timothy Findley
Text ©2002 Robert Cushman
Jacket, design, and compilation © 2002 The Madison Press Limited

Published simultaneously in the United States of America by McClelland & Stewart Ltd.,
P.O. Box 1030, Plattsburgh, New York 12901
Library of Congress Control Number: 2002103030

**National Library of Canada Cataloguing in Publication Data**

Cushman, Robert, 1943-
Fifty seasons at Stratford

Includes index.
ISBN 0-7710-2473-8

1. Stratford Festival (Ont.)—History. I. Title.

PN2306.S7C88 2002      792'.0913'23      C2001-903818-6

We acknowledge the financial support of the Government of Canada through the Book Publishing Industry Development Program for our publishing activities.

Typeset in Caslon by Madison Press Books, Toronto

Printed and bound in Canada

McClelland & Stewart Ltd.
*The Canadian Publishers*
481 University Avenue
Toronto, Ontario
M5G 2E9
www.mcclelland.com

1  2  3  4  5      06  05  04  03  02

**Fifty Seasons at Stratford**
was produced by
Madison Press Books
1000 Yonge Street, Suite 200
Toronto, Ontario,
Canada M4W 2K2

There was excitement in the air. And eager expectation — not to say an aura of suspense. In that late spring of 1953, there was even a sense of *Can this really be happening?*

As we dumped our bikes into the dust outside that barn up there in the fairgrounds — the barn where we would spend the next few weeks rehearsing — we couldn't help wondering just what would happen when we actually started to perform Shakespeare's plays in Stratford, Ontario, in a tent that did not yet exist. Was it to be a circus? Who could tell?

What we did not imagine — and could not — was that this first season would be followed by forty-nine others. Two, perhaps, but forty-nine? And yet, here we are, embarking on the fiftieth season of the Stratford Festival of Canada.

For the most part, back in 1953, we made a circle of familiar faces. Many of us had worked together on radio and television — or on the very few active stages to be found in Canada at that time. As we assembled, however, we were all keenly aware of those other faces, which, up to this time, we had seen only in photographs or in the cinema. We were going to be on stage with Alec Guinness, Irene Worth, and Douglas Campbell. We were going to be directed by the legendary Tyrone Guthrie. We were going to appear in costumes designed by Tanya Moiseiwitsch. There, too, in the barn, was tangible proof of our destiny: a replica of Tanya's innovative and daring stage. On that first day, we all stood staring at its ship-like decks, wanting to climb on board but wondering how.

The thrust stage was a challenge, but its wonders were magical. Guthrie told us to find our own way about its various levels — and by the time a week had passed, we were revelling in it.

There was a pillar on a riser more or less up centre, and it was amazing how quickly its magnetic force began to draw every actor into its field. Certainly, there was nothing wrong with our egos, just something slightly askew about our sense of how many bodies could be crowded against one pillar at one time. Should we be lashed?

Guthrie — ever resourceful in dealing with egos — devised verbal crowbars to pry us loose from this focal point, and soon we began to take pride in finding ways to avoid the pillar, dragging centre stage with us all the way down into the tunnels. Ultimately, when Tanya Moiseiwitsch redesigned the stage some years later, the infamous pillar disappeared. Problem solved.

We soon learned, too, about the hazards of rehearsing in a barn — especially a barn with a tin roof. The metal took the blazing heat of the sun and cast it down around us. Shirts came off. Shorts were worn. Guthrie, all of six foot plus, stalked around in sagging black swimming trunks and — don't ask me why — a transparent plastic raincoat. I don't like to think about the implications…. The barn's sparrow population, undaunted by the lofty words ringing in their rafters, relieved themselves with wild abandon as they flew above us. And then, of course, there was the rain. Pelting down, thundering on that metal roof. Not wanting to indulge in Shakespearean mime, we would simply give up and wait until we could hear each other again. Sometimes we lost as much as half an hour. Ciggy breaks, we called them, since in those days nearly everybody smoked.

When we began, what was to become our tented residence looked like an amphitheatre cut into the hillside above the town's baseball field. I remember visiting

# Golden Years

BY
TIMOTHY FINDLEY

*Timothy Findley as an officer in* All's Well That Ends Well, *1953*

the construction site one day, and as I headed down towards the river, walking past a baseball game, I heard someone say, "Must be an actor, his hair's so long." Meaning that the hair at the back of my head could be seen to touch the collar of my shirt…. My, how times change.

Even the baseball players got excited when the tent was finally raised — although, once it was up, I doubt if they had any idea of what it was like to rehearse inside during the heat of the day. At least the rain no longer out-shouted the actors, but it did collect in the swooping contours of the tent, causing great threatening saggings above us. At first, this brought a small brigade of men with long, thin poles that had a narrow blade mounted at one end. These would be poked through the canvas wherever the weight of the rainwater had become dangerous, which allowed the water to drain down on to the concrete tiers where the seats would ultimately be installed — and occasionally, on to us. Later, Skip Manley — another legend — and his crew of tent experts devised ways of simply pushing up on the canvas and working the collected water outwards from the centre until it ran down the outside walls of the tent.

Meanwhile, Guthrie was still pacing around the heights in his plastic mac, testing sight lines and acoustics — listening — watching — shouting commands and comments down to the stage in his own unique manner. A clap-clap of the hands, a snip-snap of the fingers, and a terse verbal pinch of salt. One day, I heard, "Findley! Not in China. Face-making. Less. Now — on!" By then I was able to translate this into: "Mr. Findley, I am not in China, I am standing right here. Consequently, the messages your face is sending me are overwhelming and vulgar. Desist — and proceed!"

Guthrie expected miracles from his actors, and very often got them, thanks to the fact that any actor has to be something of an athlete — and that working with the right director can instill a sense of daring that does not come easily. For example, in *Richard III*, three of the actors had to be thrown into a dungeon. At one late rehearsal, Guthrie came down on to the stage and had the trap door opened. As he stared down, we heard him muse — "Wonder what would happen if we pushed you backwards down the steps?" *Backwards down the steps?* "Well, there could be a mattress there — or — let's see what happens if there's someone there to catch you. Anyone good at catching falling stiffs?" As I remember it, the final solution involved both the mattress and someone "to catch the stiffs." I definitely remember thinking how lucky I was that I was not playing one of the victims.

Yes — but not for long.

My role, near the end of the play, was to bring the worst possible news to Richard. His armies are in rout and all his men and horses have fled the battlefield — prompting, of course, "A horse! A horse! My kingdom for a horse!" Given that Richard is alone on the stage at that moment, Guthrie thought it would be interesting if the messenger appeared out of thin air. Out of thin air, Tony? "Yes. Think of it! Everything in darkness — except the one light on the King. And suddenly … you're there! Like a parachute drop!" Without the parachute…. I turned and looked up at the jutting point of the balcony, high above the infamous pillar. Jump? And what's more, jump into the dark? Guinness said nothing, but I'm sure he was thinking, just don't land on me!

Thus it came about that all through that first season, at every performance of *Richard III*, my character,

Catesby, would run out on to the balcony, leap up on to the balustrade and launch himself into the dark. I was twenty-two and had trained as a dancer. Thank goodness I could work out how to land — and where! Still, the traditional pre-performance admonition "Break a leg" continued to intimidate me, although it never happened.

In one sense, the Stratford Festival of Canada — like Catesby — landed on its feet. Look at what it has become as we enter the fiftieth season, with more plays, more actors, more theatres — more audience. Think of all the imagination and all the daring that launched this incredible enterprise, not into the dark, but into the brilliance of international acclaim. Think of all the people involved, starting with Tom Patterson, whose idea it was to create such a Festival. Think of all the seasons, and all the thrilling productions and performances. What a voyage has been made since we climbed aboard the decks of that first experimental stage! Now, not unlike the questing trio of ships that brought Columbus to America, there are three unique venues: the Festival stage, the Avon, and the Tom Patterson — with a fourth, the Studio Theatre, opening this year.

Still, in another sense, the Stratford Festival has not yet landed. It continues on its adventurous voyage, heading into a future of even greater accomplishments.

In this fiftieth season, there is only one thing to say of this wondrous fleet of theatres: Bon voyage — and may the gods bless all who sail with them.

*Timothy Findley*
*Stratford, Ontario*

# Preface

This book is a celebration of the first fifty years of the Stratford Festival of Canada. I would not have accepted the invitation to write it if I did not believe the Festival to be truly worth celebrating. It is also, however, a critical book, in that it offers value judgments on plays and performances. Those judgments, unless otherwise attributed, are my own. The Festival commissioned the book, but its representatives have given me a free hand in the writing of it and are not to be held responsible for any of the opinions it contains.

My awareness of Stratford dates back to 1955, when as a stage-struck English schoolboy I read a brief account, in a theatre magazine, of the Festival's third season. Shortly after that I discovered *Twice Have the Trumpets Sounded* — the second of a series of volumes on Stratford's first three years, written by Robertson Davies, with contributions from Tyrone Guthrie and wonderfully evocative illustrations by Grant Macdonald — nestling unexpectedly on the shelves of a London public library. From then on, I read everything I could find about Stratford. I gazed in wonder at pictures of the open stage that Guthrie and Tanya Moiseiwitsch had created there; I came to know the names, and even some of the characteristics, of the principal Stratford actors as well as I knew those of performers at home.

It was twenty years before I got a chance to see the Festival for myself. Visiting in 1974, I was even more knocked out by the theatre than I had expected to be; I returned several times in succeeding years while working as theatre critic for *The Observer* in London. In 1987 I moved to Canada, but I was not able to see everything at Stratford until 1999, when I became theatre critic of the *National Post*.

Nevertheless this book deals, either in passing or at length, with virtually every Festival production, save for those of the now-discontinued Music Festival and other ancillary events. The text attempts to chronicle and analyze the events on the Festival's stages; the backstage cottage-industry aspects of Stratford's existence are covered in the sidebars and illustrations. So I have had to write reviews of productions I never saw: a stimulating exercise and less impossible than it sounds. For the most part I have known the plays (mainly Shakespeare and other classics), the actors, and the directors; and I have been able to do the math — greatly aided, of course, by the reviews of critics who *did* see the shows.

I spent the first forty-odd years of my life in Britain; there's nothing I can do about that now, and I think it may give me a useful perspective. Stratford is a vital part of the Canadian theatre — indeed, it may be said to have *started* the Canadian theatre — but it is also part of the international theatre, and especially of the English-speaking classical theatre. It drew some of its initial strength from the major Shakespeare companies in England and has continued to interact with them.

The book is divided into eight chapters, each devoted to the regime of a single artistic director, and the work of each has been treated in whatever order seemed most sensible. But I have tried to keep the central story — of an acting company and its members — going throughout. For the later, more crowded seasons this was harder; and I apologize to those actors whom I may have given short shrift, or even no shrift at all. There is always more to be said.

*Brent Carver and members of the company in* Fiddler on the Roof, *2000*

# Chapter One

# The Guthrie Years

*One of Tyrone Guthrie's first tasks as artistic director was helping his actors find vocal and physical solutions to the unique challenges posed by Stratford's thrust stage (opposite). Most welcomed the opportunity to work on a new type of stage with one of the world's great directors.*

O n July 13, 1953, the curtain rose on *Richard III*, the first production of the first Stratford Festival. Only it didn't. There was no curtain, and that is perhaps the single most important fact about the Festival. From that, sometimes in reaction to that, everything else has followed.

Today it's the rule rather than the exception for an audience to enter a theatre — certainly a theatre with any artistic pretensions — to find the set for the play all ready and staring at them. It happens even in proscenium theatres, which do have curtains to raise. A thrust or platform stage of course cannot have one, and it was a thrust or platform stage that was built for the Shakespeare festival at Stratford, Ontario. This was revolutionary. The idea had long been talked about, dreamed about, but never before put so publicly and aggressively into practice.

The two most notable Shakespearean theatres at the time — Shakespearean in repertoire rather than in design — were both, reasonably enough, in England: the Old Vic in London and the Shakespeare Memorial Theatre at Stratford-upon-Avon in Warwickshire. Both were proscenium houses, each with a small forestage built out in front of the arch as a ges-

ture towards the direct contact between actors and audience that had long been recognized as a prime element of Shakespeare's stagecraft. A gesture, though, is all it could be; whatever play was being offered at the English Stratford on July 13 (the Old Vic would have been closed for the summer), a curtain undoubtedly rose upon it.

Of the theatres erected in the English-speaking world since 1953 only a few have been designed in direct imitation of the Stratford Festival, but all — certainly if they were intended to house a classical repertoire — have had to take notice of its existence. It would be foolish to claim that the Shakespeare productions mounted on the Festival stage have been consistently more authentic or exciting than those staged anywhere else, but something about the place always suggests the possibility. And when it becomes a reality, a bond is created between actors and audience, a bond that has kept the Festival alive and loved for fifty years.

It might not have happened. It is doubtful that Tom Patterson, the trade-magazine journalist whose brainchild the Festival was, had any idea of revolutionizing the staging of Shakespeare. Indeed, it's doubtful he had much interest in Shakespeare at all. Stratford was

## "Mr. Guthrie, Canada wants you..."

### Tom Patterson

Dora Mavor Moore said, "As far as I'm concerned, the greatest Shakespeare director in the world is Tyrone Guthrie." So I phoned his home in Ireland. He lived in a very small village and the woman on the switchboard thought I was a mad Irishman, because nobody ever called from Canada. She kept hanging up on me, and I kept phoning back. When she finally realized it was Canada calling, instead of ringing Guthrie, she ran out the door and called, "Mr. Guthrie, Mr. Guthrie, Canada wants you."

The first night he was in Stratford, we got him settled in his hotel room. The next day I asked, "How did you sleep?" He said, "Oh, I had a great night." The hotel's night watchman was a retired guy from the railway shops, and Guthrie had gone down and talked to him until four in the morning — just to find out about Stratford from the ground up.

*Tom Patterson*

his home town, and his main concern was to put it more firmly on the social and economic map. Like some other pioneers — Lilian Baylis, for example, the Edwardian philanthropist who founded the Old Vic — he fell in love with theatre only after he had started one of his own. But the man to whom he turned to realize his dream was a confirmed open-stager who had been yearning for the chance to create just such a theatre. He was also attracted to the idea of helping shape Canada's still-unformed cultural identity.

The man was Tyrone Guthrie, at that time probably the foremost director of Shakespeare in the world. He had been artistic director (though the term itself was not yet in use) of the Old Vic for most of the 1930s and the Second World War years, returning often thereafter; he had also directed at the English Stratford. All the theatrical knights and dames who dominated the English theatre of the mid-twentieth century — Laurence Olivier, John Gielgud, Ralph Richardson, Donald Wolfit, Michael Redgrave, Alec Guinness, Edith Evans, Sybil Thorndike, Peggy Ashcroft — had worked with him; some had been his discoveries. Most of them worshipped him: Guthrie's actors, it was said, inevitably felt that they were making history.

The critics did not always agree: some of them found him lacking in high seriousness. Guthrie was constitutionally mischievous and irreverent, and he could never resist a joke. (Maybe it was the Irish in him.) He was also reputed to shy away from scenes of intimate emotion. (This was probably not the Irish in him.) The two essential qualities of a great director are intelligence and showmanship. Guthrie was a virtuoso of stagecraft, especially when great massed scenes were involved, and he had a

knife-edged mind. Physically, as well as imaginatively and intellectually, he was eternally restless. Since the end of the war he had been a theatrical nomad: he lived in Ireland but rarely worked there. For three years, Stratford would provide him with something like a home.

It all happened amazingly quickly. Britain's National Theatre had been discussed, debated, and delayed since 1874, and did not finally open (and then not in its own building) until 1963, a full decade after Stratford. In contrast, Patterson's dream began to take definite shape in his mind at the end of 1951 and by March 1952 he had won the confidence of enough of the members of the Stratford city council for them to fund an exploratory trip to New York, where he sought advice from Olivier. He failed, unfortunately, to make contact with the great man, but already he had made it obvious — not least to himself — that he was prepared to go to the top.

In the spring, on the advice of the doyenne of Canadian theatre, Dora Mavor Moore, who had prepared the ground with a letter, Patterson telephoned Guthrie in Ireland. In July Guthrie flew to Canada to have a look at Stratford and meet the theatre festival committee that had been convened under the dedicated chairmanship of Harrison Showalter, a local soft-drink magnate. By the end of the trip, it was understood that Stratford would have a Shakespeare festival and that Guthrie would be its director. By August, Guthrie and Patterson had sounded out, and unofficially engaged, Stratford's first leading man: Alec Guinness, the youngest of the great English actors, the subtlest and most unassuming (on-stage and off) and, by virtue of being also a certified film star, the one whose name would mean most in Canada. At the end

12

of October the Stratford Shakespearean Festival Foundation of Canada came officially into being; a board of governors was appointed in November with Showalter in the chair; Patterson became the Festival's general manager.

In December Guthrie returned to interview actors in Ontario and Quebec. (They were interviews rather than auditions: Guthrie worked from instinct.) He also found the theatre's architect, a young man named Robert Fairfield, who was asked to build a stage and auditorium rather than an entire theatre. With the opening season planned for the following year, there was no time to build a concrete playhouse and perhaps no inclination either; nobody yet knew how permanent this enterprise could hope to be. Patterson's original idea had been to mount one open-air production in a bandshell on the banks of the Avon. Guthrie, sensibly distrustful of open-air productions, persuaded him and the board that there should be a season of two plays (more would be impractical, fewer would be trifling) mounted in a tent — a tent that would house a purpose-built stage.

The purpose to which it would be built was Guthrie's own.

For years he had been dissatisfied with formal proscenium theatres as houses for Shakespeare. In 1937 he had taken an Old Vic production of *Hamlet*, starring the young Olivier, to the play's own setting, Kronborg Castle at Elsinore in Denmark. Torrential rain had washed out the show's intended première in the

*In May 1953, the financial problems facing the board (above) led to talk of postponing or cancelling the Festival (left). But two anonymous donors and the determination of board members such as Alf Bell (below, left, with his wife, Dama, in 1977) and Harrison Showalter (below, right, between Mayor Lawrence Feick and Guthrie, whose wife, Judy, is on the left) ensured its survival.*

## "He knew
## what he wanted..."

### Tanya Moiseiwitsch

It's now known as my stage, but that's not strictly true. Guthrie knew exactly what he wanted: he drew it on the back of an envelope. He drew very well, which put me to shame. I had to turn it into a half-inch-to-the-foot scale model.

He said, "We've got a Canadian architect lined up. When we get there, you'd better meet him and make sure you understand." He was very good at putting people together who he knew would get on. The architect, Robert Fairfield, was a saint. Everything that Guthrie and I asked for, Robert Fairfield interpreted and brought to life.

*Working with production manager Cecil Clarke (above) and Patterson and Guthrie (left), Tanya Moiseiwitsch played an integral part in making the Festival a reality. She turned her prodigious talents not only to the stage itself, but to costumes, sets, and props.*

castle courtyard; instead, it had been given a hurriedly rehearsed in-the-round performance in a hotel ballroom. Observing the spontaneity and the intimate contact between actors and audience, Guthrie's eyes and mind lit up: it was the closest thing he had encountered in the modern theatre to Elizabethan freedom. In 1948 he had the chance to mount a Scottish classic at the Edinburgh Festival. The play he chose was a medieval morality play, *The Satire of the Three Estates*, and the theatre the Assembly Hall of the Church of Scotland, which wasn't a theatre at all. Guthrie built a long, low platform, with the audience on three sides, and staged what was probably the biggest dramatic success the Edinburgh Festival ever had: *The Three Estates* was constantly revived, and the Assembly Hall became the festival's principal theatrical venue, though few subsequent directors proved as skilful at taming and exploiting it as Guthrie. Through all this he had continued directing in England. A production of *Henry VIII* was so successful at the Shakespeare Memorial Theatre (in both 1949 and 1950) that he was asked to re-stage it at the Old Vic (in 1953, immediately before he set off to begin rehearsing in Canada).

This *Henry VIII* was both noisily enjoyable and quietly revolutionary; it was staged in unvarying light on an unvaried timbered set, visible from the moment the audience arrived and containing all the features of an Elizabethan stage, scrambled and re-angled to fit the confines of a proscenium. The designer was Tanya Moiseiwitsch, who had first worked with Guthrie as an apprentice during the war and who was to become his most frequent collaborator.

Most of the best British theatre design of the time — in reaction to post-war austerity — was lush and painterly. Moiseiwitsch's *Henry VIII* sets were sober and architectural; her costumes, too, were rich in fabric but restrained in colour. Her similar unit set for a whole sequence of history plays at Stratford-upon-Avon in 1951 (not directed by Guthrie) marked what some think was the apex of British Shakespeare in that decade. She was — by virtue of talent, experience, and artistic compatibility — the overwhelmingly logical choice of designer for Guthrie's new Canadian stage.

The Festival stage today is, with some minor adjustments, the stage that Moiseiwitsch designed for 1953. A platform combines sweep with concentration. A graceful balcony pays tribute to the Elizabethan theatre balcony, without imitating it, jutting forward on its pillars in harmony with the platform beneath. Three levels of steps running the length and width of the platform add shape and urgency, uniting stage and auditorium. More steps run up to the balcony. Two tunnels emerge from the auditorium to give actors access to and from the front of the stage, and two facing upstage doors provide access to and from the back. Yet more steps lead up to the doors: an extravagance of levels, in fact. The audience envelops the stage on three sides and seems, on a good night, to cradle the experience in its hands.

The canvas that enfolded the auditorium that summer and for three further seasons was erected under the supervision of an American tent-master, Skip Manley. Supervising the building of stage and auditorium was a dedicated local contractor, Oliver Gaffney. His dedication was necessary because, speedy though the progress may have been from idea to realization, it was not easy. The project had been optimistically

*Local contractor Oliver Gaffney (above, at right) and his men built the Festival auditorium, designed by architect Robert Fairfield (top, at left), in just eleven weeks. Gaffney's feat was matched by American tent-master Skip Manley (below), who spent sixty sleepless hours directing the raising of the enormous tent.*

## *The Tent*

On June 26, 1953, Skip Manley's crew began erecting the tent (above) — the second largest in the world. Guthrie and his actors (below, left), including the jauntily dressed Alec Guinness (bottom, left), were anxious to see it raised. They had been rehearsing in an acoustically disastrous old shed full of mating sparrows. Over the four seasons that the tent was used, visiting stars such as James Mason (below, right, standing behind Patterson and Guthrie) were persuaded to pose hauling on its ropes.

*Theatregoers leave the tent after a performance. (Below) These souvenirs were given to Festival supporters after the tent was dismantled in 1956.*

The Stratford Shakespearean Festival
Foundation of Canada

takes pleasure in sending you, as a memento,
a portion of the canvas of the original Theatre-Tent

in appreciation of your past
in the C

The Stratford Shakespearean Festival
Foundation of Canada

takes pleasure in sending you, as a memento,
a portion of the canvas of the original Theatre-Tent

in appreciation of your past and continuing interest
in the Canadian Festival Theatre

Tent erected 1953 . . . Dismantled for
the last time 1956. To be replaced by
the Permanent Theatre summer 1957.

## *Putting Out the Welcome Mat*

Almost half the money raised for the Festival came from the efforts of Stratford's 21,650 citizens (below, left and right). Volunteers staffed ticket booths in stores (above), threw open their homes to visiting actors and playgoers, and prepared meals to help out the overburdened local restaurants. The Festival replied in kind by organizing "meet-and-greets" (bottom, left) and lectures on Shakespeare's plays for their enthusiastic supporters. More than 68,000 people attended the six-week festival, which had been extended by two weeks to handle the demand for tickets.

budgeted. Once the first flood of enthusiasm had subsided, it became harder than anticipated to extract money from the civic and government sponsors. The undertaking was logically and logistically impossible, but since the major participants — Patterson, Showalter, Gaffney — didn't know that, they went ahead and did it anyway. Guthrie, who probably did know, was wise enough not to let on. He may have found the board theatrically unworldly but, after negative experiences of boards elsewhere, he was impressed by their modesty, their practicality, their generosity, and their enthusiasm.

Certainly there were negative forecasts — from a prominent Toronto theatre critic, who had his own ideas of how the Canadian theatre should develop, and from Stratford's local newspaper, the *Beacon-Herald*, an implacable enemy of the Festival until the first productions opened, at which point it saw the light. (It had thundered in advance against the choice of *Richard III* as "unwholesome": that a respected Canadian newspaper could run such an editorial is a good indication of why the Festival was needed.) But the doubters were outnumbered by the enthusiasts: local, provincial, national, and international. Above all, the Festival provided a rallying point for the Canadian theatre.

Theatre in Canada — in English Canada, anyway — was in a trough, between the decline of the large-scale commercial and touring theatre and the emergence of a generation of new Canadian playwrights. Canadian actors had nothing much to act and nowhere much to act it. There was an abundance of talent — the first Stratford season proved that — but very little of it was able to work at a full-time professional level. Guthrie, as it happened, had no compunction about employing people who were technically amateurs — and no alternative either, if he wanted a Canadian company. He was an outsider himself (though an informed one — he

Guinness came three younger actors: the American-born Irene Worth, already an established theatre star in the West End and at the Old Vic, and two young character men, Douglas Campbell and Michael Bates, of vast experience at the Old Vic and Stratford-upon-Avon respectively. Two of this group, Moiseiwitsch and Campbell, established links with Stratford that long outlasted Guthrie's own: their work still appears there to this day. The rest of the company of sixty were Canadian.

Playing in tandem with the established stage favourite *Richard III* was the far chancier *All's Well That Ends Well*. Both, in their different ways, proved to be classic Guthrie productions.

*Richard III* thrust Stratford — thrust Canada — directly into the mainstream of 1950s Shakespearean staging. Herbert Whittaker of the *Globe and Mail*, the leading Canadian critic, said that it was such a production as nobody in Canada had ever seen before. It showed the director alternately — sometimes simultaneously — in his swirling and his sardonic modes. He was equally adept at creating grandeur and at deflating it. This being a chronicle play, featuring a coronation and a battle, Guthrie and Moiseiwitsch (and

*Actress Jo Hutchings holds the first programme on opening night, July 13, 1953.*

had visited, and even worked in, Canada before) but his vision went beyond Tom Patterson's. Patterson was committed to Stratford: to the town and, as soon as the idea began to take shape, to its Festival. Guthrie was committed to Shakespeare and the theatre, to his own ideas about them, and to Canada. This led to a paradoxical view of his role, but one suited to his roving temperament and his missionary zeal: he saw his job as being to get in, get started, and get out. In fact, he ended up staying longer than he had envisaged.

He brought a corps — or core — of British theatre people with him in 1953. Apart from Moiseiwitsch, there were supervisors of costumes and props and, to oversee the entire technical operation as production manager, an old colleague of Guthrie's, Cecil Clarke. Along with

## Flourish & Fanfare

Always the showman, Tyrone Guthrie wanted the Festival to open in a grand manner. He obtained a replica of the Shakespeare Memorial Theatre's flag (top) and asked Louis Applebaum, the Festival's first music director, to compose fanfares (bottom) to signal that the play was about to begin. Each performance began with the peal of a bell borrowed from (and later donated by) Carl Stoermer, owner of a Kitchener foundry. All are still used today.

## "This wretched nose..."

### Irene Worth

That first year was a profound experience. Nobody was looking for fame, glory, or money. We were all working for each other, and no one was working for himself. It was for the theatre.

In the first play, *Richard III*, I chose to play Margaret with a long sort of clay nose, which the boys used to make for me every night. It was so hot. I never thought I would live to hear the sound of my own sweat bouncing off the floor. This wretched nose used to slip down all the time. I'd say, "Nay, Richard" and pull my nose back on!

*Irene Worth at the tent site, 1953*

Campbell, as arranger of the fights) filled the stage with bodies, richly costumed and intricately manoeuvred. The production was in a processional style to which the stage seemed ideally suited; it was the first of many great evenings for the flourishing of banners.

*Richard III* is also a study of a mass murderer, and Guthrie happily exposed its cruelty. Three of Richard's victims, condemned to execution on trumped-up charges, were dragged on stage having clearly been tortured, and then dropped to their fate through trapdoors. When the ghosts of those Richard had murdered appeared to him before the Battle of Bosworth, the last of them — the decapitated Duke of Buckingham — was holding on his own severed head. Alec Guinness as Richard presided gleefully over the bloodshed, literally over it: he delivered the opening soliloquy sitting cheerfully astride the balcony, thus allowing the architecture of the Festival stage to declare its crucial importance from the very first moment of the very first show.

Many found Guinness's performance brilliant but lightweight. Olivier's film performance, which was to fix the popular image of the role for the rest of the century and beyond, was still two years in the future, and though more majestically satanic than Guinness's imp-with-a-limp, it was to prove equally comedic. Most later productions have veered even more emphatically towards dark laughter, though few have had Guthrie's and Guinness's genuine sense of humour: they were almost certainly ahead of their time. The Canadian response was bemused — but ecstatic. A first-night standing ovation (not the automatic event it is now) lasted five minutes: an eternity in theatre time. Everybody

knew that history had been made.

The second production proved equally important, but in a wider context. In a sense it may be the most important production Stratford has ever done, since it rediscovered — no, discovered — a Shakespeare play. *All's Well That Ends Well* was at that time rarely produced and even more rarely liked. It was one of the few remaining plays that literary critics felt safe in dismissing, while theatre critics seldom had a chance to say anything about it at all: even *The Two Gentlemen of Verona* has a more illustrious stage history.

A poor French doctor's daughter wins the hand of a disdainful young nobleman by performing a miracle cure on the sick king, then has to follow her reluctant prize to the Italian wars and win him, through love and trickery, all over again; Guthrie put this Renaissance story into modern dress and made it both hilarious and enchanting. There was plenty of broad clowning in his treatment of the play's subplot, but the predominant mood was bittersweet, a delicate side of Guthrie's talent (and of Moiseiwitsch's) that critics often overlooked. The play emerged not as a dark comedy — its traditional classification — but as an honest, unillusioned one. The term "magic realism" had not then been coined, and when it was it signified something else, but it would have fitted the production perfectly. In 1959 Guthrie was to recreate it at the British Stratford, and though he himself dismissed this revival as "cold pudding hotted up," he was in a minority: the critics mostly raved, and both actors and audience loved the show. A string of other notable productions of *All's Well That Ends Well* followed, and by the century's end the play was firmly established in the repertoire, a favourite

20

Guthrie's love of period splendour was reflected in Richard III's staging (above) and Moiseiwitsch's costumes (top) worn by Amelia Hall and Alec Guinness. The costume sketch for Richard's coronation (right) shows him holding the royal orb, which was crafted from a toilet tank float.

## "They got lost in the tunnel..."

### Donald Harron

The coronation procession in *Richard III* was led by two choirboys from Stratford's United Church choir. They got lost in the tunnel during the dress rehearsal, and for some reason Guthrie went ape. He yelled, "What are you doing? You're behaving like five-year-olds." And he was saying it to two little boys who couldn't have been much more than five years old.

The choirboys from *Richard III* also appeared in the National Film Board's 1953 film *The Stratford Adventure.*

of scholars and a magnet to directors; it had even played on Broadway. But Guthrie's 1953 Stratford production began it all, and has probably never been surpassed.

From the Festival's more immediate point of view it was the perfect complement to *Richard III*, an ensemble piece to balance that essentially one-man play. Helena, the heroine, certainly dominates, and she was dazzlingly played by Irene Worth (on alternating nights, she was the harridan Queen Margaret of the history play), but there are half a dozen other key roles. Guinness played the ailing French king and Michael Bates was Lafew, the sharp-tongued lord. Douglas Campbell inaugurated a long string of comic successes at Stratford as the braggart Parolles. They were the visitors, and expected to be good, but at least two of the Canadians were equally impressive: the veteran Eleanor Stuart as the Countess and the young Donald Harron as her son Bertram, the play's cub of a hero. It looked as if the Festival company might actually *be* a company.

In a sense, there were never any small parts in a Guthrie production: he was famous for giving every member of the crowd a separate personality to play, calling on players' enthusiasm as much as their skill. To make your presence felt in a middling or big part, however, on a middling-to-big stage — and a new kind of stage at that, both exposed and exposing — was a far greater test. Most heartening and revealing was the response of the two leading New York critics of the day, Brooks Atkinson of the *Times* and Walter Kerr of the *Herald-Tribune*, neither of whom had any vested patriotic interest in boosting a new Canadian venture. Atkinson wrote, with special reference to *All's*

*Well*, that "it would be impossible to find in North America another company so finished in comedy style and so attractive personally." Kerr, rather more temperately, reported that the "company is everywhere adequate and in many instances distinguished." The following year Kerr was roundly to declare the Canadian company superior to that at the English Stratford and inferior only to the Old Vic. As it happened, 1954 was an unusually bad year for Stratford-upon-Avon and an unusually good one for the Vic; at most points of the fifties the balance would have been the other way. But that the critics could reasonably be making such comparisons at all meant that, even in its first two seasons, the Stratford Festival could seriously be judged by international standards.

Explicit in Atkinson's comments, implicit in Kerr's, is the recognition that there was nothing comparable in the United States. Nothing has happened in the succeeding half-century to challenge that judgment. Within a couple of years of the beginnings at Stratford, Ontario, a Shakespeare festival was to open at Stratford, Connecticut; it never took off. Despite the rise of prosperous and ambitious regional theatres in the U.S., despite the heroic barnstorming of Joseph Papp and his successors in New York's Central Park, despite enormous reserves of talent and enthusiasm throughout the country, no tradition has taken hold, nothing that can be called a company has come into existence. The Festival, through good times and bad, has remained *the* theatre for Shakespeare, not just in Canada but on the continent.

Some of the Canadian actors in the first season were better known than others. In *Richard III*, for example, the key supporting roles of Buckingham, Clarence, and Richmond were played respectively by Robert Christie (who had acted for Guthrie at the Old Vic before the war), Lloyd Bochner, and Robert Goodier. All were to be pillars of the company during its first five years, all able to move easily between big roles and small ones, old characters and young, tragic and comic: a kind of unselfconscious versatility that was taken for granted then in classical and repertory theatre, in Canada as in Britain, and has gradually died out in both places. Guinness was sufficiently impressed with the potential of the company's junior players to take two of them back to London with him to attend drama school at his expense. His talent-spotting proved impeccable. One of his protégés was Richard Easton, later a leading actor in Britain, Canada, and the United States; the other, whose career was to develop spectacularly though in unexpected directions, was Timothy Findley, future novelist, playwright, and Stratford resident.

The names from that 1953 programme that now resonate most sonorously are those of three younger players, who half a century later are essentially still there. Two of them, William Hutt and William Needles, were still on the Stratford bill in 2001; the third, Douglas Rain, was not, but he has returned often in the intervening years. Hutt and Rain in particular were to become known as the Stratford actors par excellence, and Hutt is the company's undisputed leader. All three had significant small roles in *Richard III* as pawns of the hero-villain: Hutt was Brakenbury, the conscience-troubled Lieutenant of the Tower; Needles played the businesslike First Murderer; and Rain appeared as Tyrrel. These are roles

*Guthrie believed that modern dress allowed Shakespeare's plays to be "more easily understood and more vividly enjoyed." In* All's Well That Ends Well, *Alec Guinness as the King of France (above), Irene Worth as Helena (above and below, left) and a young Donald Harron (below, right) appeared in a mix of styles, including versions of 1950s clothing.*

DONALD HARRON as BERTRAM
in *ALL'S WELL THAT ENDS WELL*

*William Hutt as Hortensio (right) joined William Needles as Petruchio (top) and Barbara Chilcott as Katherina (above) in the rollicking 1954 production of* The Taming of the Shrew. *Hutt remembers Guthrie's reaction to his playing of the part: "Tony found it wildly amusing for some reason or another.... Maybe because I made something of that line about 'small choice in rotten apples.'"*

that can go for nothing but that can also make their presence felt; the same goes for the Steward in *All's Well*, played by Needles. (In this production Hutt and Rain were walk-ons.) All three actors were singled out in reviews: a cheering and accurate forecast for their subsequent careers and the identity of the company as a whole. Guthrie had predicted that it would grow its own lead actors, and it did so even more quickly than he might have envisaged.

Needles was to receive his biggest break of the fifty years in the very next season. In the 1954 production of *The Taming of the Shrew* he was cast in the star role of Petruchio, whom Guthrie wanted played as a shy, bespectacled young man with severe doubts about his prowess at shrew-taming. This interpretation might charitably be described as unorthodox, and its conflict with the original text had led to the withdrawal of the intended Petruchio, Mavor Moore, already a figurehead of Canadian drama — indeed of Canadian culture — as actor, writer, and administrator. Needles replaced him at short notice and was cordially if not rapturously received, as was Barbara Chilcott, the flashing-eyed young Toronto actress who played opposite him as Katherina, correspondingly portrayed as insecure rather than incendiary (a reading more easily sustained).

The *Shrew* was generally regarded as one of Guthrie's more waywardly farcical productions, an anything-goes romp performed in more-or-less modern dress and set vaguely in the Wild West; Petruchio might have been a cowboy newly arrived in town, except that he wore Harold Lloyd specs. The jokes and the anachronisms were strictly for fun, rather than (as they had been in

*All's Well*) the means to illuminate a difficult play. Those who shared the director's sense of humour loved it; those who did not detested it. The yea-sayers were probably right; they included Robertson Davies, whose accomplishments included being the most eloquent theatrical commentator in Canada. (An old fan of Guthrie's, he had even acted for him at the Old Vic before the war.) He spoke out not only for the production but for the play, which he called a masterpiece. That viewpoint was nearly as unfashionable then as it would be now, but it is plainly correct: there have probably been fewer boring productions of the *Shrew* than of any other Shakespeare play.

The troubles over this production, however, were indicative of troubles with the season as a whole. The number of plays was raised from two to three, and Guthrie directed two of them. He was still in artistic control, but he had relinquished the title and the post to his former administrator, Cecil Clarke. With the job, according to Guthrie, went the responsibility of directing one of the plays, and Clarke's assignment — his first as a professional director — was *Measure for Measure*. Generally catalogued among Shakespeare's "dark comedies," *Measure* might be considered a companion piece to *All's Well*: it is another searching comedy about sex (as opposed to a sex comedy). Clarke's production, richly costumed by Moiseiwitsch, was far more sombre than Guthrie's of the previous year; it was also far more straightforward. The actors, accustomed to Guthrie and devoted to him, found Clarke stiff and unresponsive. They petitioned Guthrie to take over the show which, a week before opening, he did.

Probably Clarke had done his spadework more efficiently than his cast were inclined to admit. The show was at least respectfully received, and reviewers tended to blame any dissatisfaction on the play itself. Here they were behind the times: the play, which Victorian critics had mostly found powerful but distasteful, had been gaining steadily in academic repute throughout the twentieth century, and in 1950 a legendary production by Peter Brook at Stratford-upon-Avon had vindicated it as a dynamic piece of theatre. In 1954, however, this news had yet to cross the Atlantic, though by the end of the century the play's interlinked themes of justice, power, and lust, and the ease with which it can be interpreted as a radical questioning of authority, had made it just about the most fashionable piece — intellectually fashionable, anyway — in the canon.

There were also casting problems. Once again the company was headed by an international star, this time from Hollywood. James Mason was of course British-born and even classically trained; he, like so many others, had served under Guthrie at the Vic in the thirties (though only in minor roles) and he had recently starred in a more than respectable film of *Julius Caesar*, playing Brutus as a decent, puzzled liberal. This was a mode to which his pleasant, quizzical voice admirably lent itself, and on the screen his vivid intelligence and cynical humour warded off any suspicion of blandness. But he was out of practice on the stage. In an intimate theatre, he might well have been ideal for Angelo, the puritanical deputy destroyed by desire. On the Stratford platform he was — at least early in the run — overstretched. The acting honours went to his two Canadian

## "I wanted Mason to stay..."

**Tom Patterson**

The [second] season was announced for six weeks, and we wanted to extend it to eight weeks. Obviously I wanted Mason to stay, so I called him into the office and explained the situation.

He said, "No, I've got a commitment in Hollywood. I can't stay. And besides, Tom, your actors are better than I am. This is a Canadian festival and I feel we should give every chance that we can to the Canadian actors. You don't need me. I'm not drawing anything that your company isn't drawing." This was James Mason.

*James Mason in Measure for Measure, 1954*

25

*Although Tom Patterson had his doubts about the wisdom of staging* Oedipus Rex *as the Festival's first non-Shakespearean production, the board backed Guthrie's decision to add his favourite play to the 1954 season. A visually stunning success, it was revived the following year with Douglas Campbell in the title role.*

fellow principals: Lloyd Bochner as the Duke and the young Frances Hyland, who returned from a promising career in London to play Isabella — and, as it turned out, to remain.

Mason was to be even more taxed by his other assignment of the season, the title role in the Festival's first non-Shakespearean play, Sophocles' *Oedipus Rex*. He was very moving at the last, self-blinded, self-exiled, and reaching out towards his two young daughters, but his cinematic style was not so well scaled to the pride and anger of the earlier scenes, in which Oedipus obdurately pursues his own destruction. A wholly naturalistic Sophoclean Oedipus may well be a contradiction in terms, and it would certainly appear to have been so in Guthrie's production, which was uncompromisingly ceremonial and hieratic. Stratford's semi-circular auditorium owes as much to the ancient Greek amphitheatres as its stage does to the Elizabethan playhouse, and Guthrie attired his actors in the masks, robes, and platform shoes of Athenian tragedy. No purist in any style, he took what he wanted for maximum physical effectiveness. Moiseiwitsch's design was huge in scope and meticulous in detail; the masks in particular, when seen today in photographs, seem not only impressive but emotionally affecting. When the stage and its surrounding steps were full of people — and the Festival was able to supply a large crowd of plague-stricken suppliants as well as the statutory tragic chorus — the effect was monumentally impressive: this indeed was one of the few modern productions of a Greek play in which the chorus has been an excitement rather than an embarrassment.

Guthrie (whose aversion to love scenes was notorious) was perhaps more interested in grand psychological problems than in the individual people who suffered them: he may have been one of the few people to believe that Sophocles' Oedipus actually had an Oedipus complex. His bent for psychological exploration may have explained his use of W. B. Yeats's translation which, though the work of a poet, is mainly in prose. It certainly seemed at odds with the grandeur of the production as a whole. So, perhaps, did the choice of Mason as leading man, but he worked tirelessly through the run; his farewell performance in *Measure* was a personal triumph, and he proclaimed himself extended and exhilarated by his Stratford experience. He may also have been exhausted; he rarely returned to the theatre thereafter, and never on a classic or heroic level. On the other hand, some of his best film work — *Lolita*, for example — lay ahead of him, and it would be nice to think that Stratford contributed to it.

*Oedipus* became a Stratford legend: it was revived, toured, filmed, and even — after a fashion — re-revived, decades after its director's death. Nevertheless, there was no production in this second season to match the inaugural excitement of *Richard III* or the revelatory delight of *All's Well*, nor were there any star performances like those of Guinness or Worth. Perhaps it was simply that it wasn't the first season any more. Beneath the surface, though, good things were happening: an ensemble was developing, and the three plays gave the actors room to spread themselves, especially since both the Shakespeares were essentially company pieces.

Of the previous year's British contingent only Douglas Campbell had returned, to confirm — as Pompey, the unrepentant pimp of *Measure*, and

---

## "It was a terrifying sight..."

### William Needles

Douglas Campbell had said to me, "Watch out for the day that Guthrie comes in wearing his mackintosh."

I said, "Why?"

"Well, those are usually bad days."

One day he came in wearing the raincoat and looking quite dark. He began racing up and down the stairs, shouting things like "You're overacting terribly. Never mind. Come forward, you ladies. Come forward!"

Suddenly, he came belting down from the auditorium. He ripped off his mac on the way down, and he had nothing but a tiny pair of shorts on underneath. He was a vast man, you know, and it was a terrifying sight.

But on one of his trips back up, his wife Judy whispered to him, "Tony, do put your mac on. You're upsetting the company."

*William Needles in* The Taming of the Shrew *(1954)*

## "I'd learned my lesson..."

### Hume Cronyn

Tom Patterson contacted me in New York and explained his idea, which I thought was quite mad. He asked Jessica Tandy and me if we would consider opening the Festival and I said, "Frankly, Tom, no."

Then, over a period of time, I heard that he had got Tyrone Guthrie; and then the next thing I knew he had Alec Guinness and Irene Worth. We saw that production and were very impressed, I went to Sir Tyrone — he wasn't Tony to me in those days — and said, "If you ever do this again, will you keep us in mind?"

Years went by, and I got a note from him saying, "Doing it again, in Minneapolis this time, will you care to come along, and if so, what do you want to play?" So I wrote back and said, "We're for it." I'd learned my lesson with Stratford.

*Jessica Tandy (left) talks with her husband, Hume Cronyn (centre), and Tom Patterson (right) at the site of the tent.*

Baptista, the not-too-heavy father of the *Shrew* — his robust authority in Shakespearean comedy. The promising Canadians of the first year continued to deliver. Donald Harron had the key roles of the clever valet in the *Shrew* and the waspish Lucio of *Measure*. Robert Christie as the Pedant in the *Shrew* received perhaps the only set of unanimous raves ever accorded to an actor for playing this extremely minor, and extremely drunk, character. Douglas Rain was the condemned seducer Claudio, the breathlessly voluble page Biondello (Guthrie, typically, had him accentuate the breathlessness), and the tragic messenger of Oedipus's self-mutilation — three contrasting studies in eloquence. William Hutt ranged from making the minuscule role of Froth in *Measure* a distinctive shy cameo to leading the chorus in *Oedipus*. Somewhere between these two extremes, Hutt was Hortensio, one of the two thwarted suitors in the *Shrew*; the other — another adept comedian — was Eric House. (Having a Hutt and a House playing scenes together was a rehearsal gift for Guthrie, who referred to them as "those two eminently desirable residences.")

Newcomers included two who were to make reputations at Stratford and beyond: William Shatner, later of "Star Trek," was Lucentio, the *Shrew*'s nearest approach to a romantic lead, while Bruno Gerussi, later of everywhere, gave the first in a long line of clown performances as Grumio, Petruchio's rapscallion — and, in Gerussi's persona, authentically Italianate — personal attendant.

Whatever the billing, 1954 was effectively another Guthrie season; 1955 was to be officially so, the inevitably strained relationship between him and Clarke having led to the latter's resignation. Guthrie's third and last Stratford Festival was also the last to be built around a visiting star. This was despite the fact that the actor in question was cast in only one role, and that not a huge one. But the actor was Frederick Valk, a massive bull-necked tragedian from Czechoslovakia whose flight from the Nazis had led him to a new career in Britain. He had triumphed there, during and after the war, in the two Shakespearean roles most obviously amenable to a foreign actor, Shylock and Othello. It was to play the former that he was brought to Stratford. (Before leaving Canada he was also to play Othello for a short season at the Crest Theatre in Toronto.)

The choice of *The Merchant of Venice* was greeted — as was to be the case whenever the play appeared at Stratford — with accusations of anti-Semitism. Valk, who knew as much on this subject first-hand as any of his critics, replied with a judicious mixture of sorrow and scorn ("the theatre is not a nursing home to give sedatives to biased people"), and if his performance did not still the would-be censors, it stunned everybody else. He combined impeccable technique with vocal and physical power of a force unknown in the English theatre, and his Shylock dominated the play.

It did not, however, run away with it. There was sunshine as well as thunder in the air, with the lovers expertly played by Frances Hyland and Donald Harron (the last in his string of juvenile-lead roles at Stratford and his last appearance there before going on to conquer other territories). Guthrie's production was one of his best-balanced, both exciting and enchanting, and some — who had expected to be bored or offended by the play — found it revelatory. His other contribution to the season was a revival of *Oedipus* with Douglas Campbell taking over the lead, his first tragic role at the Festival.

Guthrie was also grooming a successor, a young English director named Michael Langham, whom he had once described as "the one undoubted genius of the next lot." Langham had gone the traditional route, working at the Old Vic, where one of his productions, during Guthrie's sole post-war season as overall director of that theatre, had been an *Othello* with Douglas Campbell as the Moor. He had also co-directed a starrily cast *Julius Caesar* at Stratford-upon-Avon, and it was with this play that Guthrie tried him out at the Canadian Stratford.

It must have seemed at moments that Langham would end up again as a co-director: he ran into trouble with some of the actors and enlisted Guthrie's help at rehearsals. As with Clarke the year before, actors used to Guthrie's seemingly free-and-easy methods (Guthrie's actors, Kenneth Tynan once wrote, "were unjabbed by any spur save the spur of the moment") found Langham dictatorial and academic. Unlike Clarke, however, he was clearly a first-rate director in the making, and he already had a grip on the open stage. The production had sweep (which admittedly was easier to come by in the fifties than it is now; later directors have lost the knack), and there was plenty of praise for Langham's handling of the crowd, especially in their horrific dismemberment of Cinna the Poet.

What the critics — and Langham himself — found lacking was the acting. Lorne Greene, a Canadian near-star later to find television fame as the patriarch of "Bonanza," made a dull, stolid

Brutus, and none of the other leads — Lloyd Bochner's high-strung Cassius, the Antony of Donald Davis (Barbara Chilcott's brother and a major force in Toronto theatre) or Robert Christie's Caesar — aroused much enthusiasm. For the first time the Stratford company was found wanting *as a company*.

*Julius Caesar*, one suspects, was a play that the critics expected to like: familiar and accessible, it was a natural for the Festival stage. Indeed, the Shakespearean choices in this third season were the most mainstream the Festival had seen: the previous bills had been split between the popular-but-minor (*Richard III*, *Shrew*) and the major-but-obscure (*All's Well*, *Measure*). *Caesar* and *The Merchant* were schoolroom classics with long and uninterruptedly successful stage histories. *The Merchant*, whatever its political reverberations, has maintained that popularity, with no shortage of notable productions at Stratford and elsewhere. *Caesar* has slipped from favour, still frequently performed but seldom to any great effect. Its high-water mark in the last half-century may well have been that 1953 Joseph L. Mankiewicz film in which Mason had played Brutus to the Cassius of John Gielgud and the Antony of Marlon Brando. It seems impossible in the theatre now to bring together three actors of true star quality to play those co-equal roles, and without that chemistry the play sags; the mob, even if directors still knew how to stage a mob, can only do so much. (Neither Mason nor Brando was ideal, but they were unquestionably there.)

Then again, the play's force largely depends on rhetoric, for which most contemporary actors lack both the lungs and the inclination. And maybe the play's upstanding reputation now

*The 1955 season's Julius Caesar was Michael Langham's directorial debut in Canada. Lorne Greene, who later starred in the television series "Bonanza," played Brutus (below). Greene was joined by another future television star, William Shatner, as Lucius (above, at right). Although Greene's performance was savaged by the critics, Douglas Campbell, Donald Harron, and Eleanor Stuart were singled out for praise.*

## *The Show Must Go On*

During a heavy rain, tent-master Skip Manley had to cut the canvas with a knife to prevent buildups of water on the roof. Early audiences and ushers greeted the occasional indoor downpour with good humour. Rain during dress rehearsals was another matter. "Nobody had thought of the consequences of being in the tent in a heat wave," remembers Timothy Findley. "The rain would collect on the tent and then you'd sweat even more because it became a steambath. Tony walked around in a floppy pair of rubber shoes, wearing bathing trunks that kept falling down."

works against it. "It's such a *noble* play," said Gielgud while rehearsing an especially unfortunate production at the National Theatre, and it is about the only Shakespearean text that the editors of schoolroom editions found no cause to expurgate. The play's implications are dark — it is an unflinching study of the deceits and destruction of power politics — but its construction is remarkably clean-limbed and its style resolutely un-grubby. Most modern directors find the combination boring, and it shows.

Langham's production was a salutary reminder that a theatre grappling with Shakespeare on an annual basis must expect to run into problems, especially with the famous plays. The more often they come round, the harder they get. Stratford in its first two years had led a charmed life, but by its third year it was already becoming an institution, and institutions exist to be criticized. Guthrie himself left Stratford covered with glory, having staged no unsuccessful productions; it was perhaps the climax of his career.

There was to be an Indian summer for Guthrie in another theatre, designed to his specifications and named after him, in Minneapolis, where he pursued his fascination with Greek tragedy and revealed a previously unsuspected talent for directing Chekhov. (As an Irishman he perhaps understood those rambling country houses.) Architecturally the Guthrie Theater was son-of-Stratford, and many of his Stratford protégés — Moiseiwitsch, Campbell, Langham — worked there with or after him.

He had one more great production in him. In 1956, back in England, he staged an uproarious *Troilus and Cressida* at the Old Vic, in modern sets and costumes like his *All's Well*, but far more bitter than sweet. A brilliant satire on war, it was probably the only Shakespeare production of the fifties that might still seem ahead of its time — and ours — if it could be revived today. (John Neville, a future Stratford artistic director, played Troilus.) In 1967 he directed two productions at the National Theatre, which had finally commenced operations under Olivier, at the Old Vic. People had been saying for decades that Guthrie should run the National if ever it came into existence; now it was too late, and his productions of two plays he should have revelled in — Molière's *Tartuffe* and Ben Jonson's *Volpone* — were forced and uninspired.

Perhaps remembering this decline, people tended to patronize Guthrie after his death: Peter Hall in his published *Diaries* called him "that sad, mad Don Quixote of the theatre." But then people had patronized him in his lifetime as well, and many simply never knew what to make of him. "I am an unashamed advocate," he once wrote, "of what dry-as-dust pedagogues call 'the play way' "; and in fact, no modern director has had a firmer grasp, theoretical and practical, of what the theatre is about. He may have been both too late and too early for the National Theatre of Great Britain, but he was absolutely on time for the national theatre of Canada. They may have named a theatre after him in Minnesota (they never did in Britain), but the Stratford Festival — not just the stage, not just the theatre, but the whole buzzing organization — is his real monument.

Guthrie also, as it turned out, had an impeccable instinct in his choice of successor.

*Picnics in the park before a performance became a Stratford tradition early in the Festival's history. Here the Guthries enjoy an alfresco meal beside the tent.*

# Chapter Two

# The Langham Years

Michael Langham took over at Stratford a year before the permanent Festival Theatre was completed. The 1956 Stratford season was Janus-faced: the last under canvas, the first in what was to prove the Festival's longest-lasting directorial regime. Like Guthrie in his first season, Langham selected a repertoire of only two plays and staged both of them himself.

The plays were *Henry V* and *The Merry Wives of Windsor*, and the first was a resounding success, with two inspired strokes of casting. This was the first Stratford season to do without imported stars. Instead, Langham built his production around a repatriated Canadian star: a young firebrand from Montreal who was already established on Broadway. Even in 1953 Christopher Plummer had been enough of a known quantity to be sought out by Stratford, but no place could be found for him. (He claimed later that he had failed his audition with Guthrie.)

When he arrived at Stratford Plummer was twenty-six, so Langham was able to stage *Henry V* as a young man's progress, the French campaign a testing ground for a new monarch

learning on the job. This approach to the play almost always works, whether Henry is presented positively or negatively, as an inspiring hero or a hypocritical warlord. The best productions, of course, incorporate elements of both, but some overall choice has to be made, and Langham's approach in 1956 was overwhelmingly positive. (He was himself a young man in a testing position: he would often say in the ensuing years that taking the job after Guthrie was like following God.) Plummer's performance was not without grace-notes and insecurities, but it was, nonetheless, heroic, in the sense that it met the rhetoric head-on, an increasingly rare occurrence in the modern theatre.

*Henry V* produced in England is automatically a patriotic play, whatever the production's attitude to that patriotism. A production elsewhere can sidestep the issue but can also look a little lost without it. Why should Canadian audiences feel involved in a 400-year-old war between England and France? Even in posing the question, one senses an answer. Langham's second casting coup was a collective one: he gave the French roles to French-Canadian actors.

*Tyrone Guthrie was a hard act to follow. The company missed him and a few treated his successor, Michael Langham, badly. But as William Hutt remembers, "Michael survived, brilliantly, for thirteen years. He showed them."*

# "I'd learn my lines in the toilet..."

## William Shatner

I was playing Henry V's brother, the Duke of Gloucester, and understudying Christopher Plummer as the King. I asked, "When do we have the understudy rehearsals?" and they said, "We'll do the understudy rehearsals after we open the third play in about three or four weeks." So I'd go home and learn my lines in the toilet, because when you're renting a room in a family's house that's the only place you have any peace and quiet.

Early into the run Chris got sick and on I went. I said the words the way I had remembered them in the bathroom. And it worked out except in that last declamatory speech — "This day is call'd the feast of Crispian" — at the battle of Agincourt, I dried.

We were on a thrust stage, and there was nobody around that could help me with the line. Then I looked over and saw the actor who had moved up to play my part of Gloucester. He knew every word of *Henry V*, so I walked over to him, put my arm around his shoulders, and said, "What's the line?"

He looked at me and went, "Er...." I thought, oh my God, there's no help here. I turned around, walked back, and the line came to me.

The next day, there were write-ups all across Canada: "Understudy goes on." It was a big thing. And some of them said what a great piece of staging it was when the exhausted Henry V goes over to his brother, puts his arm around his shoulders and then walks away.

Gratien Gélinas, then and for many years to come Canada's leading francophone player, touched all spectators as the defeated Charles VI; Ginette Letondal enchanted them as his daughter, wooed and won by Henry; Jean-Louis Roux made his Stratford debut as the Duke of Orléans; and Jean Gascon made his as the Constable of France, a modest beginning for the man who twelve years later was to be the Festival's next artistic director. (The production was taken to the Edinburgh Festival that fall, in tandem with a revival of Guthrie's *Oedipus*. The British critics were sniffy about the English actors, Plummer included, but enraptured by the French ones.)

The play ends with a proclamation of harmony between English and French. In 1956 this seemed a real possibility in Canada as well. When Eleanor Stuart as the French Queen Isabel pronounced her marriage-blessing at the end of the play, people wept; they had after all just spent three hours watching the two cultures collaborating.

The Festival's early doyenne was the one anglophone entrusted with a French role, presumably because Langham knew that at this moment the verse-speaking had to be right. (Then again, Stuart was Montreal-bred and may be the only Canadian performer to have acted with the Comédie-Française).

The production was recognizably in the Stratford banner tradition but with no sacrifice of sensitivity or intelligence. After his partial failure with *Julius Caesar*, there must have been doubts as to whether Langham — a tense, shy perfectionist of a man, prone to ill health — was the right choice to succeed Guthrie. *Henry V* dispelled all such doubts.

*The Merry Wives* was far less propitious: people thought it forced. Occasionally a really delightful production of this bourgeois farcical comedy comes along, but most tend to be grisly. It is odd, though certainly not unprecedented, to find these two plays in the same season, because they have characteristics, or at least characters, in common. Both are haunted by the ghost of the fat knight, Falstaff, who bestrides the two parts of *Henry IV*. In *Henry V* he is offstage, remembered in a few patches of dialogue and poignantly celebrated in his friends' tragicomic recounting of his death. In *The Merry Wives* he is technically alive and present, but the endlessly resourceful jester of the history plays has little in common with this superannuated would-be seducer who lets himself be fooled and humiliated by the English matrons to whose beds and purses he aspires. His trio of followers, Bardolph, Nym, and Pistol, appear in both plays and spout the same catch-phrases, and each cast-list also features a Mistress Quickly, though the two ladies defy both psychological and chronological consistency.

Langham seems to have gone out of his way to emphasize the disconnection: the recurring characters were played by different actors in each play. Amelia Hall, a perennial Stratford favourite, came off especially well as the

Windsor Quickly. Douglas Campbell, by now a prized part of the Stratford furniture on stage and off, with implicit first call on the plays' more rumbustious comic roles, was Pistol in one play and Falstaff in the other. His Falstaff was subdued, though it inaugurated what was to prove a half-century's involvement with the role, in various plays and in various countries. Two admirable British actresses, Pauline Jameson and Helen Burns (Langham's wife), made little impact as the happy Windsor wives.

The first year of the new building, 1957, was also the year of Stratford's first *Hamlet*. Fittingly — not to say inevitably — the role was bestowed on Stratford's own crown prince, Christopher Plummer.

Harley Granville-Barker wrote a celebrated essay called "From *Henry V* to *Hamlet*" tracing a crucial two years in Shakespeare's development: those in which, having taken the political man-of-action hero as far as he could, he turned to the man who, when action is demanded of him, stops to think about it. The plays mark Shakespeare's transition from external drama to internal, from history to tragedy. In similar fashion, the progression from Henry to Hamlet has become a rite of passage for select young actors.

Like Richard Burton before him, and like Olivier before *him*, Plummer received better notices as Henry than as Hamlet. It was said of him, as of

*In* The Merry Wives of Windsor, *Douglas Campbell (inset) appeared for the first time as Sir John Falstaff, a role he played several times in the years that followed. His 1956 costume (below) was designed by Tanya Moiseiwitsch, as was the costume (opposite) for* Henry V.

## A Permanent Home

"The star of this year's Stratford Festival," wrote critic Herbert Whittaker in 1957, "[is] the theatre itself." Designed by architect Robert Fairfield (inset), the pavilion-like building was erected on the original tent site, with the stage at its centre. "The form of our new theatre," wrote author Robertson Davies in the 1957 Festival programme, "is experimental but not freakish; if we have led the way in a concept of theatre architecture we shall be pleased, but our first wish was to house our own Festival in the way which seemed best for both the audience and the players." Though increasing capacity by nearly 700 seats, the new building retained the intimacy of the beloved tent, the farthest seat being still only 65 feet from the stage. Winner of the Vincent Massey Gold Medal for architecture, Fairfield's theatre is surrounded by the Arthur Meighen Gardens (opposite, in the 1980s), connecting it to a unique riverfront park system often hailed as Canada's finest.

## "Hamlet bitches a lot..."

### Christopher Plummer

You can't play Hamlet properly until you're probably seventy years old. It needs a whole lifetime of wisdom and technique and maturity. Michael Langham was extraordinary. He showed me how to build vocally in certain parts and then take others lower, because it is such a huge role. You must orchestrate it with great variety, otherwise the audience would be driven out of their minds.

Hamlet bitches a lot. He's always complaining. If he was played without humour or irony, he could be called a moaner. So Michael told me a wonderful trick. He said, "When you come to a passage that could be taken as rather offensively self-pitying, just silently put before it the phrase, 'Isn't it extraordinary,' as an intellectual would: 'Isn't it extraordinary how ill this world is?'"

It changes the whole complaining note to wonderment. That was a wonderful piece of direction.

*Christopher Plummer as Hamlet was joined by Frances Hyland as Ophelia (left) and Joy Lafleur as Gertrude (right).*

them, that it was hard to believe that he would not have swooped to his revenge the moment he received his marching orders from the ghost. He was a romantic Hamlet but, by the standards of the time (still set by the introspective, lyrical, high-strung Hamlet of John Gielgud), the wrong kind of romantic. His audience, mindful of his (and their) place in Stratford history, turned to him for the instantly definitive, great Canadian Hamlet. This he could not provide: despite his stardom, he was still a comparative novice. But this may have worked to his advantage, making for a vulnerable, honest-seeming prince, tormented by the rottenness of Denmark, and he was still a Hamlet that the Festival took to its heart.

Langham, just the previous year, had mounted the play at the English Stratford on a bare Ontario-model platform with a fine sardonic actor, Alan Badel, in the lead, and he, too, had received unappreciative notices. Badel was thought to be too intellectual, just as Plummer was reckoned by some to be not intellectual enough — although both aroused fervent minority support.

Perhaps the greatest legacy to Stratford from Langham's two *Hamlet*s was Desmond Heeley, the young designer who created the costumes for both productions. For the Canadian *Hamlet* Heeley designed sets — what there were of them — as well as costumes, beginning a Stratford career that was to prove as durable and as valuable as that of Tanya Moiseiwitsch.

Unhappily, Langham never returned to the play at Stratford, nor did Plummer ever play Hamlet again in the theatre, though he appeared on British television in a heavily hyped production shot at the real Elsinore Castle. (Horatio was played by Michael

Caine — one is tempted to add "of all people," but, to adapt Tom Stoppard on Lenin, he wasn't Michael Caine then.) Plummer now played the role with far more confidence, but the delicate bloom was off.

His other Stratford role in 1957 was a complete success: a miraculous ninny of a Sir Andrew Aguecheek in *Twelfth Night*, traditionally the Shakespearean juvenile's favourite character role. (John Neville was giving one of the performances of his life in the part almost simultaneously at the Old Vic, in a season in which he too played Hamlet.) The production was directed by Guthrie, returning as a guest director for what would prove to be a memorable swan song on the Festival stage. Fittingly, for himself and for the play, it showed off both his hilarious and his melancholic sides.

The melancholy was largely in the gift of Guthrie's Irish compatriot Siobhan McKenna, best known at the time for her passionate, otherworldly Saint Joan; as Viola, her fey, brooding quality did not disguise — indeed accentuated — the play's delighted sense of its own absurdity. She was the nearest Stratford had that year to a guest star. Frances Hyland, whose Ophelia had won the supporting-player honours in *Hamlet*, was no less effectively fragile — though to very different ends — as Olivia. On the other side of the play, Douglas Campbell had one of his most distinguished comic roles as Sir Toby, and two of Stratford's home-nurtured talents, Douglas Rain and Bruno

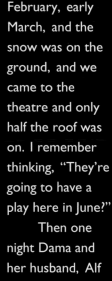

Gerussi, gave breakthrough performances as Malvolio and Feste. The ensemble in *Hamlet* had seemed, for the first time, ragged; *Twelfth Night* showed them able not just to rise to a visiting luminary's level but to meet her there on their own terms.

Programming Shakespeare's most popular tragedy and comedy in the same season was a departure (previous seasons had tended, if anything, to what were then considered minor plays), and Stratford was accused of playing it safe. This is untrue: the more familiar a play, the harder it is to do, since preconceptions weigh down audiences as well as performers. And since there are only so many plays in the Shakespeare canon, it makes no sense to avoid the popular ones. If Stratford planned to stay around — which, even without the new theatre,

it obviously did — it would simply have to take on the burden of repetition faced by every Shakespeare theatre.

Langham's first two seasons were a brace of preludes. Only in 1958, with the permanent theatre safely opened, was his regime able to establish itself on its own terms. His tenure, which lasted until 1967, was to prove the longest of any Stratford artistic director to date and is remembered as a golden age. Studied now, it seems to have been distinguished by teamwork and muscularity (as were Langham's own productions) along with an unusual sensitivity to the plays' inner and outer shapes. Better than any other director of his time, he knew his way around that stage and those texts.

Langham did have some historical advantages. The Festival was past its

teething troubles but still had the excitement of novelty about it, the sense of something being created. It also remained comparatively modest in scale: there were never more than five plays in a Langham season and rarely more than four. It is obviously easier to create a company in such circumstances than it would be with a repertoire of a dozen or more plays in production all at once, which would automatically necessitate the creation of groups within the group. And it was also the Zeitgeist. This was a time when the English-speaking classical theatre teemed with vigour and intelligence.

The sixties are thought of as a time of fervent, anarchic, experimental drama. In fact, they were a new chapter in the ongoing history of turning long-cherished and long-frustrated

*Artist Grant Macdonald did portraits of several members of the 1957 company, including Siobhan McKenna (left) as Viola in* Twelfth Night. *In 1961* Love's Labour's Lost *was performed on the Festival stage for the first time. Shown above are (left to right): Mary (Mia) Anderson, Douglas Rain, Joy Parker, Zoe Caldwell, Michael Learned, and Fred Euringer.*

dreams into reality. In 1963 Britain finally gained its National Theatre — the company, if not yet the building. Under Olivier it created a decade of glittering actor-based theatre "so good," in the words of the American writer William Goldman, "it makes you want to cry." (It wasn't always that good, but in retrospect it's hard to believe it happened at all: another reason for tears.)

In 1960 Peter Hall founded the Royal Shakespeare Company, which was to be a real ensemble, based on long-term contracts and an evolving shared aesthetic. Britain, though it may not have known it, was emulating what Canada already had; and indeed Langham was one of the directors Hall recruited at the outset. In those days Stratford directors had the time to take on outside work, and Langham's production of *The Merchant of Venice*, with the young Peter O'Toole as a magnetic and highly sympathetic Shylock, proved the triumph of the RSC's first season: a production universally acclaimed for its balance, and still perhaps unequalled.

It was as a director of the comedies, including the lesser-known ones, that Langham was to make his mark at Stratford. In his break-through year of 1958 he staged a charmingly astringent *Much Ado About Nothing*, firmly set — as the play itself is — in and around an Italian country house, though in this case the costumes and trappings were those of the late nineteenth century. (*Much Ado* must have accumulated more time-travel points than any other Shakespeare play. A production in Elizabethan costume would seem deliriously avant-garde.) Plummer played Benedick, his first and oddly his last Shakespearean comic lead, opposite the Beatrice of the British actress Eileen Herlie who, in the course of relocating

to America, had changed from a tragic actress playing parts she was too young for to an eccentric comedienne with unusual reserves of strength. She even did musicals.

The production was so successful that Langham was asked virtually to restage it for the RSC in 1961, on the heels of his triumphant *Merchant*. Plummer recreated his performance, but it seemed to have suffered an unfortunate sea-change. The production was a shadow of its Canadian self, champagne diluted to Babycham, with the British troupe (including Geraldine McEwan, a great comedienne in the making but not yet made) appearing as far under par as the Canadians had been over it. Langham was never to direct at the English Stratford again.

The same year, however, back on what was now his home ground, he surpassed his Canadian *Much Ado* with a production of *Love's Labour's Lost* that took everybody by surprise, except perhaps those who knew something about the play. One of Shakespeare's earliest, it is reputed to be obscure: it satirizes his literary contemporaries by playing verbal games that go beyond theirs, and it is packed with obscure topical references. In the theatre, this never matters. The central situation — a quartet of studious young courtiers, lured from their academic vows by a matching quartet of scintillating young ladies who know more about life than the men are ever likely to learn — is classic sex comedy, and its rustic characters are Shakespeare's funniest. Its ending, courtship deferred by an announcement of death, is the most audacious and the most moving in the canon, an uncynical satire on all happy endings that is profoundly moving in its

own right. Two superbly explicit lines confirm that Shakespeare's references to theatrical illusion were deliberate. "Worthies, away, the scene begins to cloud," Berowne, played in Langham's production by John Colicos, tells the clowns, virtually cueing the lights. His response to the news that passion is to be put on hold for a year and a day is "That's too long for a play."

*Love's Labour's Lost* has become a Stratford perennial, occasioning a series of beguiling productions. But Langham's takes priority, and not just because it was the first. John Pettigrew and Jamie Portman, in their book *Stratford: The First Thirty Years*, quote one visiting scholar as declaring it the best Shakespeare production he had seen in an international experience of forty-five years and describe him as maintaining that verdict until he died; they also say that many theatre staffers still think it the best production of anything ever mounted there. Reading such descriptions can make even those who didn't see it go misty-eyed; the play does that to people.

Langham's production — graceful, stabbing and hilarious — had no new revelations to make about the play; it merely brought out, in the sharpest relief, everything that was known to be in it. Stratford's visiting star, Paul Scofield, played Don Armado, a role for which his haggard, cracked-voiced distinction made him ideal. He crowned the production but did not dominate it, nor as it turned out was he indispensable to it. In 1964 the company took the production to England, to the Chichester Festival Theatre in the Sussex countryside. This has a platform stage built in professed emulation of Stratford's but cramped and lopsided, as if somebody had dropped the

## "I fought it..."

### Michael Langham

When I got to Stratford, I found that stage very, very difficult, and I fought it for the first years. I resisted it. It took me quite a few years before I began to realize that I had to accept it and go with it and sort of marry it. I guess it was with *Love's Labour's Lost* in 1961 that I really began to feel I could meld it to my own purposes. I realized that the front is not the front. The front is two fronts: the two diagonals. And everything on that platform has a diagonal basis to it.

*Love's Labour's* was the first time I thought it would serve what I wanted to do, and from then on I enjoyed it.

*Tanya Moiseiwitsch (above) discusses the 1962 redesign of the stage with designer Brian Jackson (left), who assisted her in the redesign, and Michael Langham (right). One major change involved replacing the old balcony's nine small pillars with five larger ones. (Opposite) The stage as it looks today.*

Stratford design somewhere over the Atlantic Ocean and the architects had tried to reconstruct it from memory. William Hutt played Armado at Chichester and was distinguished and distinctive. The production was less than it had been, but it was still fine.

Last in Langham's triumphant triptych of comedies was *The Taming of the Shrew*, which in 1962 became the first play to be given a second Stratford production. If there can be such a thing as a purist *Shrew*, Langham's was it: it was far from the Guthrie romp but it was at least as funny. Two things about it stand out. One is that, in a play offering an unusual number of acting opportunities, every one was taken: virtually every performance aroused critical enthusiasm. Stratford, as some stated and the rest implied, was a company. The other was that it was widely referred to as Langham's valedictory production. He had been repeatedly ill, and the 1959 season had had to proceed without him, with unfortunate results. What eventually kept him from leaving was the lack of a suitable successor. In fact his reign was only half over. The tone of the premature farewells, however, was gratifying and revealing: they were awed and affectionate tributes. Langham's colleagues and successors were being measured against him, both in and out of the company. It was his turn to be God.

After his auspicious start with *Henry V*, Langham returned surprisingly rarely to the histories, which still seemed naturals for that stage and, as it grew in overall strength, for that company. They were done — indeed an almost-complete sequence of them started in 1964 — but chiefly by other directors. In 1958 Langham had collaborated with George McCowan (the

first Canadian to be given a directing credit at Stratford) on a production of *Henry IV — Part One* only, and chiefly remembered for the presence of Jason Robards Jr., who, without Shakespearean voice, skills or experience, had a valiant bash at Hotspur. In 1966, when *Henry V* came round as part of the history cycle, Langham returned to it, in a production far darker (and predictably less popular) than his first version. The bilingual casting remained, with Jean Gascon promoted from Constable to King, but the prospects for Anglo-French unity at the close seemed considerably less rosy, as they were in the Canada outside the theatre.

In one of the unusually frank interviews he was in the habit of giving to the press, Langham said that Stratford had cracked the comedies and histories as groups, but had yet to succeed with the tragedies. He was right, but what he neglected to mention was that neither had any other modern theatre. Stratford's experience with the individual plays pretty much mirrored that of other companies and has continued to do so. *Hamlet* is, up to a point, an infallible play, and beginning with Plummer's the Festival has offered a series of competent and usually popular Danes, but never one for the ages. But then neither has anybody else. It may be that history has accumulated enough great Hamlets and doesn't need any more, or that our age is too fragmented for any performance to seem definitive.

*Othello* has recently slipped precipitously down the repertoire, because of the difficulty of finding a black actor to play the lead and the apparent impossibility of casting a white one. But even when this was not an issue, the play often disappointed. The necessary equilibrium between Othello and Iago

## Royal Performances

In 1958, Princess Margaret (right) was the Festival's first royal visitor. She had seen the company perform in Edinburgh two years previously. "We'd done the performance," recalls Tony van Bridge, "and I went down to the dressing room and got all my costume off except my underpants. There was a knock at the door and standing there was Michael Langham with the Princess Royal. I became famous overnight as the actor who'd been in his shorts before the Princess!" Queen Elizabeth, shown above with William Hutt (left) and Michael Langham, attended a performance of *As You Like It* on her 1959 visit to Canada.

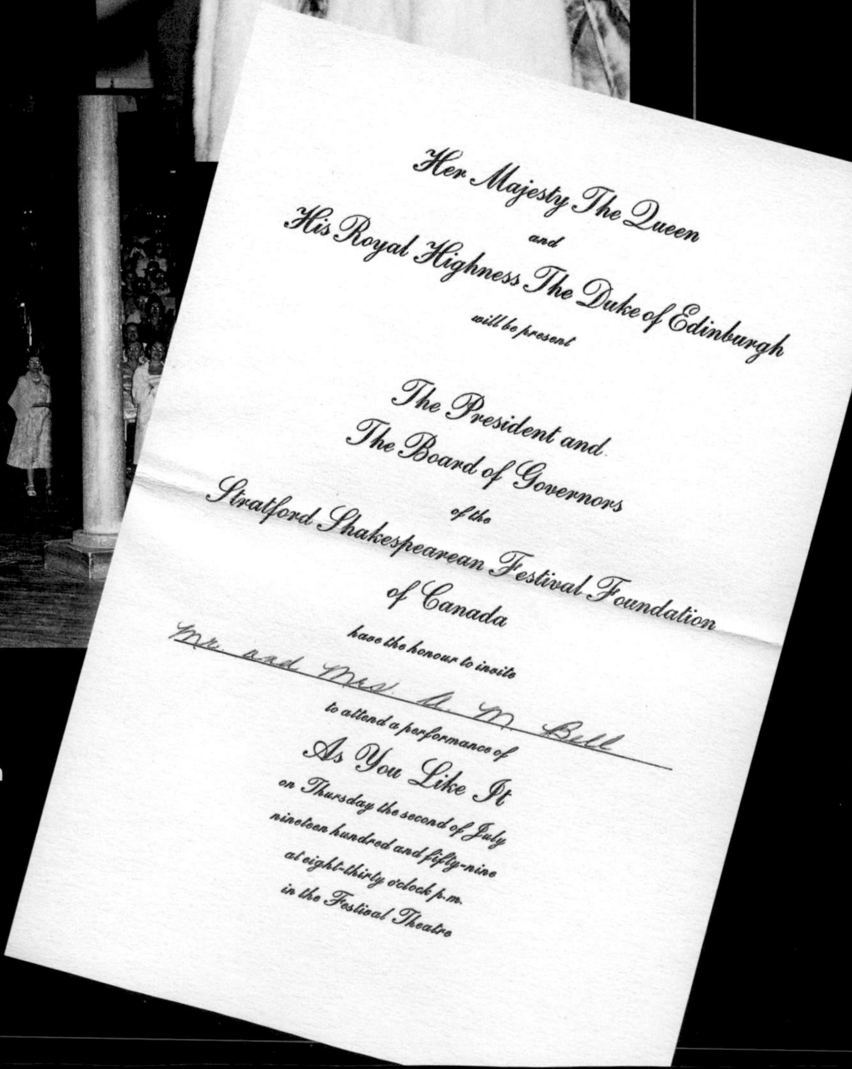

Her Majesty The Queen
and
His Royal Highness The Duke of Edinburgh
will be present

The President and
The Board of Governors
of the
Stratford Shakespearean Festival Foundation
of Canada
have the honour to invite

Mr. and Mrs. A. M. Bell

to attend a performance of
As You Like It
on Thursday the second of July
nineteen hundred and fifty-nine
at eight-thirty o'clock p.m.
in the Festival Theatre

was hard to come by, and few actors of any colour can explode as the Moor is required to do. (In fact nobody has managed it since Olivier's controversial but in practice unmatchable performance of 1964.) Lacking this, the play, short on metaphysics, has a disconcerting habit of shrinking into domestic melodrama. The British playwright Howard Brenton once said that there are only two kinds of play: plays set in rooms and plays not set in rooms. With the exception of *The Merry Wives* (which of course is also about jealousy), *Othello* is the only Shakespeare play to be set in rooms, and one feels shortchanged by it.

*Macbeth* is, by tradition and in practice, a disaster area. In the past fifty years only two actors, both at the English Stratford, have made the play work: Olivier in 1955 and Ian McKellen, in Trevor Nunn's superlative chamber production, in 1976. Stratford's extensive experience with *Macbeth* has never been rewarding, though some of the failures have been more interesting than others. The play remains, though, excellent box-office. Like *Othello* it is apt to slip into melodrama, but a kind of melodrama, involving battles and murders and witches, far easier to sell to school parties and indeed to many adults. It is one of the two or three Shakespeare plays with the greatest name-recognition value.

Which leaves, among the traditional big four, *King Lear*: supposedly unactable (thank Charles Lamb for the supposition) but on empirical evidence, at Stratford and elsewhere, the easiest of them all. Lear is a taxing role but less so than Macbeth or Othello or even Hamlet; at least when he goes mad there is no doubt about it. And though an angry and self-destructive monarch may be foreign to the experience of most of us, a self-destructive and angry parent decidedly isn't. The play's physical, emotional, and intellectual scale is dauntingly great, but that size itself calls out an answering largeness in the people who attempt it. People only do *King Lear*, as they might *The Oresteia* or *Peer Gynt*, because they want to; it isn't the kind of play that you program because it's about time somebody put it on.

Langham made his remarks about Stratford's failure with tragedy in 1962. In 1964 he went a good way towards proving himself wrong when he directed the Festival's first *Lear*. It was a moving, straightforward production, graced by the performance of John Colicos as the king. Colicos had had his first brief taste of fame a dozen years earlier in London, when he understudied the lead (and played Edmund's Captain) in a disastrous Old Vic production. When the leading actor abdicated early in the run, an experienced successor could not immediately be found, and in the interim Colicos played the role and impressed all who saw him. After coming home to Canada, he, like Plummer, worked at the Montreal Repertory Theatre and achieved success in the U.S., and from 1961 he played Stratford leads that fittingly culminated in his return to Lear, this time as the director's first choice. Lears tend to divide, using Granville-Barker's terminology again, into oaks and ashes, the aggressive and the pitifully senile; Colicos's was oaken with an infusion of ashen pathos. On the first night, when the critics saw it, his performance was sublime.

There are other Shakespeare tragedies outside the famous four, and Langham — counting his baptism of fire with *Julius Caesar* under Guthrie — directed all of them with the pardonable

*Leslie Hurry, one of Britain's leading designers, first created sets and costumes for the Festival in 1955. He worked on several productions in the Langham years, including Stratford's first* King Lear. *His costume for Regan (above) was worn by Diana Maddox. The 1964 production starred John Colicos (below).*

*Romeo and Juliet has been presented eight times over the Festival's fifty-year history. Bruno Gerussi (above) and Julie Harris (below) appeared as the star-crossed lovers in the 1960 production. It was Gerussi's first appearance in a romantic role and Harris's first appearance in a major Shakespearean role.*

exception of *Titus Andronicus*. One of his earliest successes at Stratford, the one that decisively established him in the hearts of actors and audiences, was *Romeo and Juliet* (1960), vocally a rough-edged production but boiling with youthful energies. Memory collapses these things, but Langham, like Franco Zeffirelli in a legendary production at the Old Vic the same year, directed *Romeo* in the immediate and challenging shadow of *West Side Story*. Zeffirelli's was the more authentically Italianate of the two productions, Langham's almost certainly the more authentically Shakespearean.

Its passion came from the actors rather than from their environment. In Broadway's adored Julie Harris, Langham had a Juliet with few rhetorical skills but one in whom everybody believed. And he did have a true Italian hero: Bruno Gerussi, perhaps the stockiest Romeo on record, exploding into his first romantic role after years of playing the fool. Gerussi's range and quality were unique, certainly among English-speaking actors. Others may have succeeded as both Feste and Romeo, but Gerussi is probably the only one to have taken them on in that order. Earth and fire may have seemed his natural elements, but shortly afterwards he played Ariel, proving that he could do air as well. (A watery actor he probably wasn't.) Romeo may have torn the poetry into tatters and Juliet into daintier strips, but together they tore up the stage as well.

Then there was *Timon of Athens* (1963), the bewildering unfinished satirical tragedy with which Langham, taking over the production at short notice and with Colicos as his leading actor, had a personal triumph. He inherited a modern-dress concept and a specially commissioned Duke Ellington score, and made splendid use of both. (Ellington, a great Stratford partisan, was inspired to write his superb Shakespearean suite *Such Sweet Thunder* by his experience of playing at the adjoining jazz festival.) Nathan Cohen, at the time Canada's hardest-to-please theatre critic, thought the show gimmicky, but then he thought most of Langham's productions gimmicky (and most other directors' productions as well; it's possible that he knew less about the plays than did some of the directors he trashed). *Timon* almost matched *All's Well* as a piece of Shakespearean trail-blazing: no previous director, anywhere, had ever succeeded with *Timon* — even Guthrie had only scraped by with it — and only two directors have since: Robin Phillips in London, Ontario (with William Hutt as his star), and Trevor Nunn in London, England. Of course few have had a chance: the play has remained one of the two or three most neglected. *Titus Andronicus* is a blockbuster by comparison.

*Troilus and Cressida* may not strictly count as a tragedy, but its bilious eloquence on the twin themes of war and lechery is akin to *Timon's*, though far richer and more varied. Stratford's critics and audiences certainly weren't ready for it in 1963 (one writer bizarrely dismissed its treatment of the mythical Trojan War as historically inaccurate), though it was acknowledged elsewhere as one of the greatest and, in its pervasive disenchantment, most modern-seeming of the plays. Langham gave it one of his best productions, and its democratic spread of responsibility (sixteen major roles and not a star in any of them) occasioned the best demonstration yet

# The Swans of Stratford

Whether fed by actresses in early publicity photographs (bottom inset), used in logos (left), or appearing in a 1963 parade (top inset), the city's swans have been part of the Festival since its inception. In the early 1900s, Stratford's Parks Board tore down dilapidated buildings along the Avon River, dammed the river to create Lake Victoria, and built a park along its banks. The park's first swans were donated to the city in 1918 by a railway employee, whose inspiration may have been Stratford-upon-Avon's royal swans. At last count, the flock numbered twenty-eight white mute swans and six black swans. Not to be outdone by the actors up the hill, they have even starred in their own movie, a documentary film called *Swans on the Avon*.

## *"We all jumped in..."*

### Barry MacGregor

In 1967, after the opening night of *Antony and Cleopatra*, we went to the Victorian Inn for the party. We were all dressed up: in those days you wore tuxedos and long dresses for your opening night. We were all drinking and chatting and everybody smiling. Then somebody said, "Oh, the swimming pool's open."

So we went over the passageway from the ballroom, and there in the pool was Zoe Caldwell swimming in a $400 or $500 dress, which in those days was a hell of a lot of money. So we all jumped in, in our tuxedos, except for Jean Gascon who stripped down to these tiny French bikini pants. Nobody was drunk. It was just the exuberance of what we'd just gone through.

"Isn't this wonderful?" I said to Franny Hyland. And she said, "Yes, it is. Because I can't swim."

of the company's strength. Finally, there were the two mature Roman plays: *Coriolanus* (1961) and *Antony and Cleopatra* (1967).

*Coriolanus*, done in Napoleonic costume, provided a vehicle for Paul Scofield, to balance his ensemble contribution to *Love's Labour's Lost*. Of all the visiting star actors the Festival has accommodated, including Guinness, Scofield was the only one to arrive with a worldwide reputation as a Shakespearean (his stupendous RSC Lear for Peter Brook was just a year in the future). Stratford gave him an uncompromising role to which — in his charm, charisma, ringing heroic delivery and sense of unyielding mission — he was ideally suited and that he was never to play elsewhere. (The National Theatre, years later, had him lined up for the role, but he quietly bowed out when he found that the play was to be directed by two disciples of Bertolt Brecht, in what amounted to a re-translation of Brecht's adaptation. His replacement was none other than Christopher Plummer, who also departed, more stormily, for similar reasons. The National eventually cast a rising young actor named Anthony Hopkins. It didn't do his career any harm, but the production, by general consent, was a disaster.)

Langham's last production under his own regime was *Antony and Cleopatra*, one of the greatest plays

and, spiritually and technically, one of the most difficult. Langham described the play, with its multitude of short, quickly changing scenes and its see-sawing between Rome and Egypt, as a film scenario before its time, and his staging excitingly reflected this. But the play, at least as we are conditioned to think of it, anticipates the movies in another way: it is not only a play for two stars but a play *about* two stars, and it is difficult to bring them to satisfying life. Stratford's record with the play, like that of most theatres, is one of

*Paul Scofield and Kate Reid (above) appeared in the 1961 production of* Love's Labour's Lost. *Zoe Caldwell (right), wearing one of Tanya Moiseiwitsch's elaborate costumes, starred six years later in* Antony and Cleopatra.

honourable but consistent failure. Nobody calls *Antony* an unlucky play like *Macbeth*, but most directors are terrified of it.

Langham's Cleopatra was Zoe Caldwell. Not quite a Stratford regular, not quite a visiting star, she had at least the right mercurial temperament for the role and was very impressive in flashes. His Antony was Plummer, who seemed half-hearted about doing it at all. He had been absent from Stratford for four years, and was now an established Broadway, West End, and even

Hollywood star: he had already done *The Sound of Music*.

It was fitting, however, that Plummer, who had starred in *Henry V*, Langham's first production as artistic director, should also star in his last. More than any other actor, he was identified with the Langham regime, and is still considered the poster-boy Stratford actor — no other performer has made quite the same impact both inside and outside the Festival as he did. Maybe it could only have happened at a time when both the actor and the Festival were young. Plummer, the first of his line in Canada, was perhaps the last of his line in the world: a flashing young swashbuckler of an actor, who combined earthiness and humour with a voice and presence in the classical tradition and the temper of a young iconoclast. Fittingly, the greatest success he had at Stratford was in the greatest of swashbuckling roles: as the hero of Edmond Rostand's *Cyrano de*

*Bergerac*. That production, too, was one of Langham's triumphs: by 1962, when he directed it, he had the full measure of the Festival platform and, with Moiseiwitsch and Heeley collaborating on the design, it was a breathtaking, stage-filling spectacle.

In Shakespeare, Plummer had played the great buccaneering roles — Benedick in *Much Ado*, Philip the Bastard in *King John*, Mercutio in *Romeo and Juliet* — with the Elizabethan relish that they demand and rarely get. He was perhaps the last actor not to apologize for these characters, to play them as scoundrels or as sanguinary neurotics. He would have been an ideal Hotspur, but when *Henry IV, Part One* came round for the first time, it was in a season that already had Plummer in the major roles of Benedick and Leontes in *The Winter's Tale*. In deference to repertory principles he took the minor role of Bardolph, Falstaff's purple-nosed henchman, and

turned in a comic cameo as finished and as scaled to its place in the play as any star performance he ever gave. (His then-wife Tammy Grimes was less well cast as Mistress Quickly.) Plummer, in short, had developed into both a comedian and a romantic, with a solid sense of character, and it is no wonder that his Cyrano (another nose-job) raised Stratford's roof. It was a hard act to follow, but not an impossible one; the production was revived the following year, with John Colicos scoring a considerable if quieter success in the role.

*Cyrano* was the first Stratford production to be revived — and the first production of a non-Shakespearean classic — since *Oedipus*. Nineteen-sixty had been the last year in which the Stratford repertoire was wholly devoted to Shakespeare. In 1961 — for the first and, to date, only time — a new Canadian play was mounted at the Festival Theatre: Donald Lamont Jack's *The Canvas Barricade*, a comedy about

*Stage actors are usually responsible for applying their own makeup, including fake body parts. Before each of his nineteen performances in* Cyrano de Bergerac, *Christopher Plummer applied the title character's large nose with spirit gum. Afterwards, the adhesive was removed with isopropyl alcohol.*

a trickster. (The previous year two new plays — Alfred Euringer's *Blind Man's Buff* and John Gray's *The Teacher* — had been given two performances each at the Avon Theatre). This was followed in later seasons by *The Last of the Tsars* (1966), billed as "an original play about the Russian Revolution," written at very short notice by Michael Bawtree, the Festival's first dramaturge, and directed by Langham himself, and by James Reaney's autobiographical *Colours in the Dark* (1967). Of these, only the last aroused much enthusiasm (it marked the beginning of a long-term association between Reaney and Stratford). Both it and the Bawtree play were staged at the Avon, a former vaudeville and movie house that initially was used for Stratford Festival sideshows but gradually became accepted as the proscenium-arch alternative to the main space.

Guthrie had regarded his venture into Greek tragedy as a special case and was sceptical about the suitability of the platform stage to most post-Shakespearean drama. The success of *Cyrano* would probably not have surprised him, but he was certain that Restoration comedy, for example, would be impossible: the necessity for constant movement would destroy the comic focus. Langham proved him wrong when he directed Wycherley's *Country Wife* in 1964, showing the play to be not merely an unusually explicit boudoir sex farce but a bustling study of life in a big city. It also gave Helen Burns her best-ever Stratford role as Mistress Margery Pinchwife, the rural innocent of the title happily abandoning herself to the smartest gallant in town.

Langham had an even more comprehensive success in 1967, at the very end of his reign, with a production of Gogol's *Government Inspector*: one of the very few occasions — at least in English — on which this furious satire on Russian bureaucracy has proved both as funny and as serious as it is commonly cracked up to be. Playing the role of the impoverished young clerk whose dreams of glory are suddenly realized when he is mistaken for a visiting government official was William Hutt. Appearing opposite him as the small-town mayor, desperate to fend off an investigation of his corrupt regime, was Tony van Bridge.

Hutt and van Bridge — one a Canadian who had been advancing through the company from the very first season, the other a British actor who had made his debut in the last Guthrie season and settled in Canada for life — typified the ensemble players developed by Langham over a dozen years. He advanced the actors who had been assembled by Guthrie as well as bringing in new ones. This continuity from one regime to another has proved a constant in Stratford's history, surviving even the most difficult transitions, and is perhaps the Festival's greatest intangible asset. No other English-speaking theatre approaches it, though the Shaw Festival at Niagara-on-the-Lake comes close. Company fidelity is perhaps a Canadian characteristic, though one must add that it's partly due to the lack of high-paying or high-profile opportunities elsewhere.

Langham brought in one classical star from Britain (Scofield) and a couple of non-classical stars from the States (Harris, Robards). In his last season and at short

### "Six lines on one breath..."

#### William Hutt

Michael's productions were much tighter than Tony's, and his sense of pace and tempo was much firmer. Consequently, those of us who remained throughout those years learned, slowly but surely, how to handle some of Shakespeare's language better.

Shakespeare makes enormous demands on you, enormous demands on the length of thought, the length of the emotional involvement. Guthrie used to say you should be able to speak six lines of Shakespearean verse on one breath — not simply for technical reasons, but because sometimes six lines involve one huge emotion. You cannot break that line up, that drive up, or you lose the emotion or the impact of the emotion.

*William Hutt as the Government Inspector*

## The Avon Theatre

First known as the Theatre Albert (near right), then as the Griffin and later as the Majestic, the Avon Theatre was built in 1900 as a theatre where touring plays and musical comedies could be staged. Through the years it has served as a music hall, vaudeville

house, and movie theatre (above, right). The Festival rented the theatre each summer, beginning in 1956, as a venue for presenting light operas and bought the building in 1963.

In 1964, Robert Fairfield drew up plans for the renovation of the theatre, with Tanya Moiseiwitsch in charge of its décor. Moiseiwitsch's love of dramatic colours was reflected in her choice of gold-brocade wallpaper, burnt orange carpeting, olive-green seats, and a gold curtain (below). A few years later, the exterior and front offices of the Avon were reconstructed (bottom). A major renovation in 1984 expanded the backstage area and a $15-million renovation completed in 2002 added a fourth Festival theatre — the Studio Theatre.

notice he imported Alan Bates, one of Britain's finest actors of modern plays (who else can boast of having been in the original casts of *Look Back in Anger, The Caretaker,* and *Butley* — three defining plays of the British new wave — quite apart from starring in major British and American movies?). Bates had the dark looks and the complex sensibility to be a major classical actor, and potentially he had the voice; but he had shied away from the classics at home and was not really ready to crack them in Canada. As the jealous Ford in *The Merry Wives of Windsor* he was miscast. As Richard III he was interesting but subdued.

Mostly though, Langham grew or adopted his own. Bruno Gerussi, following his startling ascent from Grumio to Romeo, went on to play Edmund in *King Lear,* in which he was ideally cast, and less happily, Mark Antony in *Julius Caesar* before leaving Stratford and, largely, the theatre. On television, he became a patriarch among Italian-Canadian actors. (His flashiest role under Stratford auspices was perhaps the least fortunate: in 1957, on the heels of his fine Feste, he played the title role in a savagely cut television production of Ibsen's *Peer Gynt,* directed by Langham. Not even Gerussi's versatility was up to the task of compressing Peer's youth, maturity, and old age into ninety minutes of live TV.) William Needles seemed to age prematurely but permanently in the Festival's service: once, as Benvolio to Gerussi's Romeo, he was allowed to play a young man, but he was more typically cast as an aged counsellor, Greek (Nestor in *Troilus*) or English (Henry IV's Lord Chief Justice).

William Hutt and Douglas Rain were eased, steadily but inexorably,

towards stardom. Hutt had his first break in 1956 as Ford in *The Merry Wives* and capped it the following year as Polonius in *Hamlet* (note the range in ages). The next big step in 1959 was Jaques in *As You Like It.* The melancholy philosopher, if not actually a star part, is a part fit for a star, and it was the first to display Hutt's voice and intelligence in all their fine-filigreed glory. Pandarus, the gloating, giggling go-between of *Troilus and Cressida,* was the first to display his genius for camp comedy, the funnier for being governed by an iron technical control that gave full value to the most scathing epilogue in Shakespeare ("Good traders in the flesh, set this in your painted cloths.") His Justice Shallow in *Henry IV* was another gem, instinct with a gentler self-deluding kind of slyness, that of an old man trying to persuade not only his hearers but himself of his imaginary madcap youth.

Hutt's first indubitable lead was Prospero in *The Tempest* (1962), a role with which he was to become identified at Stratford and that was to gather both strength and compassion each time he returned to it. In this period, though, the role that really established him was Richard II, which he played in 1964. It was a glittering, unsentimental portrait, as exquisitely spoken as dressed (people still remember his long white boots). Turn this performance inside out, play it for fun instead of for pain, and you had his Government Inspector, a man ushered into his false persona by others and taking delicious advantage of it and of them.

Rain, eight years younger than Hutt, got off to a faster start. He was already playing a varied trio of prominent roles in Guthrie's second season, and three years later he strutted firmly

*In 1967, Alan Bates (above) appeared as Ford in* The Merry Wives of Windsor. *Actor Barry MacGregor remembers the well-known English actor as "always, not experimenting, but certainly changing intentions, which is very good because it makes you go 'Ah!' and follow possibly a different path with your own reactions." Douglas Rain, a more experienced classical actor than Bates, took on a number of challenging roles during the Langham years, including* Henry V *(below) in 1966.*

## *The Music Festival*

The first official Stratford Music Festival, under the direction of Festival music director Louis Applebaum, was held over four weeks in the summer of 1955. It featured such well-known artists as violinist Isaac Stern, soprano Lois Marshall and pianist Glenn Gould. All concerts took place in the Casino on Lakeside Drive (now the Tom Patterson Theatre), which had been converted to the Festival Concert Hall for the season. Transferring to the Avon Theatre in 1958, the Music Festival's activities eventually took place in a variety of locations, including the Festival Theatre. The jazz series in particular was a huge success, featuring such greats as Duke Ellington, Dizzy Gillespie, and Billie Holiday. Although the last Music Festival was held in 1975, the Festival continues to present a small series of concerts each season.

**EXCITING MUSIC** AT STRATFORD 1968

*Cleo Laine and John Dankworth*

25/68

FOR RESERVATIONS WRITE OR PHONE STRATFORD FESTIVAL BOX OFFICE / 271-4040
FULL MUSIC SEASON DETAILS ON OTHER SIDE

**Dizzy Gillespie**

**Liona Boyd**

Festival music director Oscar Shumsky leads a workshop in the 1960s (opposite). Duke Ellington (above) plays for Rosalind Ann Knapp (left) and Martha Henry (right) in 1966. (Below) Artists-in-residence in 1960 shown with Louis Applebaum (left): Leonard Rose, Oscar Shumsky, and Glenn Gould. (Bottom) In 1966, Jan Rubes appeared in Don Giovanni at the Avon.

into the limelight (or as firmly as a man can strut in cross-garters and yellow stockings) as Malvolio in Guthrie's *Twelfth Night*. A more compact, self-effacing actor, he was even more versatile than Hutt. Hutt could adapt a wide range of roles to an unmistakable, idiosyncratic voice, stance, and personality; Rain could submerge himself. He was light but not lightweight, and age seemed to mean nothing to him. The only role that defeated him during the Langham years was that of Cardinal Wolsey in *Henry VIII*: the high greasiness of the self-made political priest calls for genuine middle-aged bulk. More affable ballooning, though, was well within his grasp, especially if it was French. As Ragueneau, the endearing poet-pastrycook of *Cyrano*, he practised up for an eventual triumph as Molière's Bourgeois Gentilhomme, delightedly aghast at the revelation that all his life he had been speaking prose.

His range during these years also took in ardent, ingenuous young love (Silvius in *As You Like It),* perky low comedy (Dromio of Syracuse in *The Comedy of Errors*), open-mouthed good nature (the Clown in *The Winter's Tale*), bilious professional misanthropy (Apemantus in *Timon of Athens*), uxorious brutality (the aptly-named Pinchwife in *The Country Wife*), seething Renaissance bloodlust (Tybalt in *Romeo and Juliet*), heroic mock-madness (Edgar in *King Lear*), the most complex political and metaphysical argument (Ulysses in *Troilus*), and spruce diabolism (Iago in *Othello*). Even in the fifties and sixties, heyday of the company actor, this was remarkable. By textbook standards, the greatest of these roles was Iago, but nobody thought it his greatest performance. He was most impressive in a far less attractive

villain's part, the devious royal weakling of *King John*, holding his own against Plummer, who had the far more glamorous (and longer) role of the Bastard.

Rain's greatest triumph, and in its way his greatest show of versatility, was in a single role spread across nine years. In 1958 he was a coolly heroic Prince Hal in *Henry IV, Part One*. In 1965 he returned to the character, in both Part One and Part Two, and the long march of events — from the prince's blithe highway robbery with his low-life friends through the test of battle and the achingly tense relationship with his father to the merciless rejection of Falstaff — inspired a more sombre, more ruthless, more moving performance: a study of a young king growing up. He completed it the following year with a Henry V who of necessity was more Machiavellian than the general run but was still a youth being tested, and in full public view — a man who groomed himself for a role and finally merged into it: a consummation partly happy, partly sad and — in the fullest and least reductive sense — ironic.

Of the Canadian actors brought into the company by Langham himself, Plummer and Colicos inevitably take precedence, the latter able to move from virtuoso showings as Lear, Timon, and Cyrano to ringing supporting work as Caliban and Hector. Gracefully poised between youth and middle age, with a clear imaginative shot at senility, Colicos was — at least until the advent of Brian Bedford a dozen years later — the nearest the Stratford Festival ever had to a traditional resident leading man.

But there were others. Peter Donat, as Florizel in *The Winter's Tale* and as Troilus, became the period's ranking juvenile, though more notable was his barnstorming cutpurse Pistol in

## Send in
## the Clowns

Throughout the years, Festival audiences have been treated to the antics of the accomplished actors who play clowns and amusing characters in productions ranging from Shakespeare to Gilbert and Sullivan. (Above) Eric Christmas in *Twelfth Night* (1966), (right) Edward Atienza in *As You Like It* (1972), and (below) Eric Donkin and Douglas Chamberlain in *The Gondoliers* (1995).

*Henry IV*: a long-range forecast of his re-emergence in the 1990s as a classical character actor, quieter now and with a touch of greatness, first with the Atlantic Theatre Festival in Wolfville, Nova Scotia (again with Langham), and then with the Soulpepper company in Toronto. Eric Christmas, already a veteran before he came to Stratford, played urban clowns (Bardolph), rural clowns (Costard), scabrous clowns (Thersites), and plain clown-clowns (Feste). For some reason Stratford actors named Eric have suffered, or perhaps benefited, from a kind of baptismal type-casting: they have all played comics (or, if no funny roles were available, old men). Eric House, for example, a comedic ornament of the Guthrie epoch, stayed on into the earlier years of Langham's.

Hugh Webster came in on a wave of comic glory as Christopher Sly in Langham's *Taming of the Shrew*, and went out on another as a fine Fool to Colicos's King Lear. And with these should perhaps be linked the Australian Max Helpmann, who specialized at this stage in the more dignified roles that generally go unnoticed: the Duke of Somewhere at the edges of a history play. He was to remain at the Festival for three decades and — in a reversal of the frequent experience of supporting actors — the longer he stayed, the less for granted he was taken. He also had a spell as company manager, thus supplying one of the first examples of a recurring pattern at Stratford whereby prominent actors either retired into or emerged from the theatre's offices and workshops.

Between Australia and Canada Helpmann had worked for a time in Britain, as had Leo Ciceri. Ciceri, a Montreal actor, began at Stratford in 1960 playing subsidiary juveniles. One of those actors who, as the saying goes, look good in a tunic, he had appeared in London in a succession of Greek-myth roles, so it was appropriate that he should have his first real break at Stratford in *Troilus and Cressida*. He played Achilles, transformed by Shakespeare from noble if sulky warrior to "great-sized coward." People never knew he had it in him, and he surprised them still more a few years later with his Malvolio in *Twelfth Night*.

Ciceri had in fact become a character actor, scoring his most significant success as Henry Bolingbroke, whom he played across three plays, from the usurper of *Richard II* to the troubled, death-haunted king of the two parts of *Henry IV*. This Henry can be played as a mere "politician," a word even more opprobrious to the Elizabethans than to us. Ciceri's Henry, though, had a conscience, and it was both his downfall and his salvation. Playing cunningly and sensitively off Hutt's Richard and Rain's Hal, he presented the Shakespearean view of kingship as something you're stuck with: hard enough if you're born to it, agonizing if you achieve it, and intolerable if it's thrust upon you.

Some tangled history is in order here. Ciceri had studied in London at the Old Vic School, which for the brief period of its existence — the late 1940s and early fifties — was probably the most highly regarded theatre school Britain has ever had. Douglas Rain had trained there, as had such future English stars as Joan Plowright and Keith Michell. The school had been started when the Old Vic itself seemed

In 1960 Tyrone Guthrie returned to Stratford to direct his first
production for the Music Festival: Gilbert and Sullivan's HMS Pinafore.
Its costumes and set were designed by Brian Jackson (centre).
The head of the property department since 1955, Jackson began
designing for the Festival in 1957. The 1960 Gilbert and Sullivan
production, featuring Irene Byatt (above, left) as Buttercup, was
followed in 1961 by The Pirates of Penzance, with Guthrie again
directing and Jackson designing. Pinafore was the first
Stratford production to appear on television.

*Leo Ciceri (above), wearing a striking costume designed by Desmond Heeley, played Bolingbroke in* Richard II *(1964). In his tenth Stratford season, Tony van Bridge (below) appeared as Exeter in the 1966 production of* Henry V.

to be on the fast track to becoming Britain's official National Theatre. When this prospect disappeared (temporarily, as it turned out), the school and associated activities were closed down. It was Guthrie, in charge of the Vic for a year during its darkest and most troubled period, who must take responsibility for the closure, and it may have been the unwisest thing he ever did.

It was ironic, too, since actors trained at the Vic School or members of the Vic company between 1950 and 1953 were to be among the vital components of Stratford's development under both Guthrie and Langham. Rain's rapid rise was no accident. Douglas Campbell, too, though hardly a Vic School type of actor (he would probably have found its rigorous European-style methods intolerably arty), was an Old Vic theatre stalwart. He had played Othello there, under Langham's direction, and was to repeat the role at Stratford in 1959, though both performances were received with respect rather than enthusiasm.

A Vic contemporary of Campbell's, who came to Stratford in 1955 and stayed to become a pillar of the company, was the invaluable Tony van Bridge. Five years older than Campbell and slighter in both lungs and physique, he would never be cast in a tragic lead, but in other respects he seemed initially to be Campbell's spiritual understudy. When Campbell played Pistol, he was Bardolph; when Campbell was Claudius to Plummer's Hamlet, van Bridge played the Gravedigger. Gradually he took on the great comic characters. He was Dogberry in *Much Ado About Nothing*, Bottom in *A Midsummer Night's Dream* (under

Campbell's direction, as it happened), and Falstaff in *Henry IV* and *The Merry Wives*. He conquered in all of them. Van Bridge's native tone is that of an English country gentleman run to seed. He could flavour it with dialect for the broader roles, dilate it with sour exaggeration for the numbskull Ajax in *Troilus*, make it sound like the accent of truth itself for the faithful Kent in *King Lear*, or play it like a keyboard in order to sound all the notes of Falstaff — an uproarious, heartbreaking performance (or pair of performances), among the most highly regarded in the Stratford record.

Powys Thomas was an Old Vic School graduate of the same vintage as Ciceri. He came to Stratford in 1957, as the Player King to Plummer's Hamlet. He was — by right of name, voice, and temperament — the company's primary Welshman: whenever *Henry IV* came round, as it did twice in his time, his right to play the proudly mystical Owen Glendower passed unchallenged. His most lasting contribution, though, to Stratford and to the Canadian theatre in general, lay in training others as he himself had been trained. In the late 1960s he became the first director of Stratford's actors' workshops, after serving from 1960 to 1965 as the first artistic director of the English section of the new National Theatre School in Montreal.

Mervyn (universally known as "Butch") Blake, like Thomas, came from the English to the Canadian Stratford in 1957. He stayed until the end of the millennium, by which point he was in his nineties, was universally loved, had appeared in every Shakespeare play, and had been in more Festival productions than anybody else. By the end of that time, of course, he was playing one-scene

# The Stratford Film Festival

The first Stratford Film Festival, held at the Avon Theatre in 1956 under the direction of Tom Patterson, showed documentaries such as the National Film Board's *The Stratford Adventure*; full-length features from around the world, including Spain's *Marcelino Pan y Vino*; and such award-winning cartoons as *Gerald McBoing Boing*. Attracting more than 6,500 spectators in its second year, the festival quickly became a major international event, the first of its kind in North America. The Avon's facilities could not handle the crowds, however, and the festival was suspended in 1962, by which time competitors had begun to spring up in Canada and the U.S. Nonetheless, the festival enjoyed a second flourishing period upon its revival in 1971, before it was finally retired in 1976. At its height, the Stratford International Film Festival combined screenings of contemporary work from more than forty different countries — including such modern classics as *Hiroshima Mon Amour*, *Sons and Lovers*, the Russian *King Lear*, and *Mon Oncle Antoine* — with a full programme of lectures, retrospectives, and symposiums with celebrated filmmakers and critics.

*The 1959 Film Festival saw former Stratford stars Alec Guinness and Irene Worth returning in celluloid form in* The Scapegoat *(above).*

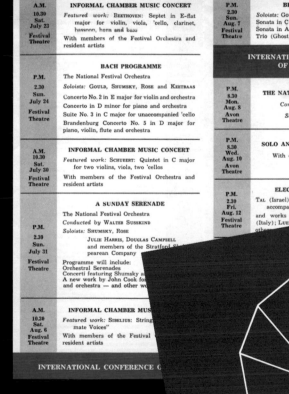

## FESTIVAL MUSIC PROGRAMME 1960

| A.M. 10.30 Sat. July 23 Festival Theatre | INFORMAL CHAMBER MUSIC CONCERT |
|---|---|
| | *Featured work:* BEETHOVEN: Septet in E-flat major for violin, viola, 'cello, clarinet, bassoon, horn and bass |
| | With members of the Festival Orchestra and resident artists |

| P.M. 2.30 Sun. July 24 Festival Theatre | BACH PROGRAMME |
|---|---|
| | The National Festival Orchestra |
| | *Soloists:* GOULD, SHUMSKY, ROSE and KEETBAAS |
| | Concerto No. 2 in E major for violin and orchestra |
| | Concerto in D minor for piano and orchestra |
| | Suite No. 3 in C major for unaccompanied 'cello |
| | Brandenburg Concerto No. 5 in D major for piano, violin, flute and orchestra |

| A.M. 10.30 Sat. July 30 Festival Theatre | INFORMAL CHAMBER MUSIC CONCERT |
|---|---|
| | *Featured work:* SCHUBERT: Quintet in C major for two violins, viola, two 'cellos |
| | With members of the Festival Orchestra and resident artists |

| P.M. 2.30 Sun. July 31 Festival Theatre | A SUNDAY SERENADE |
|---|---|
| | The National Festival Orchestra |
| | *Conducted by* WALTER SUSSKIND |
| | *Soloists:* SHUMSKY, ROSE |
| | JULIE HARRIS, DOUGLAS CAMPBELL and members of the Stratford Shakespearean Company |
| | Programme will include: Orchestral Serenades Concerti featuring Shumsky and A new work by John Cook for and orchestra — and other wo |

| A.M. 10.30 Sat. Aug. 6 Festival Theatre | INFORMAL CHAMBER MUSI |
|---|---|
| | *Featured work:* SIBELIUS: String mate Voices" |
| | With members of the Festival resident artists |

INTERNATIONAL CONFERENCE O

| P.M. 2.30 Sun. Aug. 7 Festival Theatre | BEETHOVEN PROGRAMME |
|---|---|
| | *Soloists:* GOULD, SHUMSKY, ROSE |
| | Sonata in C minor for violin and piano |
| | Sonata in A major for 'cello and piano |
| | Trio (Ghost) for piano, violin and 'cello |

INTERNATIONAL CONFERENCE OF COMPOSERS

| P.M. 8.30 Mon. Aug. 8 Avon Theatre | THE NATIONAL FESTIVAL ORCHESTRA |
|---|---|
| | *Conducted by* VICTOR FELDBRILL |
| | *Soloists:* To be announced |

| P.M. 8.30 Wed. Aug. 10 Avon Theatre | SOLO AND CHAMBER MUSIC CONCERT |
|---|---|
| | With composers in performances of their own works |

| P.M. 2.30 Fri. Aug. 12 Festival Theatre | ELECTRONIC MUSIC CONCERT |
|---|---|
| | TAL (Israel): Concerto for piano and electronic accompaniment; composer at the piano. and works by BADINGS (Nether (Italy); LUENING and othe |

Stratford 10th International Film Festival 1974

Avon Theatre September 13 - 22

STRATFORD'S 10TH INTERNATIONAL FILM FESTIVAL

## *"I perfumed the makeup..."*

### Zoe Caldwell

I was preparing for Cleopatra for about three months before, physically getting my body into proper condition — not shape, condition to do that massive role. And my voice and my emotions. I had brought some spectacular blowups of Egyptian gods, goddesses, kings, queens, everything. I had a little house in St. Marys which was absolutely chock-a-block with everything that was Egyptian and erotic. Then I perfumed the house, so I was almost drowned in Cleopatra. And I worked out a special makeup for my entire body, and I perfumed the makeup, too. So I was living with her for a long time.

I had a yellow Jeep with a red top. I drove like billy-bedamned to get away from that house that was so full of Cleopatra.

roles, like the good Old Men of *King Lear* and *Macbeth*. (He had never, it seems, played young men: even back in '54 at the English Stratford he had been cast as Nestor, the oldest man in the canon, in *Troilus and Cressida*.) In his earlier Festival years, though, he played more substantial senior parts — Quince in the *Dream*, Baptista in the *Shrew*, a couple of Chekhovian elders, above all Gloucester in *King Lear* — and gave substantial performances in them.

Everything connects. And nowhere more satisfyingly than in the fact that one of Powys Thomas's first crop of students at the National Theatre School was a young American-born actress who had gone there at his urging and whose name was Martha Henry.

Women traditionally fare less well in Shakespearean companies than men — they have far fewer opportunities — and Stratford had some trouble in building up a bank of young actresses comparable to its young actors. In a class apart was the Australian Zoe Caldwell. A leading young actress in her own country, she later won high praise at Stratford-upon-Avon and in London before arriving at the Canadian Stratford in 1961. Her dark lady Rosaline was one of the shining attractions of *Love's Labour's Lost*, and she remained in Canada, though not, to everyone's surprise, at Stratford.

Possibly great, certainly magnetic, Caldwell is difficult to categorize. She can be an eccentric husky-voiced comedienne, which is a recognized commodity, but a tragedienne in the same register is less easily accommodated. When she finally rejoined the Festival in 1967, it was to score a decisive success with an ebullient and uncommonly nuanced Mistress Page in *The Merry Wives* (success as either wife is surpris-

ingly rare, and nuance almost unheard-of) and to show tantalizing sparks of what-might-have-been as Cleopatra. By this time she had embarked on a Broadway career, having won a Tony the previous year as best supporting actress. The following year she won the major prize (for *The Prime of Miss Jean Brodie*) and was pretty much lost to Canada thereafter. She returned to Stratford only once, as a director.

Her opposite-number merry wife was Frances Hyland, happily capping a Stratford career that had begun auspiciously with Isabella and Portia under Guthrie. It had continued with a fine Ophelia and Desdemona, and a delicious Olivia in the Guthrie *Twelfth Night*, the closest, strangely, that she ever came in Langham's time to playing one of the major comedy heroines — the benchmark roles for an actress as the tragic heroes are for an actor. In the 1950s, when the Stratford powers wanted a Viola, Beatrice, or Rosalind, they sent abroad for Siobhan McKenna, Eileen Herlie, or Irene Worth. By the time these plays came round again, they were looking for someone younger. Hyland, abandoning her trademark fragility, had moved on to stronger or more riotous stuff: to Goneril, to Doll Tearsheet, to the ferocious Margaret of *Henry VI* and *Richard III*. She succeeded with all of them, as she also did with Mistress Ford and with the sad Varya of *The Cherry Orchard*. But somehow the feeling remained that the timing had been off, that Stratford's presumed first lady had never taken her rightful place. Like Zoe Caldwell, she was to return to Stratford only as a director.

Kate Reid's connection with the Festival was to prove longer but more erratic. A forceful and striking presence, only twenty-nine when she made her Stratford debut in 1959, she was immediately cast in what had traditionally been middle-aged roles: Emilia in *Othello*, the patient Katharine of Aragon in *Henry VIII*, Juliet's Nurse. The last was one of her best performances of this period, along with one of her rare chances at a comic heroine, the decidedly impatient Katherina of *The Taming of the Shrew*, a role that, characteristically and satisfyingly, she did not underplay. Her climactic role in these years was Madame Ranevskaya in *The Cherry Orchard*. Some, perhaps expecting the traditional Chekhovian mist, thought her miscast; Timothy Findley called her "luminous." By this time she too had become a recognized actress on Broadway, and she shuttled between the U.S. and Canada for the rest of her career.

Stratford needed its own girl. Martha Henry, arriving fully-fledged in 1962 at the age of twenty-four, was the answer to a prayer. She had acted professionally both before and since her training at the National Theatre School, but effectively her career began at Stratford.

Technically it began there with Lady Macduff: only one scene but, as large-part actors always say to small-part actors, while you're on you count. Two nights later, however, she was Miranda in *The Tempest*. Lightning struck and an entire audience fell in love, along with most of the press. She was a barefoot enchantress: in Walter Kerr's words "a small, clear pool of innocence in an ambiguous world." Being an innocent, Miranda may seem an ideal role for a Shakespearean debutante, but the part also needs technical authority, and it is unusual for one to be the vehicle for the other. Henry's decisive success in the role was very rare.

*Bruno Gerussi as Ariel stands on the balcony watching Peter Donat (left) as Ferdinand, William Hutt (centre) as Prospero, and Martha Henry as Miranda in the 1962 production of* The Tempest.

Promotion came quickly, inevitably, and rewardingly. The next year Henry played Cressida: in her way another innocent but one who made the fatal mistake of believing that she wasn't. Bravely and unusually, Henry's performance neither condemned the girl nor excused her; she simply was. John Pettigrew's description nailed her precisely: she "recognized that the key to Cressida's character is that she has none, a point magnificently etched by an expression of frightening vacuity on her final exit." As it happens the Troilus she betrayed, Peter Donat, had been her adored and adoring Ferdinand the year before; Stratford was advancing its juveniles in tandem. Even more interesting, from a later perspective, was her relationship in these productions to William Hutt. In *The Tempest* he played her father, counselling chastity; in *Troilus* her uncle, pushing the opposite. As the years passed she was to be recognized as his Stratford counterpart, doyenne to his doyen, and the years between them seemed psychologically to narrow so that they could — on one occasion to shattering effect (in Eugene O'Neill's *Long Day's Journey Into Night*) — play husband and wife.

Langham's aborted departure from the artistic directorship at the end of the 1962 season had been based on the assumption that he had found a worthy successor in Peter Coe, a British director riding very high on the international success of his production of *Oliver!* This plan was scuppered when Coe blotted his copy-book in fairly spectacular fashion with what was meant to be a calling-card production of *Macbeth*. This turned out to be a ritualistic staging in which the witches controlled the action from the first moment of the play, and with it the protagonist.

Plummer played him as a psychotic wreck who found some kind of redemption in surrendering to evil, while Kate Reid portrayed his lady as an enthusiastic housewife, regressing to childhood for her sleepwalking.

According to legend, the critics, without exception, hated it. But very few shows, when the record is inspected, turn out to have received the unanimous raves or pans that their subsequent "critical reputation" would suggest, and this *Macbeth* is no exception. A few critics thought it not merely wayward but incompetent, but the violence of their reactions suggests that the show must have had something going for it.

In this respect it's instructive to read Walter Kerr, the best and liveliest critic covering Stratford at the time and on this occasion the fairest. He wrote that "on its own odd, arresting, but essentially unmoving terms, the production sports its small prizes" and that Plummer's final disintegration was "extraordinarily well done." Kerr described Plummer's Macbeth in its earlier phases as "part sports hero, part potential criminal, part enthusiast, part oaf" (it sounds like the Coriolanus Plummer never got to play) and said that the performance's "surprises have something more than the fascination of novelty. They have a consistency within themselves." But, he added, "what they do not have is any consistency at all with the language of the play." The man Plummer presented was incapable of uttering the introspective speeches he was given, but he spoke them anyway. Shakespeare's text is not in itself sacred, but as long as it's being used, actors and directors had better try to make sense of it.

Coe was put on probation, so to speak, signed to direct *Timon of Athens*

the following year. This was the production that Langham ended up triumphantly taking over, since Coe backed out at the very last moment. The rest of his career was troubled, but he did finally direct a Canadian theatre, running the Citadel Theatre in Edmonton for three tempestuous years.

Other English directors were imported, with mixed results. Peter Wood's *As You Like It* (1959) elicited from Brooks Atkinson the ultimate putdown: that the director obviously didn't think it was a very good play. (That the critic seemed inclined to agree with him only made it worse.) Actually, Wood was far too smart to believe any such thing, but he was probably trying too hard. He had made his name in London the previous year with a superb production of O'Neill's gigantic *The Iceman Cometh*, following it up with a handsome staging of Schiller's *Mary Stuart* in which Irene Worth, his fine Stratford Rosalind, had played the title role. His reputation was also enhanced by his background and even, crazy though it may sound, by his name: being young, university-educated and called Peter, he was regarded as next in line to his namesakes Hall and Brook. He had the air of a classical director, but what nobody noticed was that he had never before directed a major Shakespeare production (nor has he done many since). The demanding Festival stage was not the best place to practise.

Douglas Seale, a contrastingly experienced English Shakespearean with a particular track record in the histories (he had put the neglected *Henry VI* plays on the map in the 1950s), was imported to direct the notoriously tricky *King John* (1960). He delivered, but not before incurring flak from his actors for the crime of being less intellectual than Langham, just as Langham himself had suffered for being less festive than Guthrie. In fact, Langham's principled refusal to intervene in Seale's production won him added respect and was a turning point in company morale.

Douglas Campbell, who as a director had the Guthrie gusto without his finesse, was entrusted with three plays over the twelve years. Two, *The Winter's Tale* (1958) and *Julius Caesar* (1965), were forgettable, though the latter may be remembered as the only staging of the play in which the acting honours went to the page-boy Lucius: he was played by a young actor named Heath Lamberts, later to be famous as one of Canada's (though, alas, never Stratford's) premier farceurs. Campbell did better with *A Midsummer Night's Dream* (1960), though Stratford regulars may have been surprised to find him directing rather than playing Bottom.

David William, known in Britain as a sensitive and scholarly director of the comedies, came in for a pleasing *Twelfth Night* (1966), in which Martha Henry played Viola, and a reasonable *Merry Wives* (1967). William was to be an important figure in later Stratford history, but the most consequential imported director at the time was Stuart Burge, to whom were entrusted the first three segments of the complete history cycle — *Richard II* (1964) and the two parts of *Henry IV* (the second, for audience-friendliness, renamed *Falstaff*, thus giving Tony van Bridge his one shot at a title role in his Stratford career). As with Seale, actors complained that Burge — an exceptionally nice man — gave them too little guidance, too much rope. Actors in England, where Burge has an extensive

résumé in theatre and television, have made the same complaint, but his shows usually come out well, so he must be doing something right. The Henries, indeed, might be considered the best Langham productions that Langham himself didn't direct. If lacking his rigour, they had the warmth and detail, the sense of a peopled world, that was the hallmark of his regime.

It took time, but the most exciting guest productions were directed by Canadians. In 1959 Jean Gascon and George McCowan, both former actors with the company, collaborated on the production of *Othello* in which the Douglasses Campbell and Rain squared off to no very memorable effect. Individually, the co-directors went on to better things. McCowan mounted very creditable productions of *Henry VIII* (1961) and *The Tempest* (1962). He also directed the new play *The Canvas Barricade* (1961) and had fun with it.

Jean Gascon was artistic director of the Théâtre du Nouveau Monde of Montreal, whose members had constituted the French court in Langham's 1956 production of *Henry V*. In 1956 he appeared with his company in a French programme of Molière farces at the Avon. Two years later they returned with *Le Malade*

*Martha Henry as Viola and Richard Monette as Sebastian (above) appeared in David William's 1966 production of* Twelfth Night. *(Below) Brian Jackson's design for a lady-in-waiting in the 1960 production of* A Midsummer Night's Dream, *directed by Douglas Campbell.*

N° 3
2ND LADY IN WAITING
DINAH CHRISTIE A.M.N.D.

DREAM ACT. I

FROCK OF HEAVY TEXTURED MATERIAL.

UNDERSKIRT & SLEEVES OF VELVET

LINING FOR HANGING SLEEVES OF LIGHT DULL SILK

FROCK EDGED IN VELVET & GILT BRAID

METALLIC GOLD MOTIFS ON SLEEVES & UNDERSKIRT

HANGING SLEEVES REMOVED FOR ACT II

BRIAN JACKSON 1960

*(Left) The 1961 production of* The Canvas Barricade *featured Lewis Gordon, holding the microphone, and,
from left to right, Ingi Bergman, Joseph Rutten, Douglas Chamberlain, Mary (Mia) Anderson, Anthony Robinow, and Dinah Christie.
(Right) In 1964's* Le Bourgeois Gentilhomme, *Douglas Rain (seated) appeared as Jourdain, Martha Henry (seated) as Dorimène,
and William Hutt (standing behind Henry) as Dorante.*

*Imaginaire*, a full-length Molière (also in French), which Gascon directed, and in 1963 he was invited to exercise his flair for farce on Shakespeare's own contribution to the genre, *The Comedy of Errors*. The show was inventive, the judicious thought, to the point of excess — farce on farce — but it was difficult to resist a staging that turned the endless hard-luck stories of the merchant Aegeon (Tony van Bridge) into a running gag that was still running through the curtain calls. Nathan Cohen, who hated it, grudgingly conceded that at least Gascon hadn't moved the play's setting from Italy: an odd comment since it takes place in Asia Minor. The following year Stratford took the logical next step and had Gascon direct a major Molière, in English, on the Festival stage: *Le Bourgeois Gentilhomme* with a full complement of music and dance. The show was a candy-flavoured romp, not necessarily false to its text, but audiences may have begun to wonder if Gascon could offer

them anything more substantial.

He proved in 1966 that he could. In Montreal he had directed a French-language production of *The Dance of Death*, Strindberg's most exhaustive and, in its way, exhilarating dramatization of the married state as something both intolerable and inescapable. He himself played the monstrous bullet-headed Captain, with Denise Pelletier (French Canada's foremost actress) his vindictive and — in this rendering — deceptively ladylike wife and Jean-Louis Roux as their unfortunate friend Kurt, a weekend guest in hell. Now they repeated it in English.

Strindberg was coming into fashion as black comedy, which can be used by English-speaking actors as an excuse for denaturing him. It seems unlikely in fact that he had a sense of humour: he took his own sufferings very seriously, and though he had the genius to recognize his own self-pity, that never stopped him from indulging it. Gascon and company

had the force and the daring to take the play full throttle, and in unleashing its horror they also revealed its pity. Many, Robertson Davies and Nathan Cohen among them, thought the production the greatest ever seen at Stratford.

Meanwhile, another Canadian director was establishing himself on the Festival stage. There were connections here: in 1964 John Hirsch had directed Pelletier and Gascon in a triumphant *Mother Courage* in Montreal. In 1965 Hirsch, the artistic director of the Manitoba Theatre Centre, came to Stratford to direct *The Cherry Orchard*, the Festival's first Chekhov. Chekhov's characters are islands of loneliness (or clumps of non-communication), and the platform stage, craftily used, can actually accent their isolation. It is a challenge, but Hirsch, already a world-class director, was up to it.

Douglas Campbell's performance as the rich peasant Lopahin, trying desperately to save the feckless Madame

Ranevskaya from herself, was especially notable; like his Henry VIII four years earlier, it suggested that Campbell, usually cast for buffo comedy or basso tragedy, was actually at his best — certainly his most sensitive — in the space between.

Hirsch returned the following year to take up what was left of the history cycle. This meant directing a play called *Henry VI*, stitched together from the first one-and-a-half parts of Shakespeare's trilogy of that name. The adaptation had been made by John Barton, of the Royal Shakespeare Company, to be directed by himself and Peter Hall. A second play, *Edward IV*, had taken care of the rest and the RSC had mounted both — along with their more familiar sequel, *Richard III* — in 1963 in a stunningly staged sequence entitled *The Wars of the Roses*. Cutting Barton's *Henry VI* text adrift from his *Edward IV*, however, proved a fatal error. Hirsch's production was fine as far as it went, but it didn't go far enough: literally. Lacking its companion piece, it left its audience feeling lost and baffled, wondering — as the English audience never had to — just which baron was which, and why they should care. Audience figures were disappointing, and *Edward IV*, planned for the next season, was cancelled, leaving the cycle essentially incomplete and obliging Hirsch to direct *Richard III* as a separate play.

He did this excitingly, enforcing a hard, nihilistic vision in which every man was as bad as his brother or even as his uncle, the victorious Richmond as monstrous as the defeated Richard. Alan Bates's Richard aroused controversy by virtually committing suicide on his enemy's sword. This was not as novel as some people thought. Years later, when Brian Bedford performed a similar act of self-immolation in Robin Phillips's production, nobody minded.

They'd had time to get used to it.

There was more affection, obviously, and even more true epic scope in Hirsch's production at the Avon, that same year, of James Reaney's piece of reminiscent Canadiana, *Colours in the Dark*. It was, apart from Langham's own *Antony and Cleopatra*, the last production of this great era.

Stratford had found — what might have seemed impossible a decade before — not just one but two strong, non-imported candidates for the succession. In the event they both got the job, at least for a time. Gascon and Hirsch were installed as joint directors, with a whole new set of opportunities and challenges. The Langham years had been great ones, with a freshness, range, and assurance that probably could never be recaptured. The Festival could never be so young and confident again: it would rarely find itself doing a Shakespeare play for the first or second time. Nor, it seemed, could it ever build so strong, fluent, and united a company. With the Avon now established as the Festival's second stage for drama, there were two theatres to fill; it would have to diversify.

Like nearly every one of Stratford's artistic directors, Langham would return as a guest. Guthrie, who had been *his* guest after being his employer, made no secret of the admiration he felt for his protégé, the man who had taken over his glorious, treacherous stage and made it work even better than he himself had. Writing in 1968, he described Langham's Shakespeare productions at Stratford as "in my opinion, the most consistently interesting and exciting of our time."

And, good as Langham was then, he got better.

---

## "We got to the final scene..."

### Alan Bates

One of the things I loved about John Hirsch was how he would listen to other people. In *Richard III*, we got to the final scene. The battle is about to commence, and the speeches that Richmond and Richard have are very similar. John said, "I don't know how to stage this. I don't know what to do."

My understudy, Neil Dainard, a superb teacher and actor, suddenly said, " I know what to do. You have them both on stage at the same time, and you mix the speeches."

It was a fantastic idea, because it symbolized the insanity of war: that a man standing for evil and a man standing for good can actually muster their troops by saying almost exactly the same thing. John said, "Brilliant," and we did it.

## The Making of Soldiers

Swords and armour are essential items in any Shakespearean theatre's stock of props and costumes, and in this area, as in so many others, the finely detailed work of the Stratford Festival's artisans is the envy of North America. Virtually all swords and daggers used on stage are real weapons, made (and securely stored) in the Patrick Crean Armoury, named after the Festival's renowned former fight director. To ensure the actors' safety, fights must be meticulously choreographed and rehearsed (below). In his long career at the Festival, Crean not only arranged fights for numerous productions but also helped actors prepare for their roles as soldiers. In the bottom photograph he is shown coaching John Colicos as Hector (left) and Leo Ciceri as Achilles (right) for their fight scene in the 1963 production of *Troilus and Cressida*.

*Stephen Russell (opposite) holds one of the swords used in the 1979 production of* Richard II. *Although it and the intricate dagger (top) are metal, stage armour is made mostly out of moulded fibreglass. Steel is not only incredibly time-consuming to hammer into shape, it is also heavy to wear and produces distracting clanking sounds. Jeremy G. Cox fits together the pieces of a suit of armour (above, left), and thousands of metal rings are connected to make chain mail (above, right) for a costume worn in the 1962 production of* Macbeth.

# Chapter Three

# The Gascon Years

owards the end of his tenure Michael Langham was prone to saying in interviews that the overwhelming popularity of Shakespeare evident in the 1960s might well dwindle within the next ten or fifteen years, and that the Stratford Festival would have to diversify in order to survive. Thirty years on, his prophecy seems to have been fulfilled: Shakespeare's plays now constitute only a fraction of the repertoire in any Stratford season. It was not, however, Langham but his 1968 successor, Jean Gascon, who tilted the repertoire firmly away from the Shakespearean monopoly. It was under Gascon, too, that the Avon Theatre came into its own as a dramatic stage: despite some fine productions on the Festival stage, he is more identified with the Avon than is any other Stratford artistic director. Since the Avon, being a proscenium theatre, was a non-Shakespearean space (at least according to Guthrian precepts), the two developments went together.

The planned partnership between Gascon and John Hirsch lasted only two years. It was never truly a partnership, since Gascon had been appointed executive artistic director while Hirsch was positioned one step down as associate artistic director. Hirsch, though he had

requested a lighter workload, was temperamentally unfitted to be anybody's subordinate, and he and the more placid Gascon were not compatible.

Hirsch, the greatest director ever to have grown up in Canada, was also one of the most uneven, and his work at Stratford in those two years was generally not his best. He directed two major Shakespeares. *A Midsummer Night's Dream* (1968) was somewhat influenced by the then-fashionable and extremely reductive theories of Jan Kott, at least to the extent that Theseus's court was inhabited by a collection of toothless satyrs, but the production's dark edges hardly impinged on its otherwise quite traditional funny lovers and funnier clowns.

Hirsch's *Hamlet* (1969) was less enjoyably mainstream. Its prince was a young actor, Kenneth Welsh, who had been at Stratford only three years and whose most testing roles in that period had been Hastings in *Richard III* and Octavius in *Julius Caesar*. His "hippie Hamlet" received mixed reviews (like most Hamlets), with praise for its energy outweighed by dismay at its inability to communicate the text. Welsh, clearly, had been promoted over his head, and though he stayed three more years with the company and was

*Jean Gascon (above, left, and opposite) and John Hirsch (above, right) worked together for two years as executive artistic director and associate artistic director respectively.*

## "*I tripped over the coffin...*"

### Kenneth Welsh

It was 1966. I arrived for a rehearsal of *Henry VI* about five minutes after ten in the morning, thinking I'm just going to be standing around. There was the stage manager saying, "Hurry up. There's your script. You have to get on."

I said, "Really? I have a part?"

So I went on, and there was John Hirsch: "Hurry up! You are late. Now, you come on down the stairs and you speak: 'Awake, awake, English nobility!'"

So I came running down the steps, and there was the whole contingent of Stratford actors: Bill Hutt, Tony van Bridge, Max Helpmann. And there was the coffin of Henry V. I came running on holding the script and I tripped over the coffin. Fell flat on my face. My script went sliding down the tunnel. And I was lying there, face down on the Stratford stage. My very first entrance on it.

*Angela Wood as Gertrude and Kenneth Welsh as Hamlet*

a noteworthy Edgar in *King Lear*, he was a Stratford star only by default. (He did, however, become a star in the outside world.)

Hirsch would take a shot at anything: he seemed as happy staging a nightclub revue as directing exquisite interpretations of Chekhov. His two most notable productions in this period were *The Satyricon* and *The Three Musketeers*: one was a disaster and the other a triumph. *The Satyricon*, staged at the Avon in 1969, was the disaster, a new musical based on the satirical Roman novella by Petronius. It aimed — like many other shows, before and since — both to condemn a society's supposed decadence and to entertain by showing it off: orgies topped off by moralizing. It had a talented American composer, Stanley Silverman, who had written music for Hirsch's Shakespeare productions. It was also enthusiastically performed, but its blend of silliness and pretension dragged it down. The script was written, rather hurriedly, by the Festival's new literary manager, Tom Hendry, taking over from his predecessor, Peter Raby, who had — the appropriate phrase for this production — decamped.

Earlier, Raby had supplied the text for Hirsch's great Stratford achievement, an adaptation of Alexandre Dumas's *The Three Musketeers* (1968) that filled the Festival stage, and indeed the whole house, with gorgeous swashbuckling excess.

Putting the *Musketeers* on stage was a way of recapturing all the decorative, gymnastic, and narrative delights of *Cyrano de Bergerac*, without encumbering them with anything so troublesome as a play. (Both concern seventeenth-century swordsmen from Gascony. Stratford at this time was very big on

Gascons.) Raby's adaptation could function only as scaffolding, rather like the book for a musical, though it did manage to get an extraordinary amount of the story on to the stage (most versions get as far as the affair of the diamond studs and then wrap up as quickly as possible) and also an extraordinary number of the characters. Zestfully sketched in the book, these retained at least some of their liveliness on stage. Dumas's wit suffered — the musketeers' verbal fencing took distant second place to its non-stop physical equivalent — but Hirsch never lost his sense of humour amidst the swordplay.

Desmond Heeley designed another set of glowing costumes, Raymond Pannell composed adventure-music worthy of Hollywood, and the cast had a whopping time. Douglas Rain was D'Artagnan, and Martha Henry, then his wife, had something of a career breakthrough as the fiendish Milady. An actress hitherto noted for tact and refinement, even when playing Cressida, she here plunged into full-blooded melodrama (after, apparently, some initial hesitation in rehearsal) and came joyously out the other side. The mark on her acting style was permanent. The critical response ranged from rapture to a few inevitable displays of condescension from writers who had never learned what the theatre was for.

It is noticeable that in a seven-year term of office Gascon himself directed only four Shakespeares. Two of these — *The Merchant of Venice* (1970), with Donald Davis a dignified Shylock, and *The Taming of the Shrew* (1973), funny but forced — faded into the record; the plays themselves, of course, were old familiars. (The *Shrew* was the first play to be given a third Stratford production.) The other two had never

The Three Musketeers, *with Powys Thomas as Athos (below, left), James Blendick as Porthos (below, centre), and Christopher Newton as Aramis (below, right), was a hit. Although the production's many elaborate costumes (right) looked extravagant, they were made from manufacturer's samples picked up by designer Desmond Heeley in New York for $500. Satyricon's actors, including Jack Creley as Trimalchio (bottom), gave it their best, but the quickly written musical was panned by most of the critics.*

THREE MUSKETEERS.     MUSKETEER.

HEELEY 68

*(Inset) Before a performance of* Pericles, *designer Leslie Hurry (left) chats with director Jean Gascon (centre) and actor Edward Atienza (right). The production, which featured Tony van Bridge as Simonides (above, left of centre, and opposite), Martha Henry as Thaisa (centre), and Nicholas Pennell as Pericles (far right), was richly staged and costumed. Van Bridge remembers: "The costume seemed to be gown after gown after gown of different shimmering materials. Leslie Hurry looked at me and said, 'Yes. Well, act your way out of that!'"*

72

before been dared at Stratford: they were *Cymbeline* and *Pericles*, the two rarities in the notoriously tricky quartet of late romances. Both brought out the storyteller and the magician in Gascon and proved him, in his own way, a master showman of the platform stage.

*Cymbeline* (1970) was apparently receiving its first professional production in North America. Tanya Moiseiwitsch designed the costumes and was attacked for cheerfully mixing historical periods, but that was surely her and Gascon's point. The play, a serious fairy-tale, is almost a compendium of folklore, moving from stern Roman and ancient British history to the worlds of Snow White and Babes in the Wood. It is among other things a symphony of self-plagiarism: it has a transvestite heroine out of *As You Like It* or *The Merchant*, a daughter-banishing king who has been described as a watered-down Lear, jealousy scenes that echo *Othello*, and the most complicated scene of recapitulation and reconciliation that even the mature Shakespeare ever attempted. The unveiled coincidences always get laughs; the important thing is that they should be friendly laughs.

The same charm, the same affection for narrative, and the same willingness to exploit the spectacular opportunities written into plays conceived for a courtly audience at a time when masque was king were evident in Gascon's production of *Pericles*. It is the tale of a prince's wanderings and, being straightforwardly picaresque, is easier to realize on stage than the tangled cat's cradle of *Cymbeline*. Its coincidences and revelations are ladled out one at a time, and nobody laughs at them.

It too is a play whose every episode demands to be played full out for its own value, and one scene evoked a greater response here than seems to have been recorded of any other production. Pericles' wife, Thaisa, having apparently died at sea giving birth to their daughter Marina at the height of a storm, is tossed overboard by the sailors, but is washed ashore and revived by the aristocratic physician Cerimon. Thaisa is not usually cast to strength (Marina is the obvious star role), but here she was played by Martha Henry. Powys Thomas, playing one of his gentler Celtic wizards, was Cerimon, and they brought this more whimsical resurrection scene almost to the level of the one that so movingly concludes *The Winter's Tale*.

*Pericles* proved to be something of a valedictory for Gascon: first seen in 1973, it was brought back the following year, the first Stratford Shakespeare to be so revived. It served the same farewell function for its designer, Leslie Hurry, who had previously worked at Stratford on productions by Langham and Hirsch. He had also designed the most important Stratford production never seen at Stratford: Tyrone Guthrie's revival of his legendary version of Marlowe's *Tamburlaine the Great*. Guthrie had first staged this at the Old Vic in 1951. He restaged it, in Toronto and New York, as a way of keeping the Stratford ensemble together between the 1955 and 1956 seasons.

It is possible that the francophone Gascon felt insecure about directing the more familiar Shakespeare plays at Stratford and was happier with those that were less encrusted with tradition and less open to comparison. But it is also indicative of an inquiring spirit: the Stratford repertoire during his tenure was more adventurous than at any other time before or since. There is an irony here. When the Stratford company took productions to other Canadian cities (which it did more often in these years than in any others) it was billed as "the Stratford National Theatre of Canada." It is difficult to see how a theatre can be called national when it is principally devoted to the work of a foreign playwright; but, more to the point, no country needs a national theatre as anything other than a convenient title for a major classical company. The best National Theatres have in practice been international, exploring the best drama of the world. Shakespeare did suffer

*William Hutt's costume for* Tartuffe *(below) was designed by Robert Prévost. Renowned for his work in opera, ballet, television, and theatre, this Montreal-born designer first joined the Festival in 1958; his other credits during Gascon's era included* The Threepenny Opera *and* La Vie Parisienne.

somewhat under Gascon's directorate, but it is arguable that this was more than offset by the creative attention paid to other playwrights.

Gascon's regime, coming between the blockbuster eras of Michael Langham and Robin Phillips, has been much undervalued. Three of his non-Shakespearean productions rank among the Festival's greatest achievements. All, oddly enough, were praised to the skies by critics who nonetheless went on patronizing him. Two of them, as might be expected, were of French comedies.

Georges Feydeau's bilious, spectacularly carpentered farces are the most fun you can have while still remaining cultural; since the 1960s they have been where the English-speaking classical theatre goes for a good time. Most companies have one triumphant Feydeau production lurking somewhere in their closet, and *Le Dindon*, translated here as *There's One in Every Marriage* ("The Turkey," in a North American theatre, would have had unfortunate connotations), was Stratford's. Produced in 1971, it was a team effort, but the outstanding team-player was Jack Creley as a roué who finds himself receiving an offer he cannot refuse from the respectable woman of his dreams, just after awakening from a night with a conscientious professional. The production was promptly whisked to Broadway, where it was loved by every critic except Clive Barnes. Since he wrote for the *New York Times*, that was that.

However, in 1969 Barnes's colleague on the *Times*, Walter Kerr,

had given the Festival probably the best review in its history. The occasion was Gascon's production of *Tartuffe* in the now-standard rhymed translation by the American poet Richard Wilbur. Kerr, calling the production "greater than superb" and "seriously funny," accorded this *Tartuffe* the ultimate praise by calling it a realization of the value and potential of the theatre itself: "It is the stage at peace with itself, quietly proud of itself, sensually aware of itself, uncluttered, uncompromised, securely at home with its simplest methods and most profound materials. It is the stage satisfied to be the stage, and making the magnificent most of it."

*Tartuffe* is not a play that lends itself to pageantry — it is in fact a domestic comedy, perhaps the greatest ever written — and Gascon's production bore down on the feeling of a family unit, disrupted by a grotesque but dangerous outsider. Enacting the play's skewed triangle — complacent husband, sensible wife, aspiring lover — were Stratford's very own and finest: Douglas Rain, Martha Henry, William Hutt. Kerr was especially rhapsodic over Henry's Elmire, "a good woman but never an innocent one." The production, not surprisingly, was revived the next year. It effectively established Molière as Stratford's second playwright, and that status, befitting the major classical theatre of a bilingual country, has never been challenged.

The third of Gascon's great productions was John Webster's *The Duchess of Malfi*, the first non-Shakespearean tragedy of the English Renaissance to be produced on the Festival stage and, as of this writing, still the only one. Stagings of these word-intoxicated plays have in recent years been grim, bilious, and monochromatic. The

downbeat approach fits one aspect of the plays but only one; Webster, like most of his contemporaries, obviously loved colour, especially velvet-black and blood-red. A Stratford production of *The Duchess* — certainly a Gascon production — was obviously going to go for splendour. It was, however, a disciplined kind of splendour: one in which the love and endurance of the virtuously passionate Duchess, destroyed by her brothers for the crime of marrying a social inferior, counted for as much as any of the horrors by which they sought to drive her, as their conscience-stricken agent Bosola says, "by degrees to mortification."

One scene exploded from the text and is still immediately recalled every time the production is mentioned. The Duchess with her husband and children seeks sanctuary in the church of Ancona; her brother the Cardinal has her banished from the city. Webster describes this action in a dumb-show; Gascon, taking the hint, as he did in his productions of the Shakespearean romances, turned the scene into a full-scale excommunication ceremony, the might of the Church arrayed upon the stage in full regalia, the audience's senses assaulted — as the Duchess herself was — with organ music and incense. The Festival's then resident lighting wizard, Gil Wechsler, may have done his finest work on this production.

When Stratford's junior rival, the Shaw Festival at Niagara-on-the-Lake, grew tired of restricting itself to the works of its house playwright, it found an ingenious and logical way of expanding its programme. The Niagara solution

*As Antonio in* The Duchess of Malfi *(above and below), Barry MacGregor (below, left, with Pat Galloway) was for the first time playing a character his own age. Gascon's direction notes to him ranged from "Barry, you're not only juvenile, you're boring" to "Eh, Barry, you have the balls." "Because English wasn't his first language," recalls MacGregor, "he directed you in a much more direct way — the language was straight at you!"*

consisted of including plays written by other dramatists in Shaw's conveniently long lifetime; and since he lived nearly a hundred years the riches have been embarrassing enough to keep everybody happy ever since.

Stratford might have made a similar choice, by surrounding Shakespeare's plays with those of his contemporaries and his immediate predecessors and successors. The fact that in 1971 Stratford also programmed Ben Jonson's *Volpone*, which is more or less to Elizabethan-Jacobean comedy what *The Duchess* is to tragedy, suggested that such a scheme might actually be under way. In his enthusiastic review of *The Duchess*, Urjo Kareda, who at this period was the *Toronto Star*'s excellent theatre critic and was shortly to become the Festival's dramaturge, urged Stratford to follow this course. But he himself never pursued it when he had a voice in programming, and neither did anybody else. These are not for the most part well-known plays, and as Stratford has become richer but also more financially vulnerable, the prospects of its risking more of them on the Festival stage have become increasingly remote.

There was a kind of successor to *The Duchess* in the 1972 Stratford season — a play about Medici Italy, breathing the same air of conspiracy and revenge but written during the heyday of nineteenth-century French romanticism. Alfred de Musset's *Lorenzaccio* is a textbook example of the kind of large-scale play to which only a major institutional theatre could do justice; being unfamiliar, it is also a textbook example of the kind of play that such theatres generally avoid. (Stratford beat the British National Theatre to it by nearly a decade.) It is also a discursive play,

fragile in feeling despite its physical size. Its author was not much concerned with theatrical practicalities while writing it: his stage directions call for scores of on-stage horses and the immediate appearance of a banquet for forty people. Nobody but Gascon would have risked it. He gave it his accustomed sweep, but the standard of acting was down from the previous year.

Gascon's *Tartuffe* also had its sequel: a production in his last season (1974) of Molière's last play, *The Imaginary Invalid*. If it wasn't as good as the earlier show, then neither is the play, a one-joke farce masquerading as a full-length comedy of manners. All that lingers is the memory of a wistfully subdued William Hutt — a very frisky hypochondriac earlier in the evening — intoning by rote the medical jargon with which his doctors, true and false, had been plying him all evening. This was Gascon's second attempt at a comedy of quackery: the first had been Jonson's *The Alchemist* (1969), a far greater play but a diabolically difficult one. Built like a farce, written like a dense scholastic comedy, it proceeds in effect at two speeds simultaneously, and keeping the audience both amused and abreast is Herculean work. Gascon's production, like most others before and since, became a heavy-going romp: a theatrical oxymoron.

Gascon's overall record as a director of plays on the Festival stage was a fine one. Where he faltered — and what has cast a retrospective pall on his reign — was in finding other directors to match him. He was able once to bring back Langham, for a coruscating production of Sheridan's *School for Scandal* that was up to his highest comic level. But where Langham himself had nurtured two Festival-size

Canadian directors in Gascon and Hirsch, Gascon, with or without Hirsch, found none. The nearest was the Festival's literary manager, Michael Bawtree, who distinguished himself with a warm and unforcedly funny production of that other eighteenth-century favourite, Oliver Goldsmith's *She Stoops To Conquer* (1972, revived 1973), a play that always works but not always as well as this. He followed it with another comedy, a *Love's Labour's Lost* (1974) that was equally magical but far less well received. Rumours abounded, and were never effectively denied, that the production had been taken over by Robin Phillips, the Festival's director-in-waiting. (He assumed command the following season, but was present at this one as an observer.) Whoever did it, this was a golden production, remembered by one spectator as the first occasion on which he felt the full magic of the Festival theatre and sensed the harmony it could induce between stage and auditorium.

Douglas Campbell, of course, counted by now as a Canadian. He appeared in only one play and one opera during the Gascon regime, but he directed one of its opening productions: a stolid *Romeo and Juliet*, best remembered for having an incomprehensible Juliet, the French-Canadian actress Louise Marleau. The general complaint was not so much of her accent as of her timbre: every line came out as a squeak. It wasn't even as if the production had a concept to match Langham's bi-cultural *Henry V*, with the Capulets French and the Montagues English: Juliet's relatives were all given standard Stratford casting. (Langham indeed had toyed with, but abandoned, just such a concept for his 1961 production: the one that wound up starring Julie Harris and Bruno Gerussi.) To match his Quebec Juliet, Campbell had an American Romeo: Christopher Walken, on his way to a kind of movie stardom. The dynamism of his film work, though, was nowhere apparent in his Romeo.

Gascon turned to various British directors, with disappointing results. In truth, only one of those he brought over would have been regarded as first-rate

the auditorium. Irene Worth, playing her last role at Stratford, also acted on a big scale, reminding one critic more of Medea than of "a frustrated Norwegian hausfrau." Well, why not? More to the point perhaps was that, on the platform stage, Worth was clearly much older than Hedda is supposed to be, thus turning the play into what it is

*Montreal actress Louise Marleau undertook one of her first major English-language roles when she played Juliet opposite Christopher Walken's Romeo in* Romeo and Juliet *(left).* Hedda Gabler *(below) was Irene Worth's last role at Stratford. It was a star turn by an actress who was then considerably older than the part demands.*

in his native land. This was Peter Gill, a young director who had worked his way up at the Royal Court; his rediscovery of three plays by D. H. Lawrence was that theatre's highest achievement of the 1960s.

*Hedda Gabler* (1970), Stratford's first Ibsen, with its small cast and claustrophobic domestic setting, was a strange choice for the Festival stage, and Gill, in trying to exploit the space, only made it stranger. He used the balcony as the site of Hedda's private drama, up to and including her suicide, and had characters entering through

always in danger of becoming: an excuse for a star actress to play a famous role that she has unaccountably missed on the way up. The performance, in any case, seems to have run away with, and also away from, the production. Two reviewers independently speculated on Gill's inability to control so formidable an actress, and his subsequent career bears this out: wherever possible, he has avoided working with stars, or even with actors of strong individual temperament. This may explain why in the title role of his Stratford *Macbeth*

(1971) he cast an imported actor, Ian Hogg, whose main qualification for the part was his authentic Scottishness.

Casting him seemed to be a method of taking *Macbeth* down a peg. The play was dominated by a grey-coated chorus representing the common people, expressing their (mostly silent) resentment of the kings and thanes who murder and jockey for power while the state of the nation remains as miserable as ever. As a reaction to the play's storyline, this is not unreasonable (and politicized literary criticism has since made it quite fashionable). As a method of putting the play on stage, it is defeated by the fact that most of the actual text is concerned with Macbeth and his wife — if they are boring, then so is the evening. Wholesale rewriting would be the only way out, but Gill would not have countenanced such a thing. This indeed, is the abiding puzzle of his work at Stratford: a true son of the Royal Court, with its Spartan aesthetic and its rigorous devotion to text, he was known in Britain as a purist — indeed a puritan — director; only in Canada did he become cavalier. His *Macbeth* was generally rated as perverse as Peter Coe's nine years before but slightly less fun.

Two other visiting Englishmen were

*In 1971, the Festival presented its first (and, to date, only) production of* Volpone, *by Ben Jonson, best known of Shakespeare's contemporaries. William Hutt played the title role, with Ruby Holbrook as Lady Would-Be.*

best known for their work in television, which may explain why their work at Stratford seemed rather small. In 1969, near the beginning of the Gascon era, David Giles ("The Forsyte Saga") directed a cold-porridge *Measure for Measure*. In 1974, at its end, Peter Dews mounted Stratford's second attempt at the obstinately unpopular *King John*. Like his predecessor Douglas Seale, Dews had made his reputation as a director of the histories, in his case through a BBC TV production of the entire eight-play cycle, transmitted in 1960 under the title "An Age of Kings." Criminally forgotten now, these productions were and remain the high-water mark of televised Shakespeare. In their vigour and humour they captured much of what had been best in the previous decade's Old Vic tradition and combined it with a hard, unblinking look at textual subtleties, ironies, and parallels. Little of this, though, carried over into Dews's stage work, which tended, both in Britain and Canada, to the obvious and the coarse-grained: his *King John* was standard baronial, all roast beef and declamation.

Dews's very fine television Richard II had been David William. Known principally in Canada as a director, and so frequent a visitor to Stratford as hardly to seem a visitor at all, William was also recognized in England as a mellifluous lyric actor and a very sharp farceur. His Puritan Ananias in *The Alchemist*, for Dews on television and for Guthrie at the Old Vic, was unforgettable in its quivering Cockney self-righteousness. It was fitting, then, that his most memorable Stratford production under Gascon (and far more successful than Gascon's *The Alchemist*) should have been of the other Jonsonian masterpiece, *Volpone* (1971).

Transported to the nineteenth century, the production sensually embraced the play's cold eroticism, its equation of sexual and monetary greed ("The Turk is not more sensual in his pleasures / Than will Volpone"). Volpone's opening invocation to his gold, delivered from atop a fur-laden bed, became a lubricious parody of the Mass, more Guthrian than Guthrie. It also occasioned another fine double-act from Hutt and Rain, as the titular fox feigning death to fool his legacy-hunters and Mosca, his overreaching flyweight parasite.

William also directed two of the major Shakespeare tragedies. *Othello* (1973) was a generally acknowledged fiasco. William, one of theatre's most frequent flyers, had directed the play in Tel Aviv with Nachum Buchman, one of Israel's leading actors, as the Moor. In accordance with the widespread theatrical notion that a foreign-sounding actor will necessarily make a wilder, stranger, stronger Othello than any native anglophone could manage, and possibly inspired by vague memories of Frederick Valk, Stratford agreed to let William re-direct Buchman in English. He proved incomprehensible and, perhaps worse, sluggish. *King Lear* (1972) was far happier. William Hutt, who had already played the king in a touring production (generally known as "the Eskimo *Lear*") was still some way from the stunning performance he was to give when he approached Lear's own age, but he was already both powerful and moving (less powerful, though, than the high-decibel storm laid on by the theatre's new sound system), and William built a solid, unpretentious production around him. (This was the

## "*I ran down and grabbed it...*"

### Paul Gross

My mother told me that we were going to go to Stratford one day. I think I was eleven or twelve, and I'd seen very little theatre. It was Bill Hutt's King Lear. I haven't a vivid memory of the production, but I have this powerful, overwhelming kind of general feeling about the whole event: the drive to Stratford, the parking, the grounds, the trumpets. The going into the theatre and it becoming dark.

At some point there was a war staged in the black. You could hear this clanking of pikes and swords and things. And the head of a spear came off and landed in the aisle quite near me, so I ran down and grabbed it. I still have it.

*William Hutt as King Lear (1972)*

*Eric Donkin, a versatile actor whose work ranged from classical roles to musical comedy performances, played Estragon (above, left) opposite Powys Thomas's Vladimir (above, right) in* Waiting for Godot. *(Left) A costume designed by Murray Laufer for* The Marriage Brokers. *(Opposite) Diane D'Aquila and Gordon Thomson in a scene from* A Month in the Country.

production that occasioned the most famous of all Stratford anecdotes, the one in which Hutt interrupted the storm scene to announce the hockey results to a matinee audience plainly more interested in the game than in the play.)

The list of Festival Theatre directors is completed by Hutt himself, responsible for a Belle Epoque *Much Ado About Nothing* (1971) and a Watteau-esque *As You Like It* (1972). The latter was the better of the two, with the British-born and American-based comedienne Carole Shelley making her glorious Shakespearean debut as Rosalind, to her own trepidation and most other people's delight. The popular comedies are necessarily the backbone of any Shakespearean theatre: people have heard of them, and they are guaranteed to be at least passably funny. There had always been a tendency, at Stratford as everywhere else, to treat them as romps, but these were overdressed and overeager romps, from which the true spirit and sparkle had evaporated.

Hutt's first directing assignment at Stratford had been a fine *Waiting for Godot* in 1968 at the Avon; and in 1973, he returned there with a season of two Russian comedies: one gentle, Turgenev's *A Month in the Country*, and one wild, Gogol's *The Marriage Brokers*. The latter was greeted with the derision customarily bestowed by critics on old plays they have never heard of, and the former with the mild condescension that they reserve for plays they *have* heard of but know little about. Both in fact were good productions, the Gogol boasting hilarious performances by the American actor Leonard Frey, in a poseur role not unlike the one Hutt himself had played in the same author's *Government*

*Inspector*, and by Stratford's own Roberta Maxwell — Stratford's own because she had been the Festival's first teenage apprentice back in 1957 and had been justifying that early confidence ever since 1966 when she played Olivia in *Twelfth Night*.

Gascon's laudable ambition to expand the Stratford repertoire was less happily exemplified by his habitual use of the Avon for discrete groups of plays, performed by actors separate from those in the main Festival. At its best, this policy yielded the 1971 season of French farce, in which Gascon's production of *There's One in Every Marriage* was paired with Stephen Porter's of Eugene Labiche's gentler and airier *An Italian Straw Hat*. At its worst there was, in 1970, a trio of mildly experimental contemporary plays: *The Architect and the Emperor of Assyria*, a flimsily extended fantasia by the Peter Pan of the European avant-garde, Fernando Arrabal; *The Friends* by Arnold Wesker, a verbose lament for British socialism; and, liveliest of the bunch, *Vatzlav*, an absurdist satire by the Polish Slawomir Mrozek. The respective directors, all Stratford one-offs, were Chattie Salaman, Kurt Reis, and Colin George. Even those who liked the plays (and they all had their adherents) must have found them dwarfish and out-of-place in a full-sized house at a major festival; one might have been an interesting change of pace, but three together were a non-event.

Earlier at the Avon, in 1968, Gascon had mounted a moderate production of *The Seagull*, distinguished by the Madame Arkadina of Denise Pelletier. In 1969 he staged a totally self-contained production of Peter Luke's *Hadrian VII*, based on the novel by Baron Corvo about the man who

## The Tom Patterson Theatre

In 1971, the Festival opened what was then known as the Third Stage. In leased premises on the banks of the Avon River, the interior of the theatre was disassembled at the end of each season, allowing the building (left, in 1974) to revert to its winter use as the home of the Stratford Badminton Club. Originally used mainly for workshops, concerts, and other special events, the Third Stage soon established itself as a mainstream venue, housing repertoire ranging from intimate productions of Shakespeare to new Canadian works, such as R. Murray Schafer's 1972 chamber opera *Patria II* (set shown above). Currently seating nearly 500 patrons and boasting a new façade and lobby, it was renamed the Tom Patterson Theatre in 1991, in honour of the Festival's founder.

STRATFORD FESTIVAL 3RD STAGE

Ready Steady Go

dreamed he was Pope. Its literary source and quasi-historical, quasi-religious atmosphere perhaps earned it its place at Stratford. A decent enough piece, it was still a thoroughly commercial enterprise that subsequently toured the U.S. Theatrically its main attraction is an enormously juicy leading role, which at Stratford was taken by the expatriate Canadian Hume Cronyn, inaugurating what would become a continuing relationship with Stratford. (In London, where the play originated, Stratford's own Douglas Rain had taken over the part of Hadrian from its creator, Alec McCowen, whose career it had transformed.)

Clearly, the Avon had still to find a role. It had originally been reopened to provide a home for the opera productions mounted as part of the concurrent music festival, and occasionally for dramatic productions by visiting companies. As the years went on, the distinction between what belonged to music and what to drama became harder to draw. In Gascon's time, several productions went more than half the distance between the two: *Satyricon*, obviously, and two somewhat more decorous offerings of Gascon's own, staged in the last years of his regime. One was *The Threepenny Opera* (1972), a half-success, as this clumsy, marvellous Brecht-Weill work almost invariably is, but adorned by Denise Fergusson's savage Jenny and Lila Kedrova's perversely delightful Mrs. Peachum. The other, a complete success that found Gascon happily on his home ground, was Offenbach's *La Vie Parisienne* (1974), boulevard-theatre plus.

It was also under Gascon's aegis that Stratford acquired a third stage, a 250-seat space which it called the Third Stage. Under the supervision of Michael

Bawtree, it commenced operations in 1971 and was partly devoted to small-scale music-theatre (an abiding passion of Bawtree's). It allowed at least two members of the main company to unveil projects of their own: Patrick Crean, the Festival's British-born fight arranger (and hence a vital contributor to the success of *Cyrano* and *The Three Musketeers*, not to mention numberless Shakespeare histories), returned to his roots as an actor with a one-man show about Rudyard Kipling; Tony van Bridge launched a G. K. Chesterton recital that was to stand him in good stead for many years.

Most critically, the Third Stage provided an economical testing-space for the Festival's somewhat embarrassed commitment to new Canadian plays. Among the plays presented, the two most memorable concerned iconic figures of the American West. *The Collected Works of Billy the Kid* (1973), a poetic piece adapted by Michael Ondaatje from his own novel-in-verse, went on to enjoy a long and still-continuing life in theatres across Canada. Its charismatic hero-villain was Neil Munro, who had previously played only small roles at the Festival and has not returned since; he went on, though, to a successful career as an actor and as a highly imaginative director, eventually settling at the Shaw Festival. *Walsh* (1974), by Sharon Pollock, was a decent, sober piece about the sad treatment of Chief Sitting Bull at the hands of the Canadian authorities. The play's title character, the mounted-police officer who unwillingly betrayed him, was sympathetically played by Michael Ball, another future ornament of the Shaw making his sole appearance at Stratford. Both plays were given moodily effective productions by John Wood, probably the most outstanding young

Canadian director to be recruited to Stratford during this period. In its relation to the Festival as a whole, the Third Stage's programme was even more piecemeal than the Avon's, but less obtrusively so.

With the fragmentation of the Festival company, the ensemble strength of the Langham years began to crumble. Some actors from the previous regime (and, in some cases, from the regime before that) remained and prospered. William Hutt, in addition to his Lear, Tartuffe, and Volpone, subtly modulated his mournful distinction through Don Armado in *Love's Labour's Lost*, Trigorin in *The Seagull*, and the aspiring sybarite Sir Epicure Mammon in *The Alchemist*; he repeated the last of these roles during what amounted to a two-year sabbatical in England and the U.S., in a chaotic production at the Chichester Festival Theatre that must have made him homesick.

Douglas Rain, absent for a longer period, returned to play a rather self-effacing Bastard in *King John*, hardly the swashbuckler that his still-recent D'Artagnan might have led audiences to expect and surprisingly less effective than his performance in the supposedly unrewarding title role fourteen years before; according to casting conventions for this play, he had gone from character man to juvenile lead rather than the other way about. He also played a good Bottom in Hirsch's *Dream*. The glory of this production, though, was Martha Henry's sensuous Titania; she, like her husband, missed (and was missed from) several seasons, although she was around as Desdemona to survive the shipwreck that was *Othello*.

Tony van Bridge continued to be invaluable, especially as the hospitable Mr. Hardcastle of *She Stoops to Conquer*

## "*I sat there absolutely transfixed...*"

### Stephen Ouimette

I was in grade nine in St. Thomas, Ontario, and there was a school trip to go to see *A Midsummer Night's Dream* at Stratford. It was John Hirsch's production in 1968, with Martha Henry and Barbara Bryne.

It sounds corny, but it changed my life. It was a student matinée, so the audience was pretty buoyant, pretty vocal. But that all just went away from me, and I sat there absolutely transfixed. That's where a seed got planted: that I might like to do this.

Student matinées are so hard to do, with all those unruly kids. But I keep thinking that somewhere out there in the dark, there's me.

*Douglas Rain as Bottom in 1968's Dream*

and — with less obviously rewarding material — as a sly king in *Pericles* manoeuvring his daughter and her intended into a match that both of them wanted anyway. Powys Thomas returned from his National Theatre School duties to do his finest work, culminating in his Bosola, the conscience-haunted villain of *The Duchess of Malfi*. Sadly, like the Duchess, he died young. So did his Old Vic School classmate Leo Ciceri, the suitably Italianate villain Iachimo in *Cymbeline* and an enlivening sardonic Mercutio in *Romeo and Juliet*.

Among the young actors who had been brought forward in the later Langham years were two whose presence now seems a striking coincidence: Richard Monette and Christopher Newton, at this writing the directors of Stratford and the Shaw Festival respectively. Monette, among many other things, had played Eros to Christopher Plummer's Antony; he appeared in only one Gascon season, that of 1973, in which he made as much as anyone is likely to of Lucentio, the straight man of *The Taming of the Shrew*. (He, too, had spent some of the intervening time in London, where he appeared at the Open Air Theatre, Regent's Park, outstripping most of the local talent as Lorenzo in *The Merchant of Venice*, and — talking of outstripping — was also in the original cast of *Oh! Calcutta!*). Newton had already attracted attention in the 1966 *Twelfth Night* as an Orsino who captured the right elusive blend of languor and lyricism; he stayed for Gascon's first season as one of the musketeers (Aramis, the priestly one) and as Oberon to Martha Henry's Titania. He then left to pursue an increasingly distinguished career as a director of both plays and theatres; sadly, he has never

returned to mount a show at Stratford.

Eric Donkin, another in the line of comic Erics, did valuable work in Shakespeare and out; his Prince of Arragon stopped the show (a legitimate tactic for this character) in his single casket-scene in *The Merchant of Venice*, and his Estragon, first among equals in *Waiting for Godot*, attained the special glory this role affords to first-rate actors who are also first-rate clowns.

Two British expatriates who had begun to shine under Langham continued with added brightness. Bernard Behrens, a fine comedian with a distinctively dry and understated style, had already made an impression as Fluellen in the 1966 *Henry V*; he confirmed and enlarged it as Quince in the *Dream* and Pompey in *Measure for Measure*, though in his most demanding role — the quick-changing Face of *The Alchemist* — he lacked the drive to carry the play. Barry MacGregor was to stay much longer. He had started as a boy actor in the early days of British television and later appeared with the Royal Shakespeare Company, in juvenile or character or just juvenile-character roles. He had come to Stratford in 1964, hot on the heels of an RSC world tour, to play Jack Point in a music festival production of *The Yeomen of the Guard*. Strangely, he appeared in no other Stratford musical until *My Fair Lady* in 2002. But he was very useful in plays, expanding his British range to take in romantic leads (Charles Surface in *The School for Scandal*) and secondary lovers (Hastings in *She Stoops to Conquer*) while continuing in clever-servant roles like Tranio in *The Shrew*. He also made a couple of excursions into heroic acting. One, his best performance at the time, was as Antonio, the steward who

## "The only great theatre you see is when you are young"

So Tyrone Guthrie is reputed to have said, and young people have always been a vital part of the Festival's audience. The two young women from Toronto's Loretto Abbey who saw *As You Like It* in 1959 (below, right) were among 14,000 students who attended the seven specially priced performances that were offered for schools that year. Today, nearly 70,000 students attend annually. Then, as now, school groups also enjoyed backstage tours (below, left, with Tom Patterson in the 1950s) and pre- and post-performance chats like the one shown above (in 1960, with Christopher Plummer).

PERFORMANCES TODAY

MATINEE 2·00

AS YOU LIKE IT

ASE CHECK CAMERAS
AT BOX OFFICE

courts and finds tragedy by marrying the Duchess of Malfi: a clever servant in excelsis. MacGregor's versatility extended off stage; he was to spend several years as company manager. Later, having returned to acting, he was to shuffle with what can only be called unpredictable regularity between the companies at Stratford and Niagara.

Jane Casson (Douglas Campbell's niece), whose duties in Langham's time had mainly been confined to understudying, displayed a talent for vigorous comedy, most notably as Helena in the *Dream*. James Blendick, one of those young actors who never seems young, began as Porthos and Pozzo and even as Snug the joiner, to stake out the fruity, rumbustious character market that he would corner at Stratford much later on. But of all the actors from previous years who flourished under Gascon, perhaps the most remarkable advance was made by Robin Gammell. He had been a child performer in the Guthrie and Langham seasons; his first speaking role, as good as a juvenile role gets, was the Boy in the Langham-Plummer *Henry V* (one of the few times this role can have been played by a boy, rather than a young man, making his death at Agincourt even more poignant). From there he progressed to plausibly adolescent characters, like Flute (who "has a beard coming") in the 1960 *Dream*. In 1970, after a nine-year absence, he returned a fully-fledged comedian and leading man. His hypocritical, accident-prone Joseph was the acknowledged glory of what was already a gorgeous *School for Scandal*, and he matched it as the grotesque Cloten of *Cymbeline*, a prize role, but booby-trapped. Next year he was back as the harassed bridegroom at the centre of *An Italian Straw Hat*: the charac-

ter, essential to all farce, to-whom-all-this-could-not-have-happened-at-a-worse-time. He never returned to Stratford, and he was missed.

Of the actors whom Gascon, for want of a better word, discovered, the most remarkable impression was made by Pat Galloway. She had in fact appeared during two of Langham's early seasons but without leaving much mark. Returning in 1968, she plunged into what has accurately been called the best part ever written for a maid: the managing Dorine of *Tartuffe*. Six years later she was playing the equivalent role in *The Imaginary Invalid*; she was, beyond a doubt, Stratford's most reliable soubrette. In the interim, though, she had branched out considerably. She had been a delicious Kate Hardcastle (who admittedly spends much of her time disguised as a maid) in *She Stoops*. She had ventured into villainy, wittily as the Queen in *Cymbeline*, forcefully, if without overwhelming distinction, as Goneril in *King Lear*; her Lady Macbeth was, in the circumstances of the production, hard to judge, but she seems to have suggested a nasty Mrs. Macbeth from the suburbs.

The most extraordinary thing about that performance, though, was that she gave it immediately on the heels of her Duchess of Malfi. Galloway surprised everybody with the strength and grace of her performance: qualities without which neither the part nor the play could survive, let alone triumph as they did here. The following year she was back with Gascon in another Renaissance title role, that of *Lorenzaccio*. Lorenzaccio of course is a man; those who hated the play (there were many of them) also hated the casting, sternly refusing to be swayed by the argument that Sarah Bernhardt had once done it, but those

who thought the production a brave adventure happily took Galloway's performance along with it.

Alan Scarfe made an uproarious Stratford debut as Tony Lumpkin, the good-natured young country bravo of *She Stoops To Conquer*: one of those legendary comic roles that in practice hardly ever come off. The balance of bluster and gaucherie is extremely hard to strike (not to mention that the character is supposed to be only twenty-one and passing for younger). That Scarfe was able to manage it so well put him at the top of most critical lists; his succeeding star role, as Petruchio in *The Taming of the Shrew*, dislodged him somewhat, since it was *all* bluster.

His opposite number in *She Stoops* was Nicholas Pennell as Young Marlow, congenitally shy with every woman above the rank of a barmaid. Pennell was a slim, gracious English actor whose career at home had peaked as a long-suffering suitor, and subsequently husband, in *The Forsyte Saga*. He came to Stratford initially to play Orlando to Carole Shelley's Rosalind, and romantic leads (plus the occasional hapless wooer like Hortensio in the *Shrew*) were his forte at the time, though they usually had comic aspects, which rose to the determinedly unromantic heights of Berowne in *Love's Labour's Lost*. Pennell was to become a Stratford institution, the most prominent British import since Douglas Campbell, but he was not, at this time, tested much beyond his attractive limits. Even his most apparently demanding role, Pericles, was less a matter of acting than of reacting, which admittedly is its own challenge. Pericles has little character, he simply endures: he is an apparently decent man to whom things happen. A hard part to play badly, it is

*Pat Galloway, who began taking on major roles during the Gascon years, was still acting at the Festival in the 1990s. One of her roles in 1973 was Katherina in* The Taming of the Shrew.

even harder to make memorable. It does call for a certain serenity, and this Pennell supplied.

Edward Atienza, another acquisition from Britain (Hutt had recommended him after acting with him at Chichester), never quite became part of the furniture in the same way, though he settled in Canada and had a run of important roles. At Stratford-upon-Avon, he had been best known for his clown and character roles. At the Festival, he continued in the same vein, playing Grumio in the *Shrew*, Touchstone in *As You Like It*, and the Fool in *Lear*, and he was clever in all of them, more than clever perhaps in the last. As Gower in *Pericles*, he made a charming job of a choric role composed exclusively of the most atrocious couplets ever to have been passed off in print as written by Shakespeare. His biggest test came in the title role of *King John*, in which he fell into the competently old-fashioned mould of the production as a whole: twitching on cue, ranting on cue, but never commanding the stage (as even a neurotic king like John should) or lifting the play.

Elizabeth Shepherd, a beautiful actress who had been one of the most prominent British ingénues of the early 1960s, also eventually settled in Canada (she worked a lot in the U.S. as well) but was seen less often at Stratford, then or later, than her qualifications warranted. Still, the three roles she played there in 1972 covered an impressive range. As Audrey in *As You Like It* she displayed striking good humour and even more striking décolletage; her lascivious Countess Cibo struck probably the most authoritative Renaissance note in *Lorenzaccio*; and in *King Lear* she was as fine a Cordelia as Stratford has ever seen, a heartbreaking partner for Hutt in the reconciliation scene.

Carole Shelley that same season supplemented her Rosalind (another fine casting idea of Hutt's) with the second-heroine

## Stratford on Tour

Before costs became prohibitive, national and even international tours were a proud part of the Festival's tradition. Stratford took its *Henry V* and *Oedipus Rex* to the 1956 Edinburgh Festival (above) and visited Chichester in 1964. Elizabeth Shepherd (right) was in the company that went to Moscow during a 1973 European tour which also encompassed Copenhagen, Utrecht, The Hague, Warsaw, Krakow, and Leningrad. An Australian tour followed the next year. Though the Festival's last major Canadian tour was in 1975, its 1998 production of *A Man for All Seasons* transferred to Ottawa's National Arts Centre, while two other productions from that season, *The Miser* and *Much Ado About Nothing*, went to City Center in New York — a move that company members were quick to dub "the Manhattan transfer."

role of Constance in *She Stoops To Conquer* and — perhaps her biggest stretch — Regan in *Lear*. If she must be ranked as a visiting star — she was not in fact all that famous – she was one who pulled her weight and justified her journey. Less comfortable were the importation from Britain and the U.S. of actors to play one or two roles apiece. The 1970 season, in particular, was full of them. The American Helen Carey (from, appropriately, the Guthrie Theater in Minneapolis) did well as Lady Teazle in *The School for Scandal*, and her Sir Peter did well too: he was Stephen Murray, a distinguished English actor of pre-war Old Vic vintage, who by now was working mainly on BBC radio. He had grown up playing eagle-eyed authority figures — he was one of the great actors of naval officers — but he could relax in his later years into a comic style of crinkly charm. (He had also, in 1952, been the overstretched Old Vic King Lear whose early departure gave John Colicos his first chance to shine; so his appearance at Stratford may be said to have closed a circle.) With Irene Worth in *Hedda Gabler* came two excellent British actors: Gordon Jackson, later famous as the butler of *Upstairs, Downstairs*, playing an eager, beaming Tesman, and Gillian Martell, a regular player at the Royal Court who never really got her due there or elsewhere, as Mrs. Elvsted.

It seems unlikely that actors already in the company could not have played some of these roles, but individually all these casting decisions could be defended. It was less easy to make a case for bringing over Maureen O'Brien, a regular leading player at the notoriously genteel Chichester Festival Theatre but with neither the soul nor the experience of a Shakespearean, to

play roles as choice as Portia in *The Merchant* and as overwhelmingly demanding as Imogen in *Cymbeline*. (Gascon's may be the only production of this play to have succeeded in spite of its Imogen.)

This confluence of one-stop performers in Gascon's first season without Hirsch coincided with the unfortunate quasi-experimental season at the Avon, with the strict division of the company between the two houses and with the absence, for the first time, of several of Stratford's stalwarts. The combination created an awkward, hand-to-mouth feeling that Gascon's later string of notable productions never quite dispelled. A bourgeoisification of Stratford did set in during his time (maybe it went with the Molière), and it was one of the things against which his successor set his face: not that he would have put it in those terms. He planned his revolution, incidentally, with Gascon's blessing.

*In her first season at Stratford (1972), English actress Carole Shelley played Rosalind opposite Nicholas Pennell's Orlando in* As You Like It *(above). Scottish actor Gordon Jackson (below) played Tesman in* Hedda Gabler *(1970).*

Susan Benson designed a magical costume (left) for Maureen Forrester as the Queen of the Fairies (right, centre) in the 1984 production of Iolanthe. A close-up of its skirt (above) shows the meticulous handwork involved in making this type of elaborate costume.

## "Such Stuff as Dreams Are Made On"

Festival costumes must be of the highest quality, not only to meet the aesthetic demands of the thrust stage — which relies on costumes and props rather than scenery to create the world of a play — but also to stand up to the rigours of a six-month season. Designers supply sketches for each character, usually with notes and fabric samples attached. They then work with the skilled cutters and other artisans who construct the costumes and attend fittings with the actors who will wear them. Because a newly constructed garment tends to look unnaturally flat under stage lighting, a surprising amount of artistry goes into painting costumes in a process known as "breaking them down." This enhances texture and increases the sculptural definition of such details as seams and pockets. It also makes clothes look lived-in, worn, or even ragged.

ORPHEUS

BACCHANALIAN LADY

BRIAN JACKSON 1959

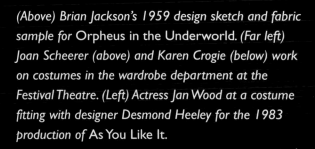

(Above) Brian Jackson's 1959 design sketch and fabric sample for Orpheus in the Underworld. (Far left) Joan Scheerer (above) and Karen Crogie (below) work on costumes in the wardrobe department at the Festival Theatre. (Left) Actress Jan Wood at a costume fitting with designer Desmond Heeley for the 1983 production of As You Like It.

# Chapter Four

# The Phillips Years

For years, Stratford had lagged behind the rest of the Shakespearean world in the matter of *Measure for Measure*. It was still being described in Canada as an "impossible" play until Robin Phillips directed it in 1975. It was his debut on the Festival stage, his first solo flight within the Stratford organization, and it bowled everybody over as surely as had Peter Brook's production of the play in England a quarter-century before. Phillips set it in the Edwardian era — a period to which he was often to return in his Shakespeare productions — in a heavy-laden late-Hapsburgian society: a physical and psychological police-state. It was a secretive society, one in which people talked in whispers. "Let no man hear me," says Angelo when confessing in soliloquy to the sin of pride, and in this production the characters' words, subtle and searching, were not so much heard as overheard.

Such quietness was a novelty at Stratford, and it was a reaction on Phillips's part to the tradition in which he had grown up. He was thirty-three when he took over at Stratford; he had had a fairly prosperous career as an actor in England and a meteoric one as

a director, mounting three successful productions for the Royal Shakespeare Company. That organization, however, had never welcomed him as one of its own. It must have been largely the RSC — not at its best circa 1970 — that Phillips had in mind when he spoke of "the semaphore style," loud and energetic acting with all emotions signalled on the surface, and he found the same disease rampant at Stratford when he came to observe the last two Gascon seasons.

In *Measure* Phillips's rigour and flair inspired superlative work from his actors. His Angelo was another newcomer to Canada, Brian Bedford, a British actor who had been part of the glorious generation of working-class heroes that had attended the Royal Academy of Dramatic Art in the 1950s, the group that also included Albert Finney and Peter O'Toole. He had played Hamlet in rep at twenty-one and Ariel to Gielgud's Prospero at Stratford-upon-Avon, but most of his career had been in modern plays. One of them, Peter Shaffer's *Five Finger Exercise*, had taken him to New York, with which he fell in love and in which he made his home. He earned something of a

*In England, Robin Phillips had been a frequent director at the Chichester Festival Theatre, whose stage was Britain's nearest equivalent to the Stratford thrust. On his first visit to Stratford's Festival Theatre in 1973, he recalls, "I was over the moon. I thought it was the most extraordinary theatre and still do."*

## "Sit up and take notice..."

### Robin Phillips

Theatre for me is a vocation. I believe that we do it for reasons other than just to entertain, and that if we do it well, we can make a huge difference to people's lives. I wanted to startle [the audience] into realizing that Stratford was more than slightly old-fashioned velvet costumes twirling around. I wanted to have people who wore clothes like we wear clothes, as opposed to *costume*. I wanted to stop them stretching out their hands from the front row, feeling the costumes, and sort of nudging each other and saying, "You could make a nice cocktail dress out of that."

I wanted people to leave with their blood pumping. I guess I was looking for things that would make them sit up and take notice.

(Above) Robin Phillips in the wardrobe department. (Right) Daphne Dare's pre–World War I costume designs for Measure for Measure.

Isabella
Miss Martha Henry.

Measure for Measure.
Stratford Festival 1975.

classical reputation there (especially in Molière), but Stratford was a new kind of venture for him; he may well have intended to stay only one season. As it turned out, he was to become an almost permanent fixture, rarely missing a season.

Technically immaculate, unwaveringly intelligent, Bedford was to prove of inestimable value to the Festival. He became best known for sparkling comic performances, but his Angelo showed his other side: it was a lacerating portrait of a man first proudly imprisoned within his own inhibitions, then devastated by his failure to live up to his own self-image. When the production was revived the following year, the role was played with equal power by Douglas Rain.

Two other Stratford veterans were rejuvenated in this production. Martha Henry, the Festival's pre-eminent player of good women, reached further into that persona as Isabella, who, once lured out of her convent and battered by real life, could never return. At the end she silently and bitterly accepted the inevitability of marriage to the Duke. William Hutt in this most ambiguous of roles was a figure of monumental suavity, a troubled character whose easy authority was, for better or worse, irresistible — notably to himself. The production dropped strong hints that Mariana, Angelo's abandoned betrothed who ends up pleading passionately for his life, had been the Duke's mistress. This is impossible to justify from the text but it made an undeniable impression. The part was given unusual presence by the American actress Kathleen Widdoes.

Equally compelling, and equally questionable, was the suggestion that the cynical rake Lucio saw through the Duke's disguise. This lent a thrilling

edge to the scene in which Lucio taunts the friar with revelations of the Duke's supposed scandalous past, but it made his final behaviour in pulling off the monk's hood to reveal the ruler beneath seem implausibly suicidal. Lucio is a gift of a part, gratefully seized by Richard Monette, who had now returned to Stratford, trailing clouds of glory from his performance as the distraught drag-queen in Michel Tremblay's *Hosanna*.

Less successful — and a persistent weakness in Phillips's work — were the scenes of broad comedy. Pompey the bawd, with his cheerfully incorrigible dedication to a life of vice, is equally part of the play's moral pattern, besides being very funny in himself, but Lewis Gordon's performance passed almost unnoticed. Phillips seemed intent on denying that the play was a comedy at all, though it ends in four marriages and the four characters sentenced to death are all reprieved. It is impossible, though, for any one production to realize all the possibilities that this sometimes maddeningly contradictory play contains. Shakespeare himself probably changed his mind while he was writing it. Phillips's dark staging knew its own mind, expressed it masterfully, and took Stratford by quiet storm. It remains the production by which he is most vividly remembered.

It was the kind of debut he needed, for his appointment as Stratford's artistic director was, and has remained, the most controversial in the Festival's history. Phillips was an Englishman awarded Canada's top theatrical post at a time of blossoming Canadian nationalism, a feeling that happened to be especially strong in the theatre. The Toronto alternative theatre, for example, despised Stratford

but thought that one of its own ought to be running it. Phillips's appointment was announced more than a year in advance (he spent the intervening period observing not only Stratford but theatre across Canada), so there was plenty of time for the nationalist backlash to express itself. In one especially notorious incident Phillips was challenged to a duel by a disaffected Canadian director.

There was, as there has always been, much talk about finding "a Canadian approach" to the classics. But there is no single recognizable British or American way of doing Shakespeare; why should there be a Canadian one? If it amounts to having the actors use their own accents: well, they had been doing that at Stratford ever since 1953. Guthrie would not have stood for anything else.

The fact is that, after Gascon's departure, only two Canadian directors had the breadth of experience to run the Festival: William Hutt, who was primarily an actor, and John Hirsch, who had not been approached, possibly because his abrupt departure from the partnership with Gascon was still fresh in memory. Phillips, who brought vision, taste, enthusiasm, and much experience on the Stratford-influenced stage at Chichester, was, to a remarkable degree, Tyrone Guthrie's natural heir. Both stood apart from the line of academically-minded British directors, especially dominant since the end of the Second World War; both were great showmen with a missionary streak. The differences between them are obvious: in the terminology once fashionable in English public schools and universities, Guthrie was a hearty and Phillips an aesthete. It is notable that the prototypical Guthrie actor, Douglas Campbell, was absent from Stratford during the Phillips years, as was James Blendick, of all Stratford's younger actors the one most plainly cast in the Campbell mould.

Both Guthrie and Phillips, however, had great choreographic and visual mastery: a rare quality among contemporary directors and one especially vital on the open stage. Both were expert at handling large groups of characters and could make every member of a stage crowd feel and act like an individual. Both could inspire their performers and theatre staff with absolute excitement and absolute loyalty. Both were artists: you could wander into one of their productions at any point, inhale the aroma of distinction, and give a confident guess as to who the director might be. Each of them brought to Stratford an artistic alter ego in the shape of a brilliant and trusted female designer; in Phillips's case it was Daphne Dare, with whom he had worked in England since his earliest productions and who became Stratford's first official head of design.

Phillips and Guthrie also shared an Achilles' heel. Their artistic sympathies stopped short at the stage door. Although both affirmed the importance of contemporary drama — Phillips programmed many new plays, and Guthrie had even written a couple — neither showed much interest in actually directing it. When they stepped outside the classics, they went for yesterday's experimentalists: for Thornton Wilder in Guthrie's case, for John Whiting in Phillips's. The bias of most contemporary drama is towards realism and, toughly pragmatic though they both were as administrators, as directors they were fantasists; they produced theatre that was essentially about theatre.

Under Phillips, the Stratford Festival achieved a new degree of integration and a new physical scale. The Festival Theatre, the Avon, and the Third Stage were no longer hived off from one another: each presented a full season, cast from the one full company. The Stratford Festival as we know it now is essentially Phillips's creation: the long season, the crowded repertoire, the cross-casting from one theatre to another. As the theatre's artistic scope expanded, so did its economy; and so, to match it, did that of Stratford the town — Tom Patterson's dream realized, perhaps, beyond his wildest imaginings. The tourist industry grew and grew, and pressure on the theatre to maintain its prosperity and the scale of its operation became intense. (It was in Phillips's time, not coincidentally, that the town acquired the first of its world-class restaurants. Stratford eating up to then had been dismal.) It happened quickly. In Gascon's last season there had been seven productions; in Phillips's first there were eleven. In his last year, 1980, there were fifteen. What was even more startling was the number of productions in any given year that Phillips directed himself. Like Langham he had a history of ill health, but his energy seemed boundless.

In his third year, 1977, the output was cut back to a mere ten shows. All the same, this season, Stratford's twenty-fifth, was perhaps the most crucial of his tenure. It was the first to feature both Brian Bedford and Maggie Smith, who may have come as visiting stars but who functioned simply as leading members of the company. It was also the first year in which the Festival made a concerted effort to invite the international critics, including a busload from Britain curious to see how their local boy was making out. They joined the Canadian and American press in sitting through seven plays in four days: an attention-grabbing concentration of openings that was to become another Stratford hallmark, though subsequently the premières were spread more humanely over an entire week.

The high point of this initial marathon was *Richard III*, Phillips's second great Shakespeare production and notable for the full-blooded seriousness with which it took every aspect of the play, starting with its psychology. Bedford, perhaps surprisingly, was one of the least humorous of Richards. He concentrated instead on the corroding resentment that informs the crookback's opening speech and dictates all his subsequent actions — and he was mesmerizing. He made his first entrance through the audience and then, with his hump to the house, surveyed the set. The image was unmistakable: one man against the world. The production never glossed over his cruelties — rather the reverse — but the man won respect, as in the theatre a great solitary always does.

The production also took the play seriously as spectacle. There were gorgeous Plantagenet costumes. Richard's coronation was a glowing ceremony with a stunted monster at its centre. And the battle, complete with flights of arrows, put to shame every other recreation of Shakespearean warfare, at Stratford or anywhere else. They talked of horses and we saw them. This early play mixes tough and witty realism — in Richard himself and most notably in the two thugs he hires to murder Clarence — with formality, and so did the production. Its ritualistic quality was embodied in Margaret Tyzack's performance of Queen Margaret — half a

# "The worst afternoon of my life..."

## Brian Bedford

The day after a very, very indulgent party, we were doing a matinee. I was sitting on my throne — terribly hung over, I'm ashamed to say — as King Richard III. Max Helpmann had said to me: "The Marquess Dorset, as I hear, is fled/To Richmond," and then I had to say to Buckingham, "Dorset is fled to Richmond." And I dried. I could not remember the name "Dorset." So I said to Max, "Who did you say had fled to Richmond?" And Max in turn couldn't remember.

A little later on, Max was offstage happily smoking a cigar (it was in the days when you could do that), and I cut four pages and said the line that was his cue. Max threw down his cigar, rushed on stage and removed his hat — because he was in the presence of the King — and with his hat came his wig.

Then, about three-quarters of an hour later, I hobbled on for my scene with Maggie [Smith], as Queen Elizabeth. The scene was played kneeling on prie-dieux: prayer stools. So I headed for my prie-dieu — and I missed it. This was just too much for Maggie, and she simply laughed out loud.

This was all in one performance of *Richard III*. It was, I think, the worst afternoon of my life at Stratford.

*Brian Bedford as Richard III in his coronation robes (left) and with (above, from left to right) Maggie Smith, Max Helpmann, Graeme Campbell, Bob Baker, Margaret Tyzack, and Alan Scarfe.*

bodeful chorus, half a real woman crazed with grief — roaming the stage in battle dress, as if still mentally reliving the Wars of the Roses. There can never have been a better Margaret.

Tyzack had come to Stratford at short notice, following the sudden withdrawal of Kate Reid. Her engagement was greeted by more nationalist protests (the Canadian actors' unions were behaving outrageously at this period), which mercifully were overruled. Had they been successful, Canadian audiences would have been deprived of three great performances: a record unmatched by any other Stratford actor in a single year. In fact Tyzack delivered them in a single week, for all three of her shows were in the season's opening batch. She had always been a loved and respected performer in Britain and was to remain so when she returned, but she never again attained the heights that she reached in that one season at Stratford; for one year, she was a great actress. She had been known for a commonsense blend of charm and astringency (both of them notably displayed in the TV series "The Forsyte Saga"); she took these qualities to a higher power when she played Mrs. Alving in Ibsen's *Ghosts*. Finely partnered by William Hutt and Nicholas Pennell (another former Forsyte) and supported by Eric Donkin and Marti Maraden, she drove the play to a devastating conclusion. This was despite ugly rehearsal clashes with the young Canadian director Arif Hasnain; the rumour, hotly denied by Phillips, was that he himself had had to take over the production.

Tyzack's wise and witty Countess similarly dominated *All's Well That Ends Well*, though Martha Henry as Helena was also in good form. The play — revived along with *Richard III* in

acknowledgement of Stratford's opening repertoire a quarter-century before — was given a competent but unexciting production by David Jones, an associate director of the Royal Shakespeare Company (where, as it happened, he had directed very little Shakespeare). At least it brought back Tanya Moiseiwitsch, who supplied handsome traditional designs very different from those she had done for the classic Guthrie staging.

A disquieting feature of 1977 was the gulf in quality between Phillips's productions and everyone else's, there being a question-mark over *Ghosts*. David William directed a *Romeo and Juliet* (his only production under this regime) that was duller than Jones's *All's Well*. It may have suffered from being housed at the Avon, a constricting environment for this youthful play, and further accentuated by a many-levelled dollhouse set of the kind that would have seemed excitingly experimental in the 1930s and had become a cliché since. What strikes us now is the presence in the title roles of two future Canadian directors, Richard Monette and Marti Maraden. Both at the time were among Stratford's more exciting young actors — Maraden had stood out a mile in Gascon's last season as one of the usually indistinguishable minor lovers of *Love's Labour's Lost* and had been steadily promoted ever since — but they seem in retrospect to have been acting as if the cares of office were already upon them.

A similar and even more drastic heaviness afflicted Strindberg's *Miss Julie*, the opening week's second Scandinavian Walpurgisnacht, directed by another young Canadian, Eric Steiner. Douglas Rain's stolid performance as the valet Jean suggested

## *Daphne Dare*

As Stratford's first head of design — a position created for her by Phillips — Daphne Dare set her stamp on the Festival in a way that no designer had done since Tanya Moiseiwitsch. By instituting a more coordinated approach to design, she and Phillips imparted something of a trademark "look" to Festival productions. Besides designing more than twenty-five of these in her time at Stratford, Dare redesigned the stages and auditoriums of the Avon and Tom Patterson theatres, and co-founded with Phillips the Festival's first designer-in-training programme. It was also in her time that — with Moiseiwitsch's collaboration — the Festival stage underwent its furthest-reaching modifications. These included making the once-permanent balcony — which Phillips found too stern a presence for the lighter and more "feminine" plays — mobile and retractable, thereby realizing an old dream of Michael Langham's.

*Daphne Dare's costume sketch (left) for the 1977 production of Hay Fever with Tom Wood, Maggie Smith, and Domini Blythe (above); a costume sketch for 1979's Henry IV, Part One (right); and a set design sketch for 1976's The Importance of Being Earnest (below).*

## "*Welcome to Canada...*"

### Robin Phillips

Maggie [Smith] was on tour with *Private Lives* and I sent her a note to say "Welcome to Canada. Would you like to escape for a weekend?" Barbara Ivey, a Stratford board member, very sweetly lent me her summer cottage on Lake Huron. It was the most magical cottage — beautiful white polar bear skin rugs, great log fires. When we arrived, Maggie said, "Bring the snows. Bring the snows. I don't want to go back to Toronto."

The next day we went for a huge walk. I didn't know until a year later that we had in fact been walking on the frozen lake. I asked her if she would like to come to Stratford and do Cleopatra and Millamant. The thing about casting is knowing what actors want to play. You have to throw the right bait. She said yes immediately, and then came for four seasons. That was the beginning of a wonderful relationship.

that there were limits even to his versatility, or at least to his capacity for shedding years; and Domini Blythe, who *was* the right age and was certainly capable of playing passion, never sounded the masochistic depths that Strindberg had dug for the heroine he both adored and abhorred. (He wrote the part for his wife, a fact that sums him up as nothing else could.) A British-born actress who settled early in Canada (her principal London credit, like Monette's, had been appearing in *Oh! Calcutta!*), Blythe was to prove one of Stratford's greatest assets.

Phillips himself staged two other plays in that opening week, both showing him in characteristic form. One, revived from the previous season, was *A Midsummer Night's Dream*, a visually ravishing production set and costumed to suggest an Elizabethan court masque. The designer was the brilliant young Susan Benson, whose sumptuous sensibility was to provide the ideal Stratford counterweight to Daphne Dare's airily stylish economy. Across the years the bewitching image remains of a double line of courtiers in the opening scene, each turning in to face his or her partner, one after another, in a rapid noiseless movement as if rehearsing some sixteenth-century equivalent of the minuet. Elizabeth I herself, in full Gloriana rig, played by Jessica Tandy in 1976 and by Maggie Smith in '77, dreamed herself into the role of Titania. It all looked lovely. What it had to do with Shakespeare's play was never made clear.

Ferenc Molnar's *The Guardsman* was the first play to present Maggie Smith and Brian Bedford in what was to be their most-loved and most-repeated Festival relationship: as witty, combustible sexual warriors. The result was

delightful, but not quite as delightful as everybody had hoped. Possibly this was because the play itself, though a kind of classic since the 1920s, is actually rather slight and strained. Concerning an actor who disguises himself as a military man in order to test the fidelity of his wife and co-star, it trades heavily on an audience's fondness for seeing famous actors playing famous actors. If they can also be famous married actors, then so much the better; in the U.S. the play had been a great vehicle for the Lunts.

The three productions that rounded out the 1977 season reinforced the mixed messages that had been sent out opening week. An experienced Canadian director, Marigold Charlesworth, mounted a *Much Ado About Nothing* that was to be her first and only Stratford production; Martha Henry's Beatrice pleased nearly everyone, and the rest of the show displeased nearly everyone. Phillips directed *As You Like It* and Noël Coward's *Hay Fever*, both of them starring Maggie Smith.

Maggie Smith is a unique figure in Stratford history. She arrived in Stratford in 1976, an acknowledged international star, and stayed for four seasons (she sat out 1979) as a fully integrated, hard-working company member. She played an average of four roles a year, and though most of them were leads, not all of them were. She had begun her career in the 1950s in revues: a historical accident that was to colour public and critical reception of her work for years. When she turned up, less than a decade later, cast as Desdemona to Olivier's Othello in the first season of the National Theatre, people raised their eyebrows, but most were impressed when they saw the actual performance. Desdemona was in

productions in this genre seemed by now to be coming off an elegant assembly line.

That was certainly the case with *Much Ado About Nothing* the same year. It had the expected glittering partnership from Brian Bedford and Maggie Smith as Benedick and Beatrice, but it made nonsense of the rest of the play. The crux of the action is a plot to pretend that the innocent Hero died of shame after being scorned at the bridal altar. Five people are in on this, and it would be impossible to keep the secret if there were any more. Phillips kept nearly the whole company on stage, in their wedding gear, as if to show off the number of actors he had at his disposal and the pretty frocks he could put them in.

The first tragedy Phillips staged at Stratford was *Hamlet* (1976), co-directed with Hutt for the Young Company, with Richard Monette and Nicholas Pennell alternating in the lead. Depending on the terms of reference, this yielded a Canadian Hamlet versus an English one; a Dionysian prince opposed to an Apollonian; a thrusting Olivier against a mellifluous Gielgud; a natural avenger compared to a born philosopher. The contrast between Monette and Pennell was accentuated by Phillips's insistence that each watch the other rehearsing; neither of them, obviously, wanted to copy the other. In strict career terms, it was a leap forward for both actors: a more surprising one, perhaps, for the thirty-seven-year-old Pennell than for the thirty-one-year-old Monette. The latter's red-hot Hamlet went down better with most people, but there was room for both — there always has been — and praise for both.

The same season threw Maggie Smith, just arrived at Stratford, in at the deep end in *Antony and Cleopatra*.

Like most Cleopatras, she was faulted for not being carnal or voluptuous enough. This is understandable, since Shakespeare failed to provide the actress with any love scenes. Writing for a boy actor, he sidestepped the issue, leaving a pretty problem for subsequent players and their audiences, who are naturally unwilling to take sex for granted. Cleopatra, as has often been observed, spends much of her time quarrelling with Antony, then regretting it, then desperately trying to repair the damage; the last desperation leads her to suicide, an end sweetened by the chance it affords her of tricking Octavius Caesar. She lives, in short, on her wits and her nerves; and Smith, who had once played a superb (and witty and nervous) Hedda Gabler, was splendidly equipped to play her. Unlike some Cleopatras, she conveyed that she was, however manipulatively, in love; like most Cleopatras, she rose superbly to the long, transcendent death-scene.

Her Antony was to have been John Colicos, which would have been a most welcome return. He opted for a movie instead, and the role went to Keith Baxter, a British actor who had all the qualities of a major classical star but had never become one, whether from his own lack of interest or that of the British theatre establishment has never been made clear. (He shared this gifted out-of-stepness with Phillips himself and with many of the English actors — Bedford, Tyzack, Pennell, even Maggie Smith and, by thunder, Peter Ustinov — whom Phillips recruited or encouraged. He gave them the chances they never got at home.)

Smith scored a similar, indeed a more decisive, success as Lady Macbeth (1978), her mannerisms totally subdued by the character's steel and

*In his first appearance at the Festival, Welsh-born actor Keith Baxter played Antony opposite Maggie Smith's Cleopatra. The short tunics and high boots designed by Daphne Dare for Baxter and the Roman soldiers were singled out for some ridicule in the press.*

## From Head to Toe

Like other costume pieces, hats, boots, and shoes are recycled as much as possible from existing stock; however, each season still requires hundreds of new items. Though hats and footwear for contemporary productions can be purchased off the shelf and modified where necessary, most period styles must be made from scratch by such artisans as Mark Fetter (above). In any case, the sole of every shoe worn on stage is fitted with a "galosh," a thin rubber covering that prevents the actor from slipping and protects the stage from marking and scuffing. Meanwhile, the Festival's millinery department produces everything from peasant caps to elaborate jewelled headdresses. While only a few hours are needed to make the simplest of hats, a more complex creation, like the one shown at left, may take several days.

the breakdown, as expected, exquisitely negotiated. The production, by Phillips and Eric Steiner, was Stratford's third outlandishly stylized *Macbeth*, lasting three hours (unusual in itself for Shakespeare's third shortest play) and given an austere Japanese-inspired staging. It boasted one tremendous effect: Banquo's death was staged in total darkness, effective enough in itself and rendered even more so when the lights immediately came up on a bustling banquet.

Phillips's most successful tragedy, beyond a doubt, was *King Lear*, mounted in 1979 and 1980 as a vehicle — there really is no other word — for Peter Ustinov. From one point of view this was a throwback to the days of Frederick Valk as Shylock: a star journeying to Stratford to play a single role. From another, it could not have been more different. Valk was a titanic actor re-creating a role that he had already made his own. Ustinov was a charmingly informal performer essaying not only Lear but Shakespeare for the very first time.

His classical credentials, in fact, were slightly more impressive than that might suggest. In the 1950s he had played a memorable Peer Gynt — live, uncut, spread over two evenings and in a rhyming translation — for BBC Television, and Peer in his old age contains strong intimations of Lear. (In his youth he recalls Hamlet and in his middle years Falstaff. It must be the best part ever written.) One of Ustinov's own early plays, *The Moment of Truth*, was about a senile military head of state modelled about equally on Marshal Pétain and Shakespeare's king, and Ustinov's original title for it had been *King Lear's Photographer*. He had been obsessed with Lear for years.

He believed the play to be about senility. This was the cause of Lear's capricious behaviour towards his daughters in the first scene; this was the real diagnosis of his madness in the central scenes. When he claimed that he would do such things, what they were yet he knew not, but they would be the terrors of the earth, the reason he didn't know was that he'd forgotten. Vocally, of course, the terrors of the earth were beyond his range. Some critics complained of his failure to release the full power of the verse, as if this were some kind of wilful omission on his part, but the obvious truth is that he didn't because he couldn't. He made no attempt to outroar the storm or to create it with his voice. "Blow, winds, and crack your cheeks," he modestly suggested, and left the winds to get on with it. He made no bones about Lear's impossible behaviour, but he was funny (as Lear certainly should be) and charming and pitiable: too easily pitiable, perhaps, to be truly moving. There seemed, really, to be nothing for Cordelia to forgive. It was understandable that Kent and the others should want to look after him, less so that they should revere him. Could he, for example, ever have been a great warrior? Then again, we were dealing here with a man, not a monolith.

In 1959 Charles Laughton, once Ustinov's colleague in corpulence in *Spartacus*, played King Lear at Stratford-upon-Avon and, despite some sublimely moving moments, failed. One reason was that he offered a small-scale performance in a traditionally scaled production: the kind that Phillips, preparing his own staging, referred to as a "Stonehenge" version. Stonehenge can work — it worked for Olivier's television performance — but it would not have

## "*The itch...*"

### Peter Ustinov

You fall to the floor and from then on, until the end of the play, everybody starts talking terribly slowly, as a deference to your recent death. And then a terrible itch manifests itself on your left ankle. You daren't move because you will destroy the illusion for thousands of people. You lie there and you think, what is 22 times 78 multiplied by 3 and divided by 17?

The next night you die slightly differently. You throw the cloak over your leg as you fall. Now if it happens again, under the great coat you can surreptitiously move one hand. The trouble is as you lie there the itch reappears in your nostril. Now what can you do? You can't throw the coat over your face. The speed they're talking, there's no chance of your being alive by the end of the evening. And those are the worst moments of *Lear*.

worked for Ustinov. Phillips cushioned him with a detailed realistic production set in his favoured nineteenth century. This was not an unprecedented idea: Trevor Nunn, three years earlier, had used the same period for a *Lear* starring Donald Sinden, another actor whom many people thought of primarily as a light comedian.

Phillips's production was more crammed than Nunn's with realistic and domestic detail: this was an epauletted, cigar-smoking Lear, addressing family and friends from his favourite armchair. It helped that these pictures were framed within the Avon proscenium: it is difficult to imagine Ustinov's Lear commanding the Festival stage. He had sympathetic support from Douglas Rain's Gloucester and Jim McQueen's Kent, and steely opposition from Richard Monette's Edmund and (in the second season) the Goneril and Regan of Martha Henry and Patricia Conolly. Above all he had William Hutt, pausing halfway through his own parade of Lears to offer a Fool whose stinging jokes were tempered by the sense that he knew — in this case from experience — exactly what the old boy was going through. Those who never saw Ustinov's Lear cannot quite believe that he brought it off. But plainly he did.

Phillips's non-Shakespearean productions covered as wide a range as his Shakespearean, though all with a bias towards comedy of manners. In his first season, 1975, he directed *Trumpets and Drums*, Bertolt Brecht's version of *The Recruiting Officer* by the early eighteenth-century dramatist George Farquhar. Farquhar's hero was mustering troops for the Duke of Marlborough's campaigns against the French; Brecht updated the offstage action to the American War of Independence, in the presumed interest of more immediate political (i.e., anti-colonialist) relevance. This may also have been why Phillips opted to produce Brecht's adaptation rather than Farquhar's very entertaining original — that and the fact that the Brecht had not been given a major English-language production before.

Phillips's direction, like Brecht's text, was a mixture of facetiousness, genuine invention, and unearned moral indignation. It contained very funny performances from William Hutt, Tom Kneebone, and especially the luminous Jackie Burroughs as the cross-dressing heroine whom Farquhar called Silvia, and Brecht — with typical lightness of satirical touch — Victoria. The show's fatal weakness, however, had been prophetically summarized by William Gaskill twelve years earlier, when he directed *The Recruiting Officer* as the first rare classic in the first season of the National Theatre. When Gaskill — himself a paid-up Brechtian — was asked why he hadn't staged the Brecht instead, he replied that he saw no reason to put on an English translation of a German adaptation of a perfectly good English play. His reward was to have mounted the first in a line of National and RSC productions that restored viable but neglected plays to the general repertoire, Stratford's very notably included. At that point Stratford had never mounted any play by Farquhar, and in the years since, it has attempted only one. Farquhar remains one of the most approachable and enjoyable playwrights in the language, and Canadian audiences deserve more chances to approach and enjoy him.

William Congreve, last and most verbally brilliant of the Restoration wits, is a far harder nut to crack, as Phillips discovered when he directed

*Bertolt Brecht's* Trumpets and Drums *received its first major English-language production at Stratford in 1975. Tom Kneebone (opposite, centre, with Robert More, left, and Rod Beattie, right) played Sergeant Kite. (Below) Grenadier costume design sketch by Daphne Dare.*

## The Art of Transformation

Though an actor's own hair can be styled for a particular role, it is far more common to wear a wig. Custom-made for their original wearers, wigs like the ones above can subsequently be refitted, restyled, and recoloured. Under the supervision of Clayton Shields (below, left) and Gerald Altenburg, they are made from real human hair, each strand painstakingly knotted into place by hand. The fine mesh at the front, where a wig meets the forehead (visible in the photograph opposite of Joy Lafleur preparing to play Gertrude in the 1957 *Hamlet*), is known as the "wig lace"; on stage, it is virtually undetectable. Facial attachments, like those worn by Douglas Chamberlain (below, right) as Merlyn in 1997's *Camelot*, are made of yak hair.

## "She's a kind of genius..."

### Brian Bedford

I've known Maggie [Smith] for a long, long time. We're exactly the same age. We met when we were twenty, twenty-one maybe. We both came into the West End at the same time.
I thought, and still do think, that she's a kind of genius.

We had both done *Private Lives* with different people: Maggie had done it in London with her then husband, Robert Stephens, and I had done it on Broadway with Tammy Grimes. But by the time Maggie and I came to do it, we sort of were those people — Elyot and Amanda. They can't live together and they can't live without each other. That wasn't quite the situation with Maggie and me, but something of it existed in real life between the two of us. We loved each other and drove each other a bit nuts at times. That was a very valuable and ready-made resource for playing *Private Lives*.

*Brian Bedford in Private Lives*

*The Way of the World* in 1976. Some of the extraordinary workload he took on at Stratford was the result of his stepping in when designated directors had bowed out. His first choice for this play had in fact been Gaskill, who in the sixties had become Britain's pre-eminent director of Restoration comedy, often with Maggie Smith as his leading lady. She was to make her Stratford debut as Millamant, the besieged enchantress for whom — by temperament and by necessity — wit was a defensive weapon, rarely sheathed and never blunted. It could have been written for her: what other actress could fulfil the text's implicit demand to come on stage and radiate? Reuniting her with Gaskill seemed ideal: part of their joint contribution to these plays had been to reconnect them to the social and psychological realities from which they had sprung. This time, however, Gaskill wanted to go one step further — or several steps back — and dress the play in blue denim, which Phillips did not see going down well with the Stratford audience. (Gaskill later admitted, with some relief, that Phillips had been right; in fact, many years later he did direct *The Way of the World*, at Chichester and in the West End, in traditional costume and with a dream cast, headed by the very same Maggie Smith. It was a big success.)

Under Phillips's direction, Smith at Stratford scored the expected triumph, one in which she was joined by Jessica Tandy, whose pathetic Lady Wishfort charmed everybody except those who, with no support from the text, insisted that the character should be vulgar, and by Tony van Bridge, returning (for just one season, alas) as the bumpkin Sir Wilful. The courtier males were less successful, with Jeremy Brett joining the long line of actors who have failed to make any impression as the supposed hero Mirabell, a character who has to do all the work while the others get the laughs. (Brett, who had played juvenile leads in England far longer and to better effect than anyone would have thought possible, was eventually to mature into television's most successful Sherlock Holmes.)

The play itself defeated many who saw it, as well as some who were in it. Its reputation as the crown of artificial comedy (admittedly an unhelpful label) rests on its having reduced the comedy of sexual combat to its purest verbal essence, unhampered by complexities or quiddities of character. Except for Millamant — and even she can be a doubtful case — none of its characters has much individual life. Also, the *idea* of pure comedy is continually hobbled by the realities of the most tangled plot in world drama.

In 1980 Phillips directed another iconic eighteenth-century piece commonly held to represent the summit of its genre, John Gay's *The Beggar's Opera*. As narrative, this work (like its Brechtian offshoot *The Threepenny Opera*) is as incoherent as *The Way of the World*, only it straggles where the Congreve convolutes. It is more easily and appealingly stageable, though, on account of its songs and its engaging thieves'-kitchen ambience, which Gay intended as satire of the better-paid political crooks of his own time.

Phillips had staged the play at

Chichester during his pre-Canadian career, and he brought over some of the trappings of that production, including some additional lyrics. The result had the air of social criticism without the content: a bit of bark but not much bite. Jim McQueen's Macheath was generally felt to be too nice by at least half. But it was a vivacious and very well-staged show, with Graeme Campbell and Jennifer Phipps giving authentically gin-soaked accounts of Mr. and Mrs. Peachum, and the on-stage deployment of the Stratford Boys' Choir adding — ironically? who can say? — to the general air of well-scrubbed tunefulness.

By common consent Phillips's two most successful productions of non-Shakespearean classic comedy — both indeed have become somewhat legendary — were the two most recent compositions. His 1978 production of Coward's *Private Lives* (co-directed with Keith Batten) was the summit of the partnership between Brian Bedford and Maggie Smith. They could just have got up on stage as the perpetually squabbling, perpetually enchained Elyot and Amanda, and coruscated to their audiences' hearts' content. Smith had done just that in an earlier London production, and the experience had made her deeply uncomfortable, but Phillips guided the actors scrupulously through the play, taking it seriously and thereby making it even funnier.

He had already taken the same obvious but uncommon tack with Oscar Wilde's *The Importance of Being Earnest*: an even harder play to make fresh, since its humour, unlike Coward's, is verbal and very famously so; it may well be fuller of quotations than *Hamlet*. Phillips staged it at the end of his first season as a *jeu d'esprit* at the Third Stage. It was so successful

that it was revived at the Avon in 1976 and again in 1979. Its sparking-point on all three occasions — indeed the main reason for reviving it — was the casting, partly at his own suggestion, of William Hutt as Lady Bracknell.

The idea may have seemed frivolous; the execution was anything but. Indeed, the keynote of Hutt's performance, not too surprisingly, was a towering dignity: furred and erect he reminded many people, himself included, of Queen Mary. While commanding from a spectacular altitude, he made similarly imperious use of all the highs and lows in the Canadian theatre's most flexible and resonant vocal instrument. Every Lady Bracknell since the Second World War has had to compete with Edith Evans's delivery of "A handbag?" — a sort of basso wail remembered even by those who have never heard it. Like most latter-day Bracknells, Hutt chose to downplay the line, thereby lulling Mr. Worthing and the audience into a brief sense of false security. Soon enough the thunder burst, hilariously counterpointed by Hutt's appalled glance at his own reticule, as if from now on all handbags were irrevocably tainted.

Hutt had a distinguished predecessor in the role: Micheál MacLiammóir, the Irish actor and raconteur, included a scene from the play in his one-man show *The Importance of Being Oscar*, playing all the parts himself and prompting the comment that he was the greatest Lady Bracknell of our time. Such statements are unprovable, but it seems reasonable to assume that Hutt ranks with Evans, MacLiammóir, and Judi Dench among the great ones: a high-strung quartet that leaps barriers of gender, geography, and physical stature.

*"I had a huge amount of fun doing Bracknell,"* recalls *William Hutt. "I'm six foot one, and then on top of that Robin put this hat with a feather sticking up, so I looked as though I were eight feet tall."*

113

A fine succession of Jacks, Algies, Gwendolens, and Cecilies (Pennell, Monette, MacGregor, Galloway, Blythe, Maraden) kept to the forefront Phillips's idea that this is a play about the perils of courtship in a rigidly corseted society. Some thought, though, that by the time of the 1979 staging, the production itself had begun to come unbuttoned: that what were originally taut pauses had become occasions for the actors to bully the audience into laughing. Gina Mallet in the *Toronto Star* made the surprising but thought-provoking suggestion that for all its stylishness Stratford — which at this point meant Phillips — lacked a sense of humour.

Phillips's range as a classical maestro was still not exhausted. In collaboration with Urjo Kareda, he directed two masterly productions of Chekhov, both in specially commissioned new translations by the Calgary playwright John Murrell that have remained the standard Canadian texts.

Murrell's *Uncle Vanya* (1978) was especially attuned to the comedy in the play; it also benefited from having Stratford's two strongest actors to play the greatest male duet in Chekhov. Hutt, with his gift for plangent farce, was ideally equipped to convey the futility, the heartache, and the occasional tragic dignity of Vanya; Brian Bedford had all the world-weariness and the battered suavity of the doctor who knows that, deep down, the two of them are brothers in defeat. Martha Henry and Marti Maraden, too, had the right chemistry for the unloving Elena and unloved Sonya, and Max Helpmann made more than most of the heartless Professor.

*The Seagull* (1980), staged boldly but rewardingly at the Festival Theatre rather than at the more obvious Avon, was even more successful, and its cast-

ing suggested unexpected but perfectly legitimate links between Chekhov and Coward. (Both have been credited with inventing subtext.) Maggie Smith's Madame Arkadina was Judith Bliss with her professional ego intact but appallingly vulnerable (or vulnerably appalling) in her private life. With Bedford as her Trigorin, the bickering relationship of the two mature lovers carried echoes of Elyot and Amanda, with the difference that these two do not appear to meet on equal terms: it's the woman here who is aggressive and obviously predatory while the man appears just to give in and go with the flow — and is in fact the greater predator. Bedford's Trigorin was the logical successor to his Astrov: a womanizer whose first allegiance, much as he had come to loathe it, was to his work.

Hutt found yet another ideal role as Dorn, the philandering physician, of all Chekhov's doctors the only one whose vice is self-love rather than self-hatred. Jay Carr of the *Detroit News* furnished a delicious portrait of the supremely poised Hutt receiving the adoration of Jennifer Phipps's adoring, frustrated Polina: "He just sits there smiling fatuously, wallowing in smugness, and is more hilarious with each passing, pregnant second."

Roberta Maxwell, now an accredited American star, returned to play Nina, her only major appearance during the Phillips regime, and scored a triumph in a supremely testing role: the aspiring ingénue whom life turns into a tragedienne almost before she has learned what either life or theatre is. Part of the achievement of Phillips's probing *Measure for Measure* had been that he directed Shakespeare as though he were Chekhov, so his success with actual Chekhov was no surprise. He had

cause to know *The Seagull* surpassingly well: in his young acting days he had played Konstantin in a BBC TV production that had achieved the impossible by being as complete an experience as the best Chekhov on stage.

Phillips did more to promote new Canadian plays at Stratford than any artistic director before him but, as already noted, he directed few new or even recent plays himself. In fact he directed four. The first, and an especially telling choice, was John Whiting's *The Devils*, which reached Stratford in 1978, a full seventeen years after its London production by the Royal Shakespeare Company as their first ever new play. (In the interim the play had become best known as the source of an especially outrageous Ken Russell film.) It suggested — what many subsequent play choices under many different regimes have confirmed — that there was a kind of accepted pedigree by which plays premièred or discovered at one institutional theatre would later be adopted by the others. In practice, this led to Stratford doing plays already seen at the RSC or the National.

Set in the seventeenth-century France of Louis XIII and Cardinal Richelieu (indeed of *The Three Musketeers*), *The Devils* juxtaposes religious fervour with sexual repression and examines how both can be exploited by power politics. Its principal drawback for most spectators is that its two central characters, carefully and elaborately built up, only meet at the very end of the play for a single gnomic exchange that can hardly repay all that the audience has by now invested in it. Nicholas Pennell seemed unsuitably wholesome casting for the libertine priest, but the role of the hunchbacked nun whose fantasies about him — attributed to diabolic possession — lead all too easily to his downfall gave brilliant scope to Martha Henry's developing talent for melodrama.

A few days later and at the opposite extreme of physical scale, though equally harrowing in subject matter, came Phillips's production of Barry Collins's *Judgement*, a more recent play that had been presented by the National Theatre. Based on the true story of a group of captive Soviet army officers abandoned by the Germans at the end of the war and reduced to cannibalism, it imagines the last survivor put on trial and explaining, if not defending, his actions. His speech, one and three-quarter hours long, is the entire play. Collins's instincts were those of a journalist rather than a playwright, and the piece suffers from its constant needling insistence that we have no right to judge this man, which is something most of the audience would have readily conceded from the outset; also, of course, the spectators became numbed by the catalogue of horrors, relayed in a single, largely unmodulated voice.

Richard Monette — fresh, if that is the appropriate word, from playing a philosophical Sewerman in *The Devils* — won even more awed respect for his performance than for his memory: he told his story as coolly and matter-of-factly as possible, on the sound principle that this would make it even more appalling.

Phillips got round to new work, previously unseen elsewhere, in his final season of 1980, with two pieces of literary origin. *Foxfire*, which he co-directed with Peter Moss, was adapted by Susan Cooper (a British writer) and Hume Cronyn from a series of oral-history books about log-cabin life in the mountains of southern Appalachia. Cronyn

and his wife Jessica Tandy — Canadian- and British-born respectively, but long-time residents of the U.S. — were two more stars in a star-studded season. They had both appeared in Phillips's 1976 season. Tandy, a lovely and glowing actress, played a widow with family problems. Cronyn was her late husband offering ghostly advice. Play and production were respectfully received, though they could not escape the curse of rural worthiness. The play did make it to Broadway in a later version, the first new Stratford play to do so.

Far more noteworthy, though, was *Virginia*, drawn from the life and writings of Virginia Woolf by the Irish novelist Edna O'Brien. Finely supported by Nicholas Pennell as Leonard Woolf and Patricia Conolly as Vita Sackville-West, Maggie Smith presented an uncannily convincing physical image of the gaunt, haunted queen of Bloomsbury and also burrowed deep into the writer's troubled psyche, mercurial sensibility, and extraordinary if sometimes blinkered intelligence. The production, exquisitely set by Phillip Silver, was marked by a kind of sensitive bravura: it was one of the great triumphs both of the Phillips regime and of his own directing career, and it also marked the apogee of Maggie Smith's work at the Festival. This was the overwhelming majority opinion at Stratford and, the following year, in London. A bored minority found it an interminable evening of cultural blackmail, trading heavily on the audience's reverence for the subject or the actress or both.

Sixty-seven separate productions were presented on Stratford's three stages (two in some seasons) during the six years of Robin Phillips's directorate. Of these, he himself directed or co-directed a staggering (in several

### "My knees were shaking..."

**Richard Monette**

It took me three months to memorize *Judgement*. I could never do that now. I'd learn ten pages for every time we had a rehearsal. And every time I started, my knees were shaking. And Robin said, "Richard, you know you don't have to do that." I said, "This isn't an acting choice. I'm terrified!"

What was extremely difficult was having only one move in the entire piece. If you stand for one hour and forty-five minutes, your joints, everything starts to go. In one performance, I just leapt into the air — involuntary muscle spasm.

I'm glad I did it. I'm glad I never have to do it again.

Olga, Miss Martha Henry.
3 Sisters. 76. Stratford Festival.

Act I    Acts II & III    Act III

*Daphne Dare designed the turn-of-the-century costumes (above) for the 1976 production of Chekhov's* Three Sisters. *(Inset, seated from left to right) Marti Maraden appeared as Irina, Maggie Smith as Masha, Martha Henry as Olga, and, in her fifteenth season at Stratford, Amelia Hall (standing) as Anfisa the nurse.*

senses) twenty-nine. But that, of course, still left a heavy demand for guest directors. Finding them, at Stratford as at other big institutional theatres, has always been a headache. Phillips cast his net wide and, on average, successfully. He was especially anxious to bring in young directors from the burgeoning new theatre movement across Canada. These, as was to be expected, were usually less happy with classics than with new plays, where they were likelier to share the author's mindset and where they were less exposed to awkward comparisons. (As a leading British director once observed, "The production of a new play always looks definitive.") By the same token they were usually more successful at the Avon or at the Third Stage than at the Festival.

Phillips was able, in 1976, to secure the return of John Hirsch, who directed a magnificently lived-in *Three Sisters* that eclipsed all other Chekhovs — his own, Gascon's or Phillips's — seen at Stratford. He was given the best talent of the Phillips era, including Phillips's own designer, Daphne Dare, and he drew the best from them. Martha Henry, Maggie Smith (her only Stratford appearance for a director other than Phillips),

and Marti Maraden were the sisters, Keith Baxter Vershinin, and William Hutt the last and most desperately vodka-sodden of Chekhov's doctors. Hirsch was not, however, invited to return; he quarrelled with Phillips, and Stratford had to resign itself to not being big enough for both of them.

Unfortunately, there was no one else, not on that level. Probably the closest was John Wood, who had directed two Third Stage productions for Gascon and was promoted to the main stages by Phillips. He came through in 1975 with a very taut production of Arthur Miller's *The Crucible*. The role of Elizabeth Proctor, the Puritan wife who in trying to save her husband's good name inadvertently condemns him to hang for witchcraft, was a further stage in the reinvention of Martha Henry, and there were strong performances from Stephen Macht, an American actor, as the husband, from Douglas Rain as the merciless deputy-governor, and from Odetta — yes, the folk-singer — as Tituba. Eric Donkin was rewardingly stretched as the conscience-stricken Reverend Hale, who furnishes the play's moral centre. Wood proved that he could find all the excitement in a highly theatrical text.

He was less successful with *Julius Caesar* (1978), his first Stratford Shakespeare. This actually sacrificed the most obvious excitement by keeping the Roman mob offstage, thus making life difficult for the audience and for the actor playing Antony. It was a determinedly unromantic production, peopled by ignoble Romans. But there were atmospheric thrills: a dark stage, lit up only for the murder of Caesar, and an ominous sound-score. Cassius (Alan Scarfe) emerged as the play's most interesting character, which often happens, and Casca (Frank Maraden) as its most entertaining, which always happens.

Directing talent was also recruited from within the higher echelons of the acting company. The very first production of the Phillips era, Shaw's *Saint Joan*, was actually directed by William

Hutt, and the production was generally excoriated as reminiscent of the previous regime at its stodgiest. The word "Edwardian" was bandied about; Hutt mildly replied that the play *was* Edwardian. In fact it is difficult to imagine an avant-garde production of Shaw's jolly, talkative chronicle play on the Festival stage. Radical re-interpretation is largely a matter of décor, and the platform stage doesn't allow for much of that.

This was the first Shaw play that Stratford had presented, and almost the last; for obvious reasons the Festival had no wish to trespass on the preserve of the rival concern at Niagara-on-the-Lake. (As Groucho Marx said of the houseflies: "They don't practise law and I don't walk on the ceiling.") *Saint Joan* was to be Hutt's last major solo production at Stratford; two days later, however, his Duke in Phillips's *Measure* launched a brilliant new chapter in his acting career.

The same production did the same thing for Brian Bedford, but in his case the acting rejuvenation led to a new career as a director. He made his debut, in startling fashion, with the horrific *Titus Andronicus* (1978), spectacularly restored to circulation by Peter Brook and Laurence Olivier in 1955 but still unseen at Stratford. Like Brook, Bedford stressed the ritual elements in the play and kept most of the bloodshed out of sight, while letting its impact hang vividly and musically in the air. Also like Brook, he performed his own extensive surgery on the text. A later RSC production by Deborah Warner proved that it was possible to do the play uncut and with sober realism, but in its own terms Bedford's production was superb, exposing a society at the breaking point — Rome past decline and well into fall — without gloating over it.

Besides, all the reality that anyone could want was there in William Hutt's soldierly, maddened Titus, surely as fine as Olivier's. The combination of iron and silk in this actor's voice and personality can seldom have been more subtly and rewardingly combined. (Like his Fool, it looks now like a way-station between his various Lears.) When the production was revived in 1980, Pat Galloway took over the role of his voluptuous antagonist Tamora, Queen of the Goths, and gave probably the finest of her latter-day Stratford performances: her Duchess of Malfi turned stunningly inside-out.

That *Titus* came into its own in the second half of the twentieth century is hardly surprising. It was the only Shakespeare play left to rediscover, but more than that, what we have learned and what we have lived through have made any description of its action as "impossible" or "excessive" seem naive. It needs discipline and ability, though, to turn this realization into more than a trendily sadistic wallow, and Bedford's production ranks with Brook's, Warner's, and the Julie Taymor film among those that have brought it off.

Although Bedford was to direct more productions in the post-Phillips years, he remained, like Hutt, primarily an actor. Of those who might be called director-directors, the most prolific was Peter Moss, a young Canadian who had moved to England but was lured back to work at Stratford, despite initially having serious doubts about the place. His test-drive was a piece as tricky as *Titus* but for opposite reasons: the doggedly farcical *Merry Wives of Windsor*.

Moss did the three things most necessary with this play; he made it warm, he made it funny and he gave it a recognizable small-town setting, slightly

117

*"Thou dost give me flattering busses," Falstaff (Lewis Gordon) tells Doll Tearsheet (Martha Henry) in this tavern scene from* Henry IV, Part Two *(above). In the same production, Richard Monette appeared as Prince Hal (below).*

updating the play's period from the Elizabethan to the Restoration: the residents as Puritans, Falstaff and company as somewhat bedraggled Cavaliers. Hutt scored yet another success, pretty much in the vein that would have been expected of him: dignified, delicate, rueful, with links both to the Falstaff of *Henry IV*, whom he regrettably never played, and to the deluded, impervious losers of Molière, whom he did.

A new comic talent, Tom Wood, impressed himself in the sweet but often neglected role of Master Slender (Richard Eder of the *New York Times* called him "a Woody Allen without desire"), and Alan Scarfe was properly manic in Hutt's old role of the jealous Ford. Above all, and by no means to be taken for granted, the production had two authentically and infectiously merry wives. Domini Blythe was the quieter of the two as Mistress Ford; Jennifer Phipps's Mistress Page spread outrageous joy without ever losing her grip on the truth of the character. A character actress with a rare combination of force, subtlety and freshness, she was soon to switch festivals and embark on two decades' worth of impeccable work at the Shaw.

After dealing so happily with what Harold Bloom calls the pseudo-Falstaff, Moss moved on to the real thing, *in extenso*. He directed both parts of *Henry IV* (1979), this time with Lewis Gordon as Sir John. Gordon, a much-loved and much-valued actor, was part of the

Stratford fabric; he had acted there since 1960, and before that had worked in the props department. He had never before been given a part this large — in any sense — and he suffered from the fact that, however much padding he put on, he still registered as thin. But in other respects he offered a hugely intelligent performance, presiding with great actorly cunning over an Eastcheap tavern enlivened by Martha Henry's Doll Tearsheet.

The production was equally successful with the royal and baronial scenes. Most notable was Douglas Rain's king, a far more interesting role than is usually admitted, rendered as fascinating by the man's deep flaws — his pettiness and unscrupulousness — as by the real concerns for his son and his country that torment him almost to his death. Rain realized all of this, in his finest performance of this period. He was matched by Richard Monette as a barbed-wire Hal moving steadily away from his disreputable friends and towards the inevitable, depersonalizing acceptance of his royal role.

It seemed logical that the following year Moss would direct Monette in the sequel, *Henry V*. Surprisingly, though, the continuity was compromised by having two alternating Henries. Even more surprisingly, it was the newcomer who proved the better of the two: Jack Wetherall, although too soft-grained for the warrior-king, at least brought off his more spiritual and self-doubting moods. As with the Monette-Pennell *Hamlet* of four years before, audiences were offered one tender protagonist and one tough. In Monette's Henry, however, the man's humanity seemed to have sunk so deeply within his official role that it was impossible for the actor to dig it out. He had also developed jerky,

## *The Jewels in the Crowns*

All of the opulent-looking adornments shown here were made in the Festival's bijoux department. After meeting with the designer of a production, an artist like Polly Scranton Bohdanetzky (right) will cut outlines of the required items from sheets of brass or other metal. Once shaped, the pieces are built up with layers of enamel paint, with found materials such as beads and pieces of filigree, or with "jewels" of glass or plastic tinted with a mixture of powdered dye, alcohol, and shellac. The department also makes extensive use of donated costume jewellery: some items can be used intact, while broken ones can be taken apart and used as components in anything from cufflinks to crowns.

mechanical speech-patterns of a kind often heard at the English Stratford but rarely at Canada's.

The production seriously misfired, with only a few bright spots. Diana Leblanc, a future director of distinction, continued the theatre's line of authentically French princesses; Rod Beattie, a young Festival veteran of seven years' standing, made his first strong comic mark as Ancient Pistol.

Moss had also been blessed through this cycle with a magnificent trio of Mistress Quicklies. In *The Merry Wives* he had had the ultra-reliable Mary Savidge. (Savidge was an expatriate British actress who in the 1950s had been leading lady at the Oxford Playhouse. When Maggie Smith, who was raised in Oxford, first came to Stratford she greeted Savidge and said, "My father told me, if you ever become half the actress Mary Savidge is, you'll be doing all right.") In *Henry IV* Jennifer Phipps was a harried Hostess whose speech, protesting her respectability despite all evidence to the contrary, was like a muddied stream of consciousness. In *Henry V* the Festival's beloved Amelia Hall, the first actress to appear on that stage (she had been Lady Anne to Guinness's *Richard III*) and already a multiply qualified Quickly, delivered the infallibly moving account of Falstaff's death.

Moss, in collaboration with Urjo Kareda, directed one other large-scale production: *The Woman* (1979) by Britain's most virulently uncompromising left-wing playwright, Edward Bond. A virtual free compendium of Greek legend, the play is the second of two epic variations by Bond on literary or mythological themes. The first was *Lear*, on the face of it a more obvious choice for the Festival.

Bond himself had directed *The Woman* at the National Theatre, and the sweep and boldness of his staging had taken everyone by surprise. He never equalled it in his subsequent productions of his own plays, which tended to be crabbed and awkward, and the Stratford directors of *The Woman* failed to equal it too. Without that strength and eloquence the play, a sustained assault on the cradle of male-dominated western civilization, can seem naggingly didactic and one-sided.

Martha Henry was properly scaled for Bond's craftily avenging Hecuba; Clare Coulter, a heroine of the Toronto new-theatre scene, was underpowered for his Ismene. More precisely, perhaps, she was underpowered for the Avon stage; it would have been interesting to see what she might have done at Stratford in later years, when she matured into one of the best actresses in Canada, capable of handling all the rhetoric any playwright might throw at her, though admittedly still in small spaces. *The Woman* was well worth Stratford's time, but along with *Henry V* and a disastrous version of Goldoni's *The Servant of Two Masters*, it lowered Moss's stock as a Festival director.

In 1979 a brace of star actresses from earlier seasons returned as directors. (Jamie Portman has observed that "no male artistic director in Canadian theatre history was as hospitable to woman directors as Robin Phillips.") Frances Hyland staged a good straightforward *Othello*, with Alan Scarfe in the title role. Stratford's previous two *Othello*s had mainly been noted for fine Desdemonas, one of them Hyland herself. Domini Blythe fitted honourably into this tradition, but it was Nicholas Pennell who upheld a far older tradition by walking off with the play as Iago. His

acting had often been polite to a fault; playing the greatest of villains obviously released something in him. He hinted at a few motives for Iago's malignity but did not stress them; what counted was the sheer dogged glitter of evil.

Zoe Caldwell's production of *Richard II* might also be called straightforward, since it took a definite path and kept to it. It might even be called conventional, although the conventions it adhered to were not the customary ones. It was a rigidly formalized production in the "Japanese" mode of Phillips's *Macbeth*. Phillips had intended to direct it himself, but ill health caused him to cut back on the number of shows he undertook in this, his penultimate season. The spareness of the staging was intended to concentrate attention on the text and the principal performances, of which there were no fewer than six. Upping the ante on Phillips's *Hamlet* and Moss's *Henry V* with their alternating protagonists, this production offered an embarrassment of Richards. (The phrase is Kenneth Tynan's when faced with a mere two performances of this play in one week.) Three kings were paraded on separate nights, each one teamed with a different Bolingbroke. A saintly Nicholas Pennell was matched against an overparted Rod Beattie. A hysterical Frank Maraden was paired with a steely Jim McQueen. A handsome Stephen Russell was seen off by an efficient Craig Dudley.

Of these half-dozen performances, not one made any kind of history. Phillips's multiple-casting concept had now reached the point of mannerism. It seems in retrospect unfair to the actors, to the audience, and even to the director. True, she knew what she was getting into, but it would have been good to see Caldwell direct her one

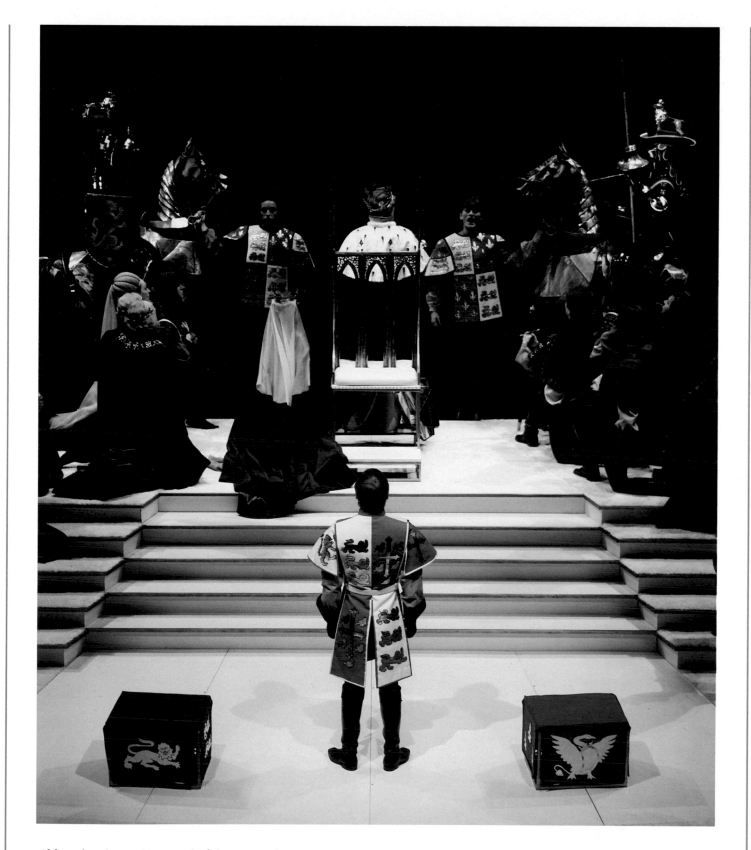

*Although enlivened by wonderful props and costumes, Daphne Dare's severe set design for the 1979 production of* Richard II
*— five white steps on the bare stage with a plain screen at the back — found few admirers among the critics.*

*The characters in the 1975 production of* Kennedy's Children *wait out a storm in a Lower East Side bar by remembering the sixties (above), while* The Gin Game's *Douglas Rain and Kate Reid reminisce and play cards in a retirement home (below).*

Hume Cronyn's uncompromisingly villainous Shylock alone excepted.

Glassco might have fared better if he could have directed Shakespeare, too, on the far less demanding Third Stage; two later Shakespearean debutantes did very well there. The first was Pamela Hawthorn, from the Vancouver New Play Centre, who staged a breezy in-the-round *Taming of the Shrew* (1979). Giving this play to a woman director has come to seem a reliable way of pre-empting criticism; what is surprising, though perhaps reassuring, is how often this results in a traditional romantic interpretation, slightly modified. That was the case here: Jamie Portman described the relationship of Graeme Campbell's Petruchio and Margot Dionne's Kate as "sexually charged" and "a meeting of intellectual equals." In other words, this was the good old love-at-first-sight story, reinvigorated by a strong older actor and a vibrant young one.

In Michael Langham's day, Stratford had embarked on the three *Henry VI* plays, compressed into two, and pulled up stakes halfway through. In 1980 any possibility of this history repeating itself was smartly forestalled by cramming the trilogy into one four-hour play. Pam Brighton, a recent immigrant from Britain, was entrusted with adapting and directing it, and she came up with an exhausting, exhilarating production (Ray Conlogue in the *Globe and Mail* called it "a splendid ordeal") of a kind that Stratford had not seen before.

This *Henry VI* was rough Shakespeare, regarding its royal warmongers with jovial cynicism rather than highly polished irony. There was excellent if scrambled storytelling. There was also a democratic mix of seasoned

Stratford production on her own terms.

Bill Glassco, founder of Toronto's Tarragon Theatre, had made an auspicious Third Stage debut in 1975 with the American playwright Robert Patrick's riveting tone-poem *Kennedy's Children*, five intercut monologues, by turns hilarious and moving, for survivors of the Camelot sixties. Glassco then made an inauspicious Festival Theatre debut with *The Merchant of Venice*, a production that became the season's critical whipping-boy just as Hutt's *Saint Joan* had the previous year. Hutt's production, though, was able eventually to rise above it; Glassco's sank with all hands, actors and beginners. It accommodated two contrasting studies in bloodlust: veteran Nicholas Pennell as Richard Crookback, striding (or limping) with obvious delight still further from his accustomed virtuous image, killing for ambition, and new boy Stephen Ouimette as Young Clifford, killing for revenge. Casting a Quebec actress, Luce Guilbeault, in the dominating role of Margaret of Anjou was a less fortunate idea. Peggy Ashcroft had played the role with a French accent, but she was Peggy Ashcroft; French Canadians had played French roles in other histories, but they had not had to handle nearly as many iambic pentameters.

A new strain of production began to appear in the second half of Phillips's reign: call it Broadway Stratford. A respected New York director, Mel Shapiro, staged two recent American plays in 1980. One, D. L. Coburn's *The Gin Game*, had been a big hit and won a Pulitzer Prize (the latter honour being more of a warning than a recommendation). A play about two old people in a retirement home, it had titillated Broadway audiences with the revelation that senior citizens can lose their tempers and even swear, but that they can be cute as hell while doing it, especially when played by a well-loved real-life couple like Jessica Tandy and Hume Cronyn. Though both these actors were now in the Stratford company, the slumming expedition was undertaken this time by Kate Reid and Douglas Rain.

Nothing in Stratford's later ventures into Broadway repertoire was to be quite as unforgivable as *The Gin Game* (well, maybe *Man of La Mancha*). Still, it brought Kate Reid back to Stratford to appear in John Guare's *Bosoms and Neglect*. Guare, who was later to write the superb *Six*

## "*I'm a little fish out of water...*"

### Andrea Martin

I don't think I'd ever actually been to Stratford when I was asked to play Sybil in *Private Lives*. I was a little cocky, because I was quite successful in Second City. And then the first day of rehearsal we did a read-through, and I was thinking, "Gee, I'm a little fish out of water, but I'll be okay because I'm funny."

I did the first line and Robin Phillips said, "No, I wouldn't do it in an English accent." From that moment on I knew I was in trouble. I'm a girl from Portland, Maine, who's done some sketch accents, and all of a sudden I'm trying to do an English one, and I really don't know how to be a person underneath the accent. When I look back on it, I don't know how I dared to do what I did.

*In addition to her role in* Private Lives, *Andrea Martin played the Old Lady in the musical* Candide *in 1978.*

*Degrees of Separation*, was already recognized as one of the wittiest and quirkiest playwrights in America, and the play gave Reid the role of her career (she had played it in its first, New York production the previous year), as a blind and dying woman still set on controlling the life of her middle-aged bookworm son. She was extraordinary. The play, incidentally, was a comedy.

"Stratford," wrote Stephen Godfrey of the *Globe and Mail* in 1978, "is not the kind of place where you expect the rejuvenation of the big-budget musical to take place." Little did he know. However, the first Broadway-pedigreed show to be staged at Stratford constituted a very tentative start. *Candide* had as impressive a set of cultural credentials as any classical theatre could hope to advertise: source by Voltaire, music by Leonard Bernstein, lyrics by Richard Wilbur (Stratford's own Molière man) and Stephen Sondheim, and original 1956 staging by Tyrone Guthrie himself. However, it was always a problematic show despite a wonderful score. This production, by Lotfi Mansouri of the Canadian Opera Company, fell flat; even Andrea Martin, the then-rising Second City comedienne, made no great splash as the easily-assimilated Old Lady, a role she was to repeat on Broadway years later.

Worse still, far worse, was *Happy New Year* (1979), an ill-advised attempt by Broadway veteran Burt Shevelove to graft some little-known Cole Porter songs, some of them excellent, on to the trunk of *Holiday*, a 1928 comedy by Philip Barry. The text and the tunes came from roughly the same period and milieu, but breaking up a still-viable play with songs that weren't even written to fit it is an invariable recipe for

disaster, and Shevelove's production acted like it knew it. (It marched on to ritual failure in New York, nonetheless.)

Robin Phillips's determination to stage new Canadian plays at Stratford bore fruit in his very first season. *Fellowship* by a Toronto playwright, Michael Tait, was somewhat ahead of its time (though based on a true incident); it dealt with a religious cult in a run-down house. It was directed by a familiar member of the company, Bernard Hopkins, though Phillips had originally thought of staging it himself. There were certainly elements of theatricality in it that might have attracted him: they culminated in the on-stage crucifixion of a crazed Anglican priest. (He was valiantly acted by Neil Vipond, who had played walk-ons in the Festival's first three seasons. This was some homecoming.)

Nobody thought the play made much sense. Still, it was a beginning. The new-play policy was placed on a more systematic footing at the end of 1975, with the arrival of Kareda as literary manager, and was further reinforced in 1977 by the appointment of Peter Moss as director of the Third Stage, where the plays were produced.

The policy encouraged not only new plays but also commissioned new translations — more strictly, since the playwrights were rarely bilingual, adaptations — of old ones. John Murrell's versions of Chekhov were outstandingly successful examples of the latter, but there seemed to be a curse on Stratford productions of Murrell's own plays. Three of them — *Parma*, *Memoir*, and *Waiting for the Parade* — were announced and then cancelled. It was years before a Murrell play was produced at the Festival. By contrast, Tom Cone's adaptation of *The Servant*

*of Two Masters* proved unfortunate, but his own brief, lyrical piece *Stargazing* was put on in 1978, under the sensitive direction of Pamela Hawthorn, to beguiling effect.

Most — no, all — of the new plays have proved ephemeral, but then so do most plays. High among those that seemed exciting at the time was Larry Fineberg's *Eve* (1976), based on a novel by Constance Beresford-Howe and starring Jessica Tandy, who in fact suggested the project, much as her husband was later to suggest *Foxfire*. It gave her a virtuoso and determinedly un-elegant role as a sixty-five-year-old woman who turns her back on a long marriage to live her own life in a Montreal basement, and — under the direction of the Anglo-American Vivian Matalon — she gave a heart-lifting performance. A really first-rate play, though, should resonate beyond its own borders, and this one seemed very wan when it was mounted a few years later in London. Fineberg's subsequent Stratford entry was a pointless rewrite of *Medea* (1978) directed by John Palmer.

Sheldon Rosen's *Ned and Jack* (1978), directed by Moss, was the only new Third Stage play to be brought back a year later at the Avon. It imagined a 1922 encounter between John Barrymore, at the height of his success, and Edward Sheldon, a once-successful playwright, now blind and crippled; this being Barrymore, it was a drunken encounter. Alan Scarfe played Barrymore. Many of his performances during this period (in roles ranging from Bottom to Othello) were coarse or stolid, but this outstandingly juicy role gave him his biggest success since his early Tony Lumpkin. Gina Mallet, reviewing the Avon transfer, thought the play would work better as Scarfe's

## And On to Broadway

The renowned husband-and-wife team of Jessica Tandy and Hume Cronyn, having regretted turning down Tom Patterson's invitation to join the first company in 1953, both acted in Stratford during the Phillips years. In 1980 they appeared in the première of *Foxfire*, co-written by Cronyn. Tandy played the widow Annie Nations (far right, top), and Cronyn the ghost of her late husband, Hector (far right, bottom). The cast also included Richard Monette and a young Brent Carver as the couple's son. A later Broadway production of *Foxfire* won a Tony Award — an achievement that was echoed many years later when Christopher Plummer received a Tony for his performance in *Barrymore*, another new play that had premièred at Stratford.

*(Inset) In 1980 Cronyn and Tandy appeared in a programme of readings and songs with the Stratford Youth Choir, a short-lived addition to the Festival company.*

FESTIVAL STAGE

28th Season
June 9 to November 8

Stratford Festival
Canada, 1980

JESSICA TANDY
HUME CRONYN
and
The Stratford
Youth Choir

## "*My performance was too self-conscious...*"

### William Hutt

One night Robin came back to my dressing room and he said, "Bill, I want you to take your subconscious on stage tonight." So I asked him what that meant. It meant that my performance was becoming too self-conscious. It's the old thing of nudging the audience slightly and saying, "Look, folks, what I am doing," instead of just doing it.

In the final act of *Long Day's Journey Into Night*, there came one line for which O'Neill's stage direction is "Tyrone, in guilty confusion," and I did all sorts of funny things with it. And Robin said, "Stop, Bill. I don't believe you." In other words you're *telling* me you're in guilty confusion instead of *being* in guilty confusion.

one-man show; she might have been foreseeing Christopher Plummer's *Barrymore*, nearly twenty years later. In truth, something about the play's one-on-one confrontation sounds glib, but of all these plays it might be the most worth reviving.

The least might be *Victoria* (1979) from a Vancouver playwright, Steve Petch, and director, Kathryn Shaw. It concerned a highly dysfunctional Canadian family living in squalor in California. The play elicited an endearingly spluttering review from McKenzie Porter, the notoriously conservative critic of the Toronto *Sun*, who pronounced it "pretentious, offensive, Canada Council-ish taradiddle."

In a category of its own was *Barren/Yerma*, officially described as "an improvisation inspired by Lorca's *Yerma*." Federico García Lorca's play concerns an infertile Spanish woman shunned by her extremely fecund neighbours. Pam Brighton, the assigned director, balked when confronted with the text (a not unprecedented reaction) and had her actors improvise a contemporary counter-play about an Ontario woman suffering from "intellectual sterility," an affliction less easily pinned. Confusingly, she seemed still to be suffering from physical sterility as well; according to David McCaughna's pointed description in the *Toronto Star*, the upshot was "like a *Cosmo* story about a woman searching for selfhood."

It did get points for enterprise, and it paved the way for Brighton's cheeky *Henry VI* the following year. It also focused attention on two young actors of considerable importance to Stratford's

long-term future: Diane D'Aquila as the former Yerma ("like a wailing banshee," said McCaughna) and Peter Donaldson ("quite funny playing a student whose essay is late").

A few more or less literary odds-and-ends, spread out across the six Phillips seasons, complete the record: the celebrated one-man play *Brief Lives* with Douglas Rain playing John Aubrey, the antic antiquarian; a quadruple bill of Samuel Beckett brevities, one of them marking the directorial debut of Richard Monette; an unaccountable entertainment called *Heloise and Abelard* in which Ted Follows and Dawn Greenhalgh, veterans of earlier Stratford seasons, stood up and read the luckless lovers' listless letters.

Phillips's swan-song was *Long Day's Journey Into Night*, and it might have made a magnificent, if defiantly unfestive, finale. And in fact, at the very end, it did: Jessica Tandy's Mary Tyrone was as fine as everybody had expected, and her delivery of the final reverie, in which the drugged wife and mother mentally retreats into girlhood, was very moving. Tandy, both tough and delicate, was ideally equipped among actresses to conjure both ages at the same time. But in general the production was disappointing, ladling out gloom as if that were enough to make a tragedy.

William Hutt had played James Tyrone before, and was to do so — magnificently — again; this intermediate performance, though, was excessively tight and cold. Graeme Campbell, enterprisingly cast, livened things up as Jamie, the elder brother, and the auto-biographical Edmund — Eugene O'Neill himself — was hauntingly played by Brent Carver, by all odds the most exciting young actor in Canada.

This was Carver's first season at

*Jessica Tandy (opposite and above) as Mary Tyrone, William Hutt as James Tyrone, Brent Carver as Edmund, and Graeme Campbell as Jamie appear in a scene from the 1980 production of Eugene O'Neill's autobiographical masterpiece,* Long Day's Journey Into Night.

Stratford and his most important role in it. He was to do extraordinary work there in future years, though he was never a long-term pillar of the Festival: he was an actor around Stratford rather than of it. But his presence points up a disquieting feature of the Phillips regime: its failure to recruit and develop striking young actors from outside its existing ranks. There were Carver, Richard McMillan, Peter Donaldson, Stephen Ouimette — very few others and these were huge companies. The situation with young actresses was brighter — Domini Blythe, Goldie Semple, Margot Dionne — but, unfair though it may be, a Shakespeare-based company needs a

preponderance of men, and too many of these, including some entrusted with leading roles, were bland.

Perhaps this is quibbling. Phillips was able to attract Brian Bedford and Maggie Smith, and to keep them attracted. He inherited many actors from Gascon and his predecessors and provided an environment in which they could, on a continuing basis, excel: William Hutt and Martha Henry, obviously, but also such dependables as Max Helpmann and Mary Savidge and such comparative youngsters as Marti Maraden and Richard Monette. He had a huge vision — the sheer expanding bulk of the three theatres' output bears

witness to that — which he filled out, both on the stage and behind it, with extraordinarily painstaking detail.

Michael Langham probably maintained a higher overall standard of production, but Phillips's imprint on the Festival remains greater than that of any artistic director except Guthrie. One of the nicer things about Stratford is its continuity: the directors, after their terms of office, have consistently returned as guests and have often, in that more relaxed capacity, done their best work. Some of Phillips's finest Stratford productions still lay ahead.

Before he reached them, though, a lot of blood had to flow.

Five carousel animals — a rooster, a pig, a rabbit, and two horses — were constructed for Brian Macdonald's 1991 production of the musical Carousel (inset). One of the horses was later donated as a prize in a fundraising event for charity; the other (above) remains in storage in the Festival's Burritt Street warehouse, along with thousands of other props and costumes.

## From Simulated Soup to Imitation Nuts

Every kind of stage property from scrolls to severed heads, from mechanical monkeys to fake foodstuffs, is made in the Festival's workshops. (Right, top) Propmakers Ken Dubblestyne and Stewart Robertson (in background) build a rocking horse for Robin Phillips's 1987 production of *The School for Scandal.* (Right, below) Jennifer Macdonald works on a giant hibiscus for Richard Monette's 1994 production of *Twelfth Night,* designed by Debra Hanson. (Below, left) Brian Jackon, then head of props, designer and prop-maker Marie Day, Michael Langham, and Christopher Plummer examine a shield used in Douglas Campbell's 1958 production of *The Winter's Tale.* Plummer played Leontes in the production, which was designed by Tanya Moiseiwitsch.

*(Inset) "Soft props" used to dress dummy figures in 1989's Titus Andronicus. (Left) Prop-maker Jacqueline Cundall (left), designer Tanya Moiseiwitsch, and Tyrone Guthrie examine the chain of office worn by Alec Guinness in the inaugural production of Richard III.*

# Chapter Five

# *The Hirsch Years*

Robin Phillips was so hard an act to follow that Stratford tried its hardest not to follow him.

To be more precise, the Festival's board of governors did its best to eliminate the necessity of having him followed. They had received plenty of warnings that Phillips would not stay forever. In both 1976 and 1978 he announced his resignation, citing demoralization in the face of continuing nationalist sniping on the first occasion, and illness and exhaustion on the second. Theoretically, 1979 was a sabbatical year for him, though he still ended up directing three plays; 1980 was a personal tour-de-force that he undertook on the assumption that it would be his last as artistic director. The board, however, seems to have made no serious effort to recruit a successor. It floated various complicated schemes for multi-person directorates that would involve Phillips at least in an advisory capacity. These eventually resolved into a plan for a two-tier committee ("working collectively," according to a press release issued by the board in August 1980) whose members would be Brian Bedford, Len Cariou, Martha Henry, Pam Brighton, William Hutt, Urjo Kareda, Peter Moss, Peter Roberts (the Festival's production manager), Douglas Rain, and Phillips.

It may have seemed comforting to have all those familiar names on board, but it is impossible to believe that so cumbersome a mechanism could ever have worked. Many of its constituents seem to have come to the same conclusion; by October 1980 all had resigned except for Kareda, Henry, Moss, and Brighton. This quartet, universally known as the Gang of Four, prepared — with the stated public support of the board — a programme for the 1981 season that still looks, on paper, unusually appetizing. It was never put to the test on stage.

What happened next is somewhat murky and wholly disgraceful. Stratford had recently appointed a new executive director, an Englishman named Peter Stevens. He advised the board that the Gang of Four's programme was economically unviable and persuaded them to approach the world-famous British director John Dexter to take over the Festival. It is conceivable that, having been deprived of the opportunity of working with one famous British director, Robin Phillips, Stevens had his

*John Hirsch, actor James Blendick remembers, "wanted you to be as real as possible, whatever that took. It didn't matter to him as long as he got that — the reality of it." An outstanding Canadian director, Hirsch had often been proposed as a successor to Phillips, but it took a crisis to give him the job.*

heart set on working with another. After ten days during which the four directors-designate were left in ignorance to work on their season, they were informed that they were out, with no right of appeal, and that Dexter was in.

Scandal and pandemonium ensued. For the first time in Stratford history, the cultural nationalists — spearheaded by Canadian Actors' Equity — truly had something to protest about, though the Gang of Four themselves were at pains to point out that the issue was not one of nationality but of unfair and underhanded treatment. The Stratford actors, speaking through their Equity deputy, Rod Beattie, made the same point: "We feel as if we have made the right stand on the wrong ground." In any event Dexter was denied a visa to work in Canada. And Stratford, on the brink of 1981, found itself without an artistic director and very possibly without a festival.

There may be some doubt as to how long rule by quadrumvirate could have lasted. None of the Four was at this time a front-rank director of plays, though Martha Henry would become one. (At this point, though, she was the least experienced, having only directed her then-husband Douglas Rain in the monologue *Brief Lives*.) However, all except Brighton, who shortly returned to the United Kingdom, were to become successful directors of Canadian theatres. So they may be said to have had the last laugh on Dexter, a great director of plays, who for a time was director of productions at the Metropolitan Opera in New York but would go to his (premature) grave without ever having headed a dramatic theatre of his own.

One name that had cropped up repeatedly as a possible successor to Phillips was that of John Hirsch, generally acknowledged as the finest director to hold a Canadian passport, though by now working much of the time in the U.S. In the hour of severest crisis he was approached by a hastily reconvened Stratford search committee and offered the job. So it was that after months of damaging, agonizing, and bitterly farcical drama, the new artistic directorship of the Stratford Festival was taken on by the very man who should have had it in the first place.

Whether he was now in a position to do justice to it is another question. Hirsch accepted on the understanding that he would oversee the 1981 season but not stage any shows himself until 1982. The 1981 season was a hastily assembled patchwork whose primary achievements were that it existed at all and was not a disaster when it did.

Hirsch and his producer, Muriel Sherrin, reached back to the pre-Phillips years and engaged Jean Gascon to direct two productions. He opened proceedings on the Festival stage with Molière's *The Misanthrope*, a prettily decorated but harshly lit production that was a distinct let-down after his famous *Tartuffe*, even with Brian Bedford playing Alceste.

He did far better at the Avon with Friedrich Dürrenmatt's *The Visit*, the paradigm of the post-Expressionist parable plays prevalent in mid-century middle-Europe: dark moral comedies set in symbolic townships whose inhabitants have job descriptions — the Schoolmaster, the Mayor — where their personalities should be. The Canadian theatre, especially its French sector, has a direct line to this style, and Gascon handled it masterfully, aided by John Ferguson's artfully artificial sets, on which a train station, for example, looked the very picture of itself.

Gascon's company gave him the anonymously competent performances that the play's supporting roles require. Of the leads, William Hutt (making what was to prove his only contribution to the Hirsch regime) was good, not great, as the man ritually killed by his impoverished fellow citizens at the behest of the fabulously wealthy grande dame whom he seduced and abandoned when she was far from grand and nothing like a dame. This part was played by Alexis Smith, the 1940s movie starlet who in 1971 had confounded all expectations on Broadway with her performance in the Stephen Sondheim–Harold Prince musical *Follies*, in which she both looked and sounded stunning. She looked stunning in *The Visit* too, at least on first appearance, but this time there was no iron beneath and surprisingly little glitter.

Back from Gascon's last season came Peter Dews to direct two of the earliest and most farcical Shakespeare comedies. His *Comedy of Errors* was fair, a conventionally slapstick production in a nineteenth-century setting. It had a rowdy pair of young Dromios: John Jarvis (a future reliable actor) extroverting all over Ephesus and Miles Potter (a future reliable director) spreading balm with a grin. The plum role of the jealous wife Adriana went to Fiona Reid, one of Toronto's brightest young actresses, then best known for her starring role in CBC's "King of Kensington." An obvious candidate for Stratford (she had been part of the Gang of Four's plans), she was to stay there for two largely unfulfilling seasons and has yet to return. Susan Wright, another newcomer and one who *was* to remain at the Festival, played her sister Luciana.

Dews had greater success with *The Taming of the Shrew*. He defused some

John Hirsch's first year as artistic director saw Jean Gascon return to direct The Misanthrope *(above),* which was designed by Desmond Heeley, *and* The Visit, *in which Canadian-born Broadway star Alexis Smith (left) made her only Festival appearance. (Right) John Jarvis and Miles Potter gave lively performances as the Dromios in* The Comedy of Errors, *another 1981 production.*

of the piece's potential problems by framing it firmly as a play performed by strolling actors for the hoodwinked tinker Christopher Sly; he included not only the Shakespearean prologue that sets this up but also an epilogue, found only in an anonymous play with nearly the same title, that rounds it off. As always, some critics greeted this as a revelation, though nearly all productions include it in some form. Indeed Dews's production was pretty much an anthology of standard English approaches to the text, from the appearance of a string of sausages at Petruchio's inquiry "What dogs are these?" to the final happy accommodation between the two principals: Len Cariou's large, robust Petruchio and Sharry Flett's small, wily Katherina.

There was no complete break with the Phillips regime: some actors stayed, and more might have done had the season been assembled earlier. The most distinguished survivor was Brian Bedford, who had intended to take at least a year away from Stratford, but whose feelings of responsibility towards the Festival drew him back. As well as acting in *The Misanthrope*, he directed two plays. After his success with *Titus Andronicus*, he tackled a later and far more complex Roman tragedy, *Coriolanus*. He again showed his mastery of atmospherics and movement.

His protagonist was Len Cariou, who had played small parts at Stratford in three of the Langham years and had subsequently become both a commercial and classical star in the U.S. He had also run the Manitoba Theatre Centre in Winnipeg, and his name had figured among those in a possible post-Phillips group directorate. He seemed, in many ways, to be the home-grown star Stratford was looking for, perhaps a new

Plummer. Like Alexis Smith, he had scored his greatest Broadway success in a Sondheim-Prince musical: in his case it was *Sweeney Todd*, in which he gave a performance of anguished, tragic stature. It had, though, unfortunate after-effects: the near-operatic demands ravaged his voice, as was demonstrated in his later singing roles, while playing in musicals seemed to have broadened and desensitized his acting. This hardly hindered his Petruchio (most audiences at the *Shrew* would rather be watching *Kiss Me, Kate* anyway), but even so rhetorical and pugnacious a tragic hero as Coriolanus has his nuances. Cariou was tremendous when defying his killers at the end, and he split movingly apart before the entreaties of his mother (returning veteran Barbara Chilcott), but he missed the irony that runs not only through the play but through the character. Still, he was a presence.

There was very little presence in Bedford's production of Sheridan's *The Rivals*. This was the one play in the season that had also been planned by the Gang of Four, and the new regime took over their casting of Pat Galloway as Mrs. Malaprop. This unanimity was justified: she was a bright spot. Other welcome familiar faces were Richard Monette as the sensible hero Jack Absolute and Mary Haney as the conniving maid Lucy. The English actor David Langton was imported to play the choleric Sir Anthony and proved not half choleric enough. The play, which can be a delight, here never escaped its reputation as the most dispiritingly wholesome of schoolroom classics.

Surprisingly, *The Rivals* was one of two eighteenth-century comedies on the bill that year. The other, far less familiar, was John O'Keeffe's *Wild Oats*, rediscovered a few years earlier by the RSC (and

(Opposite) An impressive Len Cariou (left) as Coriolanus battled Scott Hylands — later a star of the award-winning TV crime series "Night Heat" — as Tullus Aufidius in the 1981 production of Coriolanus. Two eighteenth-century comedies were staged that year: The Rivals (above) and Wild Oats, with Keene Curtis (below) stomping about the stage as Sir George Thunder.

## *"John and I were in constant battle..."*

### Roberta Maxwell

ohn wanted me to be bright and glamorous. But I was forty-two and the great Irene Worth had been forty-two and her Rosalind had been very mellow. And then, of course, there was the great Miss Smith and she was forty-two when she played it. And Robin had allowed her to be this pining, anguishing Rosalind. But Hirsch wanted me to be joyous, to be — felt — less of what I internally was.

In many ways I suppose after Robin my work changed. And what I felt I could bring to a part changed. So John and I were in constant battle. I think he felt I had betrayed him. But I was old enough, and had invested enough in my own life, to say no. And John didn't like to hear no at all. For a while, John and I lost our friendship.

Roberta Maxwell as Rosalind in As You Like It (1983)

their then-dramaturge Ronald Bryden, by now on the Stratford board). This is a joyous piece, written by a performer and dealing with people who make performing their life, professionally or otherwise; actors always take to it, and so as a result do audiences. Derek Goldby, a British director with a carefully nurtured Canadian reputation for outrageousness, especially at the Shaw Festival, staged it with aplomb and kept himself on a comparatively tight rein.

Scott Hylands, who had already made a very strong impression as Aufidius to Cariou's Coriolanus, now had the leading role of Rover, a strolling player whose conversation is made up of remembered scraps of former roles and who, for reasons too complicated to unravel, is brought to believe that everybody he meets is actually an ill-rehearsed character in a play. ("Well done, old Abrawang," he calls out encouragingly, as a testy naval officer stomps about the stage like a man impersonating a testy naval officer.) The Festival must have longed to hang on to Hylands, an actor able to smile or snarl to equally glowing effect, but he was never to return. Fiona Reid as Lady Amaranth, a moderately susceptible Quaker, gave her clearest Stratford forecast of the high-comic skills she was later to exhibit at the Shaw and elsewhere, and Nicholas Pennell, coming increasingly into his own as a farceur, stole several scenes as Ephraim Smooth, a more hypocritical Quaker, feeling his own oats.

It was not a great season, though it was better than many people had expected (or possibly, in some quarters, hoped). But even with Hirsch fully in charge over the four ensuing seasons, his regime never took on a confident identity of its own: the awkwardness of

the manner of his appointment hung heavy over it throughout. There was good work, though, and Hirsch, contrary to legend, proved that he could be a superb director of Shakespeare.

The key production here is his *As You Like It* (1983). This was much criticized for its presentation of the usurper's palace as a jackbooted police-state HQ, governed by a duke (Graeme Campbell) who relieved his own guilty torment by torturing others. Perhaps it was overstated, but it was powerful; and the play is after all about the contrast between a tyrannical court and a comparatively idyllic forest — comparatively, because this production, like the play, was always on guard to puncture over-idealistic bubbles. This spirit, bittersweet without being cynical, was beautifully realized, and the last scene of hard-won happiness bewitchingly staged, in a wood suddenly full of lanterns. Hirsch had an excellent cast — Roberta Maxwell's Rosalind, Rosemary Dunsmore's Celia, and Pennell's Jaques were especially notable, while another name that now rises from the programme is that of Graham Abbey, the Henry V of Stratford's 2001 season, then a local schoolboy appearing as Second Page — but what counted was the superbly unforced way in which the whole production unfolded. It had the priceless feeling of inevitability.

This was both the pinnacle and the prototype of Hirsch's comedy productions. He geared up for it with *The Tempest* (1982), a production generally damned for the luxuriance of its spectacular effects, starting with an "utterly stunning" shipwreck. (Desmond Heeley was the designer.) In fact the text calls, explicitly and repeatedly, for spectacle. Shakespeare was a showman, and

136

## "As There Comes Light from Heaven"

Lighting is a crucial part of a production's design; indeed, an evocative setting can often be created by lighting alone. A lighting designer begins by drawing up a "lighting plot": a diagram showing what instruments should be used and where each should be placed. Colour is added by mounting tinted plastic transparencies or "gels" in front of lights, while shadows cast by cut-out silhouettes called "gobos" can create the effect of light streaming through tree branches or window frames. The lighting designer works with the director to establish lighting cues for each scene. A lighting change can be almost imperceptible, like the gradual fading of an afternoon sun, or dramatically abrupt, like the sudden appearance of Ariel (Ian Deakin, inset) in the 1982 production of *The Tempest*, lit by resident lighting designer Michael J. Whitfield.

FAIRIES - ATTENDING
TITANIA.

HEELEY '84

A MIDSUMMER NIGHTS DREAM, STRATFORD ONTARIO.

*John Hirsch directed* A Midsummer Night's Dream *in 1984 and* King Lear *in 1985. (Above) Desmond Heeley's costume design for fairies attending Titania in the* Dream. *(Left) Nicholas Pennell played the Fool to Douglas Campbell's Lear. Hirsch wrote that doing* Lear *was "a little like climbing Mount Everest. I don't think it is possible to approach this play without some measure of fear and trembling."*

Robert Fulford, writing in the *Toronto Star*, called this production "a showman's *Tempest*," adding, "Hirsch has taken that part of his artistic personality that responds to show-business and applied it to Shakespeare's most graceful, delicate and eloquent magic play."

Len Cariou's unyielding style brought out the anger in Prospero but none of the grace notes, so the equation failed to balance properly; but there were compensations in the clown scenes (Pennell as Stephano, Miles Potter as Caliban) and, some thought, in the lovers. Ray Conlogue wrote that Sharry Flett's Miranda had "the brows of a storm-trooper," which hardly suggests your average ingénue, and that Jim Mezon's Ferdinand was "loopy with love." Those who know this fine actor's later work (sensitive-benevolent or sensitive-creepy) have difficulty crediting that this casting ever happened, but everybody was young once.

Hirsch's second *Midsummer Night's Dream* (1984) followed the trajectory of his *As You Like It* from violence to rejoicing, but with considerably less support from the text. It started with an unscripted battle between Theseus and the Amazons, leading to an undertow of bitterness in the defeated Hippolyta's acceptance of her conqueror's wedding plans. Directors are always trying to read this into the play — though few as determinedly as Hirsch — but there is precious little support for it in the lines. After Nicholas Pennell and Patricia Conolly had performed the now customary morphing from these roles into Oberon and Titania, the bitterness was ratcheted up: Pennell delivered Oberon's "I know a bank" as if, according to David Prosser of the Kingston *Whig-Standard*, he'd once been mugged there. His co-conspirator was the young Diego

Matamoros, taller and thinner than the average Puck, and rather effective.

The wood they inhabited (Heeley again) was stiflingly uninviting. Hirsch's interpretation again took off from the already outmoded theories advanced by Jan Kott in *Shakespeare Our Contemporary* but had the good sense not to follow them all the way. Titania may have seemed at the point of copulating with the ass-headed Bottom before the audience's very eyes, but Brian Bedford, both within and without his mask, was still a traditional stage-struck weaver, one of nature's scene-stealers operating with gloriously quiet assurance. Jamie Portman commended Hirsch for having, in pushing the play to extremes, "the courage of his excesses"; Conlogue, weighing the balance of grimness and beatitude, acutely noted that Hirsch "admits the idea of reconciliation but can't quite trust it."

Hirsch would have been the first to acknowledge — indeed proclaim — the mark left on him and his work by his childhood as a Jewish orphan in a devastated Europe. His vision of Shakespeare may have been partial, but it was not false or externally imposed: it was heartfelt, not trendy. The changeling boy, usually unseen, was an important figure in his production of the *Dream*. His *As You Like It* started with a bemused child alone on stage. A similar image late in his production of *King Lear* (1985) had the audience catching its breath: a small boy, caught between the advancing armies of France and England, holding up his hand as if to ward them off.

On the face of it, *Lear* was a better fit for Hirsch than any of the comedies, but in fact his work was diminished without a comic edge. There seemed, too, to be a disjunction between the director and his leading actor, the returning Douglas Campbell. There were imaginatively monumental touches — the play began with the literal image of Lear's "wheel of fire," a huge torchlit cartwheel hung aloft and metamorphosing into a chandelier — but Campbell's performance was monumental in another, frankly old-fashioned way. This was one Lear who had no difficulty outstorming the thunder, but the very relentlessness of his vocal power prevented him from being moving. The actor's son, Benedict Campbell, had one of his first substantial Stratford roles as a too-lightweight Edmund, but James Blendick, another pre-Phillips refugee, was universally praised as Kent.

Hirsch directed few non-Shakespearean classics at this time. His Avon production of Schiller's *Mary Stuart* (1982) featured an overpowering set by the Broadway designer Ming Cho Lee, suggesting the imprisonment of all the characters by historical forces, and an American translation by Joe McClinton of the kind sometimes described as "vigorous": i.e., determinedly unpolished. Margot Dionne played Mary Queen of Scots as a romantic martyr, and Pat Galloway played Elizabeth I as a jealous tyrant; this seems to have been pretty much how Schiller saw them, but the production pushed it to extremes. The play centres on an imagined confrontation between the two queens, who historically never met. It should reveal the weaknesses in both, but here the scales were tipped firmly in Mary's favour. R. H. Thomson, already an acclaimed young actor in Toronto, played the dashing Mortimer in an overwrought style that dismayed everybody, not least Thomson himself. Maybe Hirsch was

## Writers in Our Midst

Since the first three seasons, when Robertson Davies (below, circa 1953) wrote eloquently about the productions on stage, the Festival has cultivated relationships with some of Canada's — and the world's — best writers. Davies was one of the guests (along with scholar Northrop Frye, novelist Hugh MacLennan, and playwright Arthur Miller) in the Festival's first writers' lecture series in 1982. He also participated, as did noted feminist author Gloria Steinem, in a series of weekend seminars that was introduced in 1990, and in the "Celebrated Writers Series" of lectures and readings that replaced it in 1993. This latter series has also included appearances by such renowned authors as Margaret Atwood, Timothy Findley, Rohinton Mistry, Joyce Carol Oates, Michael Ondaatje, Mordecai Richler, Peter Shaffer, Carol Shields, Jane Urquhart, and Kurt Vonnegut.

Designed by Debra Hanson, the metallic-mesh mask at left (modelled here by Daniel MacDonell) was worn by George Chiang in Richard Monette's 1994 production of Twelfth Night. In 1984, the carnival revellers in The Merchant of Venice (top) wore papier-mâché masks designed by Christina Poddubiuk. (Above) Propmaker Ken Dubblestyne applies finishing touches to masks of sized gauze for the 1997 re-creation of Tyrone Guthrie's legendary Oedipus Rex, originally designed by Tanya Moiseiwitsch. (Right) a mask designed by Susan Benson for the 1974 production of the medieval morality play The Summoning of Everyman.

## *"You Shall Play It in a Mask"*

An essential element in all kinds of drama from ancient Greek tragedy to commedia dell'arte, masks are often worn in Shakespearean scenes of revelry or magic. The first step in making a mask is to take a cast of the face of the actor who will wear it. This is done by carefully applying plaster bandages, leaving gaps for the actor to breathe through. (Festival mask-makers say that straws are not inserted into the nostrils during this process!) The resulting negative mould is used to make a positive cast, which in turn becomes the armature on which the mask's features are modelled, using Plasticine or clay. From that sculpture another plaster cast is taken that can be used to produce a finished mask in papier-mâché, latex rubber, or any other desired medium.

pushing for a grandeur his actors could not deliver.

Like Gascon, Hirsch had his finest hour with a production of Molière, and indeed of the very same play. *Tartuffe* (1984) was as tight, searching, and stylish a production as has been seen at Stratford, ever. There were two palpable links to the previous version: the use of Richard Wilbur's translation and the presence of Pat Galloway in her old role of the maid Dorine. As Jamie Portman observed, the cast and crew summed up thirty years of Stratford history. Tanya Moiseiwitsch designed a handsome and useful setting in dark oak. Douglas Campbell, whose power (like Hirsch's own) was always best harnessed in comedy, played a massively credulous Orgon, crushing everybody under the weight of his blinkered benevolence. Other Stratford foundation stones included Amelia Hall and William Needles, with such bright newcomers as Seana McKenna, Andrew Gillies, and Shaun Austin-Olsen. In the solid middle there was Nicholas Pennell, giving full cheerful value to the sensible brother-in-law, and as Tartuffe there was Brian Bedford.

Bedford was less of a Dickensian hand-wringing hypocrite than William Hutt had been: he was personable and contained and, when he finally turned on the victimized family and angrily accused *them* of betraying *him*, truly frightening. This Tartuffe may not have believed in his own religious pretensions, but he certainly believed in his own righteousness. It was the crowning performance in Bedford's line of puritans, hypocritical or otherwise.

His first Elmire was Roberta Maxwell; when the production, like Gascon's, was brought back for a second season, she was succeeded by Domini Blythe. The seduction scene

between Blythe and Bedford, with Campbell hidden under the table, reached a level of contact, concentration, and sheer intimate grownupness very rare in the Festival Theatre's wide-open spaces.

At the beginning of his tenure, Hirsch told Ray Conlogue, with only slight exaggeration, that the only directors to whom a thrust stage was "natural" were those "with a choreographic sense, twenty years of repertory experience, nine *Shrew*s and five *Hamlet*s behind them." Such directors did not, of course, exist; and whatever his intentions, Hirsch did little to invent them. Regressively and regrettably, only one new Canadian director was asked to stage a major classical production in Hirsch's time. This was Des McAnuff, on his way to being famous in California and on Broadway, but here coming up with another disappointing Stratford *Macbeth* (1983), with Nicholas Pennell and Roberta Maxwell respectively stolid and freezing in the leads. As in Phillips's production, one visual effect stood out, and it came at the same point in the play: at the spot on which Banquo had been murdered an altar arose, which in turn was transformed into the banqueting table.

American directors also came in, to no great effect. Robert Beard, young and fairly untried, staged a moping *Merry Wives of Windsor* (1982). Mark Lamos, from Hartford Stage, directed 1984's *Merchant of Venice* in an eighteenth-century setting, mostly indifferent but with some stark moments: especially vivid was the forcible-conversion image of Richard Monette's Antonio hanging a crucifix around the neck of John Neville's powerful Jew. Lamos, in an interview, offered a telling description of the Festival Theatre space and the

## "*This Shakespeare stuff is really not for kids...*"

### Colm Feore

[Playing Romeo] was terrifying but extraordinary. Hirsch wanted us to be passionate, to be lively, so there was an awful lot of dashing around. I remember after the first run-through of the first act, I simply passed out. I didn't faint, but I lay down on a table, heaving. This Shakespeare stuff is really not for kids. It was then that I got a glimmer of an understanding about the stamina required to do this stuff properly.

And then I got stronger and stronger. I thought, oh this is fun. I mean if there's a runner's high — I don't run long enough to find out — I know there's a Shakespeare big-show high. And it comes from throwing yourself at these parts with abandon and if you can come out on the other end of it, you've really learned something.

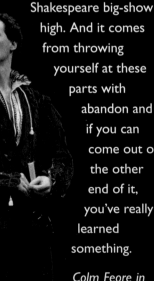

*Colm Feore in*
Romeo and
Juliet *(1984)*

way it had of forcing an untried director into the processional style: "a sculptured space, with the blocking already sketched in by Tony Guthrie."

Hirsch continued to fall back on British directors, many of them by now old-guard. Peter Dews's last Stratford production was probably his best: a *Romeo and Juliet* (1984) which, though conventional, had genuine fire in it. It also, as this play and this theatre should, gave birth to a couple of stars from right within the company. Colm Feore, after three years of supporting roles, gave Romeo a quiet sense of wonder that made his love almost a religious quest. Seana McKenna, with two seasons' seasoning, was fresh enough to show the child in Juliet and skilled enough to play the woman, and broke her audiences' hearts as both. There was also an unusually sexy and commanding Lady Capulet from Patricia Conolly.

David Giles returned to Stratford for a pleasing enough *Twelfth Night* (1985) in the currently approved sombre vein. Nicholas Pennell walked off with yet another play as Malvolio, sharing comic honours with Edward Atienza's practised and acerbic Feste. McKenna paradoxically found less joy in Viola than she had in Juliet, though her Romeo was now her Orsino: witty casting, allowing Feore to present more romantic mooning, with the satire turned up to maximum. Their onstage courtship continued in *She Stoops to Conquer* (1985). His shyness came in very handy for Young Marlow, and she pertly blossomed when Miss Hardcastle went into barmaid mode, but their comic relationship never really combusted. David William's production was otherwise a heavy-going affair in which the player who attracted most attention

was an anonymous fellow in a bear suit. (It was a walk-on role).

Most interesting of these traditionalist stagings was a *Richard II* (1983) from Richard Cottrell, who some fifteen years earlier had directed the English production of the same play that had made a star of Ian McKellen. McKellen had played a king ecstatically wedded to the idea of his own kingship and undone by the failure of his rebellious subjects to play the game by his rules. Brian Bedford's Richard started from the same point but allowed the gap between appearance and reality to open wider, and then filled it up with irony. His Richard, mischievous in power, was twice as mischievous in defeat, laughing sardonically at his own foibles and maliciously at the machinations of his enemies. He had to give in to their brutal politics, but his intellect was his revenge: he practically *embarrassed* Bolingbroke on to the throne. This was not an unprecedented idea, but no other actor had ever taken it quite so far. Having played the least humorous of Richard the Thirds, Bedford now gave the most humorous of Richard the Seconds; and even if it was sometimes hard to distinguish the actor's wit from the character's, it was a fascinating performance.

Around it Cottrell built an intelligent production in which Cedric Smith stood out as Bolingbroke, a startling reversion to age-appropriate casting for a young actor whose previous Stratford success had been as the septuagenarian Shallow of *Henry IV*. Unfortunately, Smith then played an unaccountably limp and sanitized Mr. Horner in Cottrell's Avon production of *The Country Wife*.

Of the theoretically more radical Britons, Derek Goldby returned in 1982 to direct a *Julius Caesar* high on violence, which was reasonable, and low on character, which wasn't. Len Cariou's Brutus came across as a booming mouthpiece, and R. H. Thomson, not at this stage a natural orator, made Antony into a nice, sorrowing guy, which is probably only half of him. Cassius, often the most rewarding because the most obviously neurotic role, was so again in the hands of Nicholas Pennell; and as Cinna the Poet, who dies protesting that he is not Cinna the conspirator, Richard Monette was memorably dismembered.

Most eagerly awaited was the advent, in Hirsch's last season, of Michael Bogdanov, associate director of Britain's National Theatre. His production of Howard Brenton's *The Romans in Britain*, an epic play including one graphic scene of homosexual rape, had brought him notoriety and the threat — from England's most celebrated cultural vigilante, Mrs. Mary Whitehouse — of prosecution and even imprisonment. He had channelled his feelings of rage against the forces of puritanism into an interpretation of *Measure for Measure*, which he vigorously proclaimed to be an indictment of repressive government with the Duke as its hypocritical villain. As it happens, *Measure*'s title and its theme derive from a passage in the Sermon on the Mount, whose upshot is "Judge not that ye be not judged." This is weird: a director approaches a play that explicitly tells us not to go looking for villains and then announces that he

has found one. The idea has, of course, a simplistic attractiveness, and Bogdanov was certainly forceful. His *Measure* attracted immediate attention for a prologue set in a leather bar, designed to shock and/or titillate the bourgeoisie. Shakespeare's view of the way of all flesh, as expressed in this

*Patricia Collins played Mistress Overdone (above, second from right), while Eric McCormack, Eric Zivot, and Howard Rosenstein made a kinky rock-band trio (left) in 1985's controversial* Measure for Measure.

play's dialogue, is far more nuanced and much funnier.

Alan Scarfe returned to play the gleefully manipulative Duke demanded by the director. Nicholas Pennell's creepy Angelo was allowed some measure of complexity, since in this scheme he functioned as both Vienna's oppressor and the Duke's victim; it also, coinciding with his Malvolio, enabled Pennell to repeat Brian Bedford's 1975 feat of playing both the great Shakespearean puritans

in one season. In so cynical a production it was inevitable that Isabella (Barbara March) would sink more or less without trace, and that the star role would be Lucio, especially as played by Richard McMillan, returning to drama after a few seasons of Gilbert and Sullivan productions at the Avon.

Certainly nobody slept during this *Measure*. But it was shown up by the work the same season of a maturer English maverick. Ronald Eyre's production of *The Government Inspector* was remarkable for its intermittent savagery and unremitting hilarity, the two modes coming powerfully together in the scene in which the Russian town's oppressed petitioners overwhelm the supposed inspector with their grievances, bearing down on him like (Ray Conlogue's description) "a horde of shambling corpses." It's all in Gogol's text, at least

143

in embryo. So is the dazzling multiple focus in which Richard McMillan presented the title role: the gawky impostor who comes half to believe in his own imposture, the penniless loser suddenly empowered to soak the rich. Peter Donat, the juvenile of twenty years before, returned to give a superbly uninhibited account of the Mayor who is both chief tyrant and chief gull. He was accorded a first entrance of Tamburlaine proportions (after all, both characters are Tartars): "in an enclosed steam bath dragged by sweating minions" (Robert Crew in the *Toronto Star*). Its sides were let down and the comedy of corruption began. With gluttonous designs by Tanya Moiseiwitsch and a cast incited to fever pitch, this show was a rare example of purposeful grotesquerie hitting its target.

The scale of the Festival stage was probably a stimulus: this is a play that often falls flat in English, but this was its second triumphant production at Stratford. Michael Langham, who had directed the first, made a long-overdue return with *Arms and the Man* (1982), a compact and infallible play that on the face of it needed neither him nor that stage, but in the event profited handsomely from both. Shaw's satire on romantic militarism in the Balkans gave Desmond Heeley the cue to turn the acting area into a miniature Ruritania: even the centre balcony, which Hirsch had ordered restored to its pre-Phillips position, though in removable form, was swathed in operettish timber. This provided a perfect environment for Len Cariou's strutting (and self-spoofing)

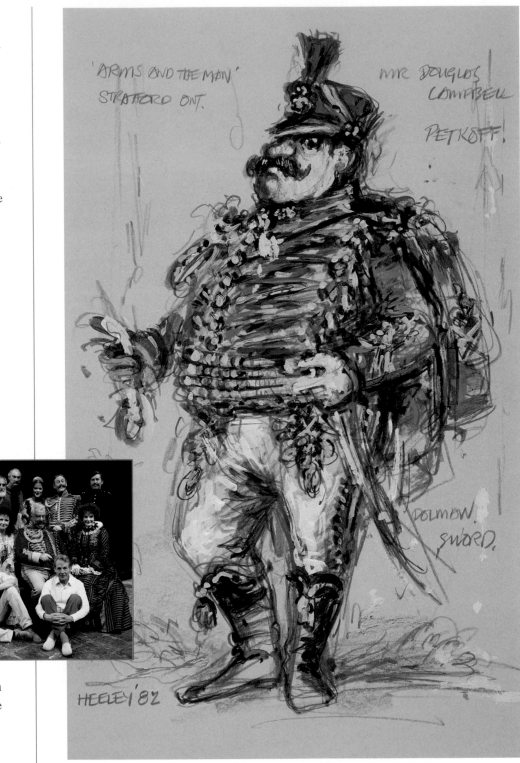

*In 1982, the Festival made a rare foray into Shavian repertoire with* Arms and the Man. *(Inset) Top row, left to right: designer Desmond Heeley and actors Colin Fox, Susan Wright, Len Cariou, and Brian Bedford. Middle row: actors Helen Carey, Douglas Campbell, and Carole Shelley. Bottom row: assistant director Elliott Hayes and director Michael Langham. The sketch is by Desmond Heeley.*

Sergius. It was also the right rustic setting for some old Stratford favourites: Douglas Campbell as the complacent Major; Carole Shelley, luxury casting as his wife; and Helen Carey as Raina, the deceptively starry-eyed heroine. Susan Wright was the delicious and ambitious maid, and Brian Bedford, preternaturally relaxed, put them all into realistic perspective as Captain Bluntschli, phlegmatic prophet of common sense and chocolate creams.

Bedford directed Coward's *Blithe Spirit* at the Avon at the end of the same season, also putting a quizzical shine on the wife-haunted hero Charles. Carey was properly knife-edged as his present wife, Ruth; Shelley was expectedly enchanting as the late and ghostly Elvira; and another returning throaty charmer, Tammy Grimes, cast a refreshing new light on Madame Arcati. To Stephen Godfrey she suggested "a jaunty real estate agent, rather than a medium," but that was the point: this briskly happy medium pursued her business *as* a business.

*Blithe Spirit* is a late Coward comedy, written during World War II, and it ushered in a new emphasis on the "modern classic" repertoire that was to become increasingly important at Stratford. Phillips had toyed with it; Hirsch dived into it. The playwright most usually linked with Coward, Terence Rattigan, was represented with a production of his 1950s double-bill *Separate Tables* (1984), twin studies in sexual and social failure. David William prefaced his production with a burst of rock music, as if in acknowledgement of how much had changed from the plays' shabby-genteel small-hotel world. It was all very English, with John Neville and Domini Blythe impeccably delivering the widely differentiated double performances on which the evening's interest depends and Ann Casson in grande-dame overdrive as the imperious permanent resident who makes their lives a misery, twice over. (It was a part her mother had once played: Casson was Sybil Thorndike's daughter and Douglas Campbell's ex-wife.) Both this production and *Blithe Spirit* were transferred to the Royal Alexandra Theatre in Toronto, and seemed very much at home there.

More important were the revivals of American plays from just after the war. Guy Sprung, one of the founder-directors of the new Toronto theatre movement, had a half-success with *Death of a Salesman* (1983), in which both the play and the characters were dwarfed by another grimly monumental set from Ming Cho Lee. It was largely cast from outside the regular Stratford pool, and the two stars were Americans familiar from the movies. Kim Hunter moved everyone as Linda and so, ultimately, did Nehemiah Persoff as a hulking Willy Loman, groping his way into the light, though some people found his unmistakable Jewishness hard to accept. Willy is a favourite role for Jewish actors, but they don't usually stress the point. In fact, Persoff's rhythms went well with those with which Arthur Miller, perhaps unconsciously, filled his text.

Hirsch himself directed the two most famous Tennessee Williams plays. In *A Streetcar Named Desire* (1984) a Chicago actor, William L. Petersen, came in to play Stanley Kowalski and battled valiantly with the memory of Brando, whom he rather resembled. Patricia Conolly extended herself as Blanche, whom she played not as a pre-destined fragile martyr but as a woman of considerable if strained reserves; and there was fine work from Rosemary Dunsmore as Stella and Les Carlson as Mitch. Hirsch was admirably equipped to bring out both the cruelty and tenderness in Williams, and he did even better with *The Glass Menagerie* (1985). Again his approach was tougher and funnier than the norm, with American actress Sada Thompson brandishing Amanda's Southern-belle memories like weapons. Scott Wentworth, another American and with a Stratford future, similarly avoided wispiness as the narrating son and Susan Coyne drove hard at Laura's fragile mental state.

These three shows confirmed what other theatres had been discovering: that the best Broadway plays of the late forties are the most solid chunk of recent dramatic capital that the English-speaking theatre has to call its own. People will go to them because they are famous and accessible titles, but they are big enough to yield new insights every time.

The modern-masterpiece category obviously accommodates Beckett's *Waiting for Godot*, and it returned (at the Third Stage, 1984) in a production taken over at short notice by a young English director, Leon Rubin, who had assisted on the RSC's magnificent *Nicholas Nickleby*. Some liked Brian Bedford's Vladimir and some Edward Atienza's Estragon, but few claimed that there was any great chemistry between them.

A later Irish playwright, Brian Friel, had seen his play *Translations* accorded instant classic status when it was premièred in Britain in the early 1980s. That judgement is probably overblown: the play's project — to dramatize colonialism by showing the imposition of English place names on a rural Irish community — is original and haunting, but the story and characters

145

are rather faint. But it is a work of distinction, as well as being appropriate meat for a classical company; it appeared at the Avon, in 1982, in a strongly cast production directed by Guy Sprung.

Sprung, the Canadian director most firmly encouraged by Hirsch, also directed — that same year, at the Third Stage — Aldyth Morris's *Damien*, a surprisingly compelling one-man play, featuring Lewis Gordon, about a priest who gave his life to ministering to lepers in the Caribbean. There were two more solo triumphs in 1983: Edward Atienza's in *When That I Was*, a reverie by John Mortimer about the last surviving member of Shakespeare's own company, and Douglas Campbell's in *Blake* by Elliott Hayes, basically a poetry recital but one in which the actor shed all bombast and arrived at simple grandeur; it was probably more Lear-like than his Lear. John Wood directed the first, and Richard Monette the second.

Mostly, though, the Third Stage in Hirsch's time was devoted to the revival of Phillips's long-abandoned idea of a Young Company. It seemed to undergo a different incarnation every year. In 1982 it was known as Shakespeare 3, a name that was quickly and fortunately dropped, and mounted modest, well-spoken productions of *A Midsummer Night's Dream* and (more interestingly) *All's Well That Ends Well*, directed by Peter Froehlich and Richard Cottrell respectively. There were some outstanding young players involved — Fiona Reid, Nicky Guadagni, Seana McKenna, Diego Matamoros — with a few older actors as leaven: Charmion King made a charming Widow (né Peter) Quince. But nobody got very excited.

In 1983 the scheme was given a higher profile and placed under the direction of Michael Langham, some of whose post-Stratford years had been devoted to running the Juilliard theatre school in New York. Desmond Heeley designed a new stage (with an asymmetrical balcony), and he and Langham revisited two of their earlier triumphs. *Much Ado About Nothing* (co-directed with Helen Burns) was a disappointment, though Colm Feore pulled off the rare feat of making Claudio sympathetic. *Love's Labour's Lost*, on the other hand, recalled Langham's early, legendary production.

Admittedly, much of the glory in this Young Company (and young play) went to the older actors. John Neville enraptured everyone as the quixotic Don Armado, though there were some who muttered that all he had to do was to turn up in his tattered grandeur and mournfully intone the lines in his beautiful voice. He shared his triumph with his British compatriot John Frankyn-Robbins as Holofernes: the two played rich duets of self-satisfied verbosity. Probably the best of the juniors was Diego Matamoros as Holofernes' sidekick Nathaniel. But the romantics, the roles in which youth should logically have had its day, were muted. Joseph Ziegler as Berowne had intelligence and even wit but lacked verve. An American actress, Maria Ricossa, made an agreeable impression as the Princess of France, and the King of Navarre was Garrick Hagon, who as a *very* young company member had been one of the Princes in the Tower in that very first *Richard III*: continuity in excelsis.

*Love's Labour's* was transferred to the Festival stage the following year, predictably losing some of its charm en route. Nicholas Pennell now played a bottom-scratching Holofernes. Douglas Campbell came in as a massively genial and discreetly lustful Costard; his son Benedict now played the King, thus enjoying the rare pleasure of sentencing his old man to testing and penance; and his *other* son, Torquil, aged twelve, made very fluent work of Armado's page Moth. The show's status as a Young Company production was now somewhat in doubt, though some of the actors were still officially members of it.

Leon Rubin's punk-styled production of *The Two Gentlemen of Verona* made New Wave seem like old hat. Launce's dog, immune to fashion, was the liveliest character, though John Dolan, who had to share the stage with him, put up a good show. The ladies showed promise: Maggie Huculak, Michelle Fisk, and — as the waiting woman — Lucy Peacock. Langham's return to *Henry IV, Part One* was far more distinguished, though with Douglas Campbell (Falstaff again), John Franklyn-Robbins, Nicholas Pennell, Graeme Campbell, and Mary Haney all prominently cast, it began to seem as though the mentors were outweighing the students. Youth was served by casting Joseph Ziegler as Hotspur, for which he was ready, and David Ferry as Hal, for which he wasn't quite; but much of this casting could equally well have happened on the main stage. The production itself, perhaps, couldn't. Langham's Third Stage productions seemed to be less about forging new talent than about exploring the possibilities of high-end Shakespeare in an intimate space: a valuable initiative and at Stratford, frankly, an overdue one.

Anyway the pendulum swung back in 1985 when John Neville, already announced as Hirsch's successor, took over direction of the Young Company. He banished Shakespeare for the year and put the accent firmly on youth. This

*Michael Langham directed John Neville (left) as Don Armado and Torquil Campbell (right)
as Moth in 1984's* Love's Labour's Lost. *Langham set his sixth production of this play in the park of an Edwardian
estate, beautifully brought to life by designer John Pennoyer.* •

147

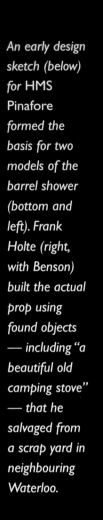

An early design sketch (below) for HMS Pinafore formed the basis for two models of the barrel shower (bottom and left). Frank Holte (right, with Benson) built the actual prop using found objects — including "a beautiful old camping stove" — that he salvaged from a scrap yard in neighbouring Waterloo.

## *Benson's Inventions*

For many Festival patrons, designer Susan Benson (above) will forever be associated with the boats, balloons, flying machines, and other weirdly wonderful contraptions she dreamed up for Brian Macdonald's Gilbert and Sullivan shows — including the shipboard shower-in-a-barrel for *HMS Pinafore* in 1992. Frank Holte, head of properties for the Festival Theatre, recalls that the inspiration for this particular item came from the whimsically inventive drawings of Rowland Emmet, a cartoonist for the British humour magazine *Punch* in the 1950s.

did not work too well for Sophocles' *Antigone*, directed by David William. Farquhar's *The Beaux' Stratagem*, however, last and most human of the great Restoration comedies, came off splendidly.

Edwin Stephenson, an experienced director from Victoria, mounted a sparkling production. Lucy Peacock emerged, almost from nowhere, as a high comedienne, expert in asperity and how to melt it; her Mrs. Sullen (sullen by marriage, not by nature) was matched by the acute high spirits of John Moffat as Archer, the fortune-hunter caught. Ted Dykstra also caught various eyes as Gibbet, the highwayman. The senior members of the company were now just two: William Needles, who inspired real awe as Sophocles' Tiresias, and Patricia Conolly, who inspired real affection as Farquhar's Lady Bountiful. After five years the precise function of the Young Company (not to mention its future existence) remained in doubt: was it to be a strenuous training-ground or a full-value experience for paying customers? *The Beaux' Stratagem* suggested that it might be both, but in this it was unique.

One other component of the Hirsch regime was to prove perhaps the most important to the Festival's future identity. In 1960 and 1961, with Gilbert and Sullivan fresh out of copyright, Tyrone Guthrie had directed sparkling Stratford productions of *HMS Pinafore* and *The Pirates of Penzance*. These became international successes, but they were really part of Stratford's music festival. This ceased to exist in 1975, and when musicals began to reappear at the tail end of the Phillips era, it was as part of the regular repertoire. The first Hirsch season in 1981 featured another *HMS Pinafore*, directed by

Leon Major. It was a heavy-handed production, and it looked extremely ugly, but it did very well at the box office. It was also well sung (Michael Burgess was the Captain) and boasted one excellent comic performance, from Eric Donkin as Sir Joseph Porter. It was determined that the next year Stratford would try and capitalize on the good things about this show and eliminate the bad.

Hirsch called in Brian Macdonald, whose choreography had been the best thing about Stratford's unfortunate *Candide*. He staged *The Mikado* and it went through the roof. It was taken to London and brought back to Stratford for two more consecutive seasons. In 1983 it shared the Avon stage with Macdonald's production of *The Gondoliers*, and in 1984 they were both joined by *Iolanthe*. In 1985 the cycle was rounded off with *The Pirates of Penzance*.

Macdonald's productions had, obviously, many things in common. They were all gloriously designed by Susan Benson. They were all dynamically conducted by Berthold Carrière and excellently sung: *Iolanthe* even mustered Maureen Forrester as the Queen of the Fairies. They all had rich comic performances by Donkin and Richard McMillan in the Ko-Ko and Pooh-Bah lines of roles. Douglas Chamberlain's appearance in *The Gondoliers* as the Duchess of Plaza-Toro emphasized how closely the style could approximate to camp — though, as Gilbert said of the House of Lords, he did it very well. There were choreographic values such as the Savoy operas had never known. Still fondly remembered is the cachucha in *The Gondoliers*, which started out vigorous but conventional, mainly notable for the swirl of the costumes; then one dancer, then another, then all,

149

## The Magnificent Mikado

Revolutionary in its fluid integration of song, dance, and storytelling, and exquis-itely designed by Susan Benson, Brian Macdonald's 1982 production of Gilbert and Sullivan's *The Mikado* was an immediate sensation that became one of the biggest success stories in the history of Canadian musical theatre. Revived in 1983 and again in 1984, the production enjoyed a long life beyond Stratford when Macdonald toured it independently to such cities as Toronto, Montreal, Ottawa, Winnipeg, Vancouver, Boston, Milwaukee, Baltimore, and Detroit. It played at the Kennedy Center in Washington, D.C., and the Old Vic in London,

Suzanne Benson '82

Christina James

Katisha

The Mikado '8[

England; and on Broadway it was nominated for two Tony Awards. At the Festival it was revived for an unprecedented fourth season in 1993. Although many cast members changed with each revival, two members of the original 1982 cast — Karen Wood as Pitti-Sing and Eric Donkin as Ko-Ko — retained their roles throughout the production's many incarnations. By October 30, 1993, when the last Festival revival closed, both actors had logged a remarkable 512 performances. (Main photo, from left) Marcia Tratt, Aggie Cekuta, Jean Stilwell, Glori Gage, Gwyneth Walsh, and Allison Grant in 1983. (Upper inset) Christina James as Katisha in 1982. (Lower inset) Avo Kittask as the Mikado in 1984.

## "Old pals from Montreal…"

### Brian Macdonald

Maureen Forrester and I were old pals from Montreal. We were both working in New York and I took her to a smart lunch at a hotel and said, "I'd like you to do this role and I just happen to have the score right here. What do you think? Would you like to play the Queen of the Fairies?"

She said, "Well, do I have jokes?"

"Yes, you have lots of jokes," I said. "And I'll make sure Susan Benson gives you a beautiful costume."

She said, "Sure, I'm in." Just like that.

I think part of the trick of making these things successful is very, very careful casting — people that you know are going to enjoy a summer of doing singing and dancing, and being funny people.

picked up dummies as partners and swung them about like the most ruthless of apache dancers. It built and built, into the wildest, funniest, and most intoxicating of production numbers.

Most controversially, there was rewriting of the text — and especially the lyrics — that went far beyond the customary finessing of obscure references. Gilbert's satire was mostly replaced by jokes specific to the 1980s and to Canada. The effect of this varied. Gilbert, like Lewis Carroll, wrote nonsense, but nonsense absolutely relies on strict adherence to its own rules. Gilbert and Sullivan, contrary to popular belief, did not keep writing the same show under different titles, and the rules change from piece to piece. No great damage was done to *The Mikado*, which is a gigantic anachronistic joke to begin with: a cartoon of Victorian society dressed up in the clothes, and a few of the customs, of a mythical Japan. Great harm was done to *Iolanthe*, which is a very specific and still entertaining satire on the British political system. This was not a modern-dress production, and the plot was left intact, but suddenly the English peerage was singing about Brian Mulroney. Some of the new lines were actually very neat ("Bow, bow, ye not-so-well-connected; Bow, ye who have to get elected"), but the total effect was patronizing to the authors and to the audience.

*Iolanthe* was the least well received of the series. Critics decided that the opera was second-drawer G&S anyway; this must have surprised traditional Savoyards, who have always ranked it just after *The Mikado* and *The Gondoliers*, which is precisely where Stratford scheduled it. But all was forgiven when *The Pirates* sailed in, shorn of desperate updates and

riotously entertaining. Brent Carver returned as the Pirate King, debonair but accident-prone, a dizzying mixture of Errol Flynn and Danny Kaye. Carver's great career in musical theatre was yet to come, but he shared the honours here with an already established Canadian musical star, Jeff Hyslop, who gave bags of personality to the super-conscientious hero Frederic, plus a dancing ability that the Slave of Duty (as he's described in the opera's subtitle) can never have known he had.

*The Pirates* was in fact a last-minute choice — Stratford had hoped to do *Guys and Dolls* but it proved unavailable — and it was almost a last hurrah. John Neville, perhaps irked by the extent to which Macdonald had created a company within a company, remarked tartly that Stratford was "never meant to be a Gilbert and Sullivan festival" and announced that it would now turn to more recent musicals. Which it did.

Hirsch's regime is difficult to characterize. Far less prolific in output than Phillips's had been, it yet appears more diffuse. In its five years it presented a fair cross-section of the Shakespeare canon, though it steered clear of the obscurest plays. Hirsch's choice of other classics was also reasonable, and occasionally brave. (Surprisingly, he avoided Chekhov, generally reckoned his strongest suit.) He established a firm beachhead in the modern repertoire and discovered a populist strand, the extent of whose success may have taken him by surprise. ("Robin Phillips," he said, "had Maggie Smith; we have Gilbert and Sullivan.") He had been known as a champion of Canadian work, but he insisted that it was not the Festival's role to do new Canadian

*(Above) Susan Benson's set model for* The Gondoliers. *(Inset, from left) Marcia Tratt, Aggie Cekuta, Glori Gage, Karen Wood, Stephen Beamish, and Richard March in the 1983 production.*

plays. He was far more persistent than Phillips had been at bringing in promising new actors: many of the current leaders of the Canadian theatre passed through his companies. "Passing through," though, may be the operative phrase; few of them — Feore and McKenna are obvious exceptions — stayed or were nurtured. A significant number (Fiona Reid, Jim Mezon, Simon Bradbury, William Vickers) were to find more of a home at Niagara-on-the-Lake. Like Phillips, though, Hirsch was good at developing those who were already there: Bedford, Pennell, Blythe, Monette all extended themselves, and so did such an old reliable as Max Helpmann, who pumped life into functional roles (Vincentio in *The Shrew*, Nym in *The Merry Wives*, Egeus in the *Dream*) that have reduced most actors to talking waxworks.

Perhaps the strangest thing is how slight a mark Hirsch's own productions, as a group, left on the Festival. They were just *there* alongside those of a myriad guests. The eras of Guthrie, Langham, and Phillips were all defined by the shows that they themselves directed. With Hirsch, this stopped.

153

# Chapter Six

# The Neville Years

*"John Neville got us out of debt, which was great, but he also gave me my chance to direct," recalls Richard Monette. "I thought he was mad to give me that responsibility. He took a big chance on me, as he did on many young people."*

John Neville had had a unique career. He had first made his name as an actor at the Old Vic in the mid-1950s. His fair good looks and remarkably resonant and melodious voice had made him natural casting for romantic roles, from Romeo on down. He used the same gifts in notable performances of Hamlet and Richard II, and excelled — on the rare occasions when he was given the chance — in such varied comic roles as Ancient Pistol and Sir Andrew Aguecheek.

Like generations of actors before and since, Neville would sit in pubs talking about the neglected role of the actor in shaping theatrical policy and the necessity of bringing the theatre to the people and vice versa. Unlike most, he proceeded to put his talent where his ideals were. He started directing plays, mostly for regional repertory theatres, eventually becoming artistic director of the Nottingham Playhouse in the mid-sixties. Neville's regime there was a flaming success in terms of staging old plays, encouraging new ones, and reaching out to the community. He ended up, though, clashing with the theatre board and tendering a resignation which, somewhat to his discomfiture, was accepted.

He returned to acting in plays and films, but he had already made a decisive break with London by going to Nottingham, and he soon broke with England as well. In 1971 he was invited to Ottawa to direct a guest production of *The Rivals* and essentially he never went back. He became a Canadian citizen, and artistic director in turn of the Citadel Theatre in Edmonton and the Neptune in Halifax. He vitalized both theatres artistically, and economically he took them decisively out of the red. Still a star, he remained outside the establishment and had shown little interest in working at Stratford.

All the same, Robin Phillips had suggested that either Neville or John Hirsch might be the ideal man to succeed him. When Neville finally came to Stratford, it was under Hirsch's banner: to act with the Young Company in 1983 and on the main stages in 1984, and to take charge of the Young Company in 1985 while supposedly working alongside Hirsch as director-designate.

In fact, the two men loathed each other, Hirsch prophesying that Neville would lead Stratford into middlebrow mediocrity, and Neville charging that Hirsch had already done just that. "I hate the guy," he told Lawrence DeVine of the *Detroit Free Press*, adding

Patrick Clark designed the richly
coloured costumes (left) for
Pericles in 1986. Geraint Wyn
Davies (inset, below), in his first
season at Stratford, played the title
role, while the character of Gower
(historically, a medieval male
poet) was unconventionally
portrayed by actor-singer Renée
Rogers (inset, above).

A PRINCE OF MACEDON
PERICLES STRATFORD
FESTIVAL 1986

that he intended to bring in "the younger, zippier actresses that Stratford has lacked recently — hand-picked by me." Neville, DeVine noted delicately, was "the first married man to lead Stratford in more than a decade." "Sex-appeal," said Neville, incontrovertibly, "is a definite quality in Shakespeare" — and, he might have added, in all theatre.

It is also, of course, a remunerative quality; and the Stratford board, mindful of Neville's track record, hoped that he would save the Festival from bankruptcy. Under Phillips Stratford had been very prosperous, but his expansionist policies rendered that prosperity precarious: as Phillips himself knew and warned, it would take one bad season to push the theatre over the brink. The Festival has always received very little government subsidy and is extremely dependent on the box office, at least compared to equivalent theatres in Europe. Hirsch's last-minute opening season lost a lot of money, which was forgivable in the circumstances; his later seasons did the same and there was less forgiveness for that. In any case Neville pledged to eradicate the deficit, and he succeeded.

He did not do this — at least not initially — by playing safe. He accused Hirsch of a conservative choice of Shakespeare plays on the main stages. It could even, he claimed, be self-defeating, since audiences might well rebel against being offered *A Midsummer Night's Dream* year after year. That sounds reasonable, but in fact the audience's appetite for this particular play appears to be, so to speak, bottomless. Meanwhile, the public's indifference to the obscurer plays seems only to increase; and Neville found himself programming the *Dream* and *The Merchant* in one season soon enough.

In 1986, however, when he started, his repertoire was genuinely bold. The Festival stage was that year largely given over to three of the four late romances, omitting *The Tempest*, the one crowd-pleaser in the group. *Cymbeline* and *Pericles* were each receiving only their second Stratford productions, *The Winter's Tale* its third. And none of them has been seen on the main Stratford stage since.

There were no formal links between the three productions, but the juxtaposition provided its own excitement and all, in different measures, were well received. Richard Ouzounian, who had established an exuberant reputation in Vancouver and Winnipeg, arrived to direct a Turkish-delight *Pericles·* a whirlwind tour in which each exotic stopover seemed to thrust the hero (an eloquent and attractive Geraint Wyn Davies) and the audience into not only a new ethnic subgroup but also a new historical period. The production was heavily musicalized, with the choral role of ancient Gower recast as a female blues singer (Renée Rogers). This, as Ouzounian himself pointed out, echoed an English Stratford production of the fifties in which Gower, though still a man, had sung calypso, and both versions ran into the same problem: the music, plus muddy diction, obscured the words. Gower's execrable couplets may well deserve obscuring, but unfortunately they carry the story.

*The Winter's Tale* was considerably more sober, but then this play has more to be sober about. It began with the haunting image of Father Time —

who textually appears only halfway through the play to carry the audience over a sixteen-year break — appearing on stage attended by his children. He was played, just as he had been eight seasons earlier, by the indestructible Mervyn Blake, giving a new meaning to the idea of Time standing still. Many were moved by the intensity of Colm Feore's Leontes, the passion of Goldie Semple's Hermione, and the formidable forthrightness of Susan Wright's Paulina.

The crown of the three romances, beyond a doubt, was *Cymbeline*, which in itself embodied the theme of reconciliation by marking the sudden return of Robin Phillips (and also, as his assistant, of Martha Henry). Phillips did, as was expected of him, the unexpected. He took a literally fabulous play that most directors strive to make either as remote or as scenically neutral as possible, and set it in a period not only specific but recent: Britain, in the years leading up to the Second World War. Eric Donkin and Susan Wright, as Cymbeline and his evil-stepmother spouse, looked like George V and Queen Mary. The war between Britain and Rome, usually one narrative strand among many, became the dominating action and, in a surprising way, it anchored the play. Shakespeare's Romans in *Cymbeline* are, despite the occasional pious references to Julius and Augustus Caesar, Renaissance Italians; in Daphne Dare's designs they turned, smoothly enough, into modern Fascists.

It was best perhaps not to take this too literally; the play ends, after all, with a victorious Britain voluntarily resubmitting itself to Rome. But the fact of peace is more dramatically important than the details of it, and it was all the more moving for following on a recognizable war. Jupiter descended in the cockpit of a bomber rather than on the back of an eagle, and the last scene of multiple reunions was set in a Red Cross hospital. At its close the cast dispersed into the lobby singing "It's a Long Way to Tipperary"; the spectators, if they chose, could join the singalong. (Audience participation was a new weapon in Phillips's armoury.)

Within this environment, the characters flourished. What Ray Conlogue called Martha Burns's "egoless, almost distracted quality"

## "He looked absolutely green..."

### Robin Phillips

I saw Johnny Neville looking wretched in the Belfry Bar at the Church Restaurant. He looked absolutely green, and I said to him, "Is anything wrong. Can I help?"

He was in trouble because he'd lost his director for *Cymbeline*. I said, "If there's anything I can do to help, please ask me. I know the problems and I know the agony, trying to get through these seasons, so please ask."

And he said, "Will you come and do *Cymbeline?*"

I cannot tell you the terror of going back into that building. It was like going back to a home that you no longer own. It's full of memories. Everything about it was very emotional.

literally took me by the hand into the theatre. He couldn't have been more generous or more understanding. The company likewise were very sweet.

established Imogen as a crystal surface in which the whole play was reflected. Colm Feore was a brilliantly insinuating Iachimo, whose furtive, erotic soliloquy in Imogen's bedchamber was murmured into a body-mike, drawing the audience into disturbing complicity. Nicholas Pennell, one faithful servant playing another, was Pisanio, Benedict Campbell a hoot as Cloten, and Joseph Ziegler a passionately, even painfully, believable Posthumus. This production was the true if belated heir of Guthrie's *All's Well*: teasingly anachronistic, elegantly moving, and heart-stoppingly beautiful.

It was one of two Shakespearean triumphs that season: both, as is so often the case, in the little-known plays. The Avon had a separate company, but one of its productions was a pendant to the Festival romances: *Henry VIII*, Shakespeare's (probably collaborative) swan song. Brian Rintoul, who had been an assistant director under Hirsch, justified his promotion with the best production of this play, anywhere, since Guthrie's in England. The play is a pageant, and Rintoul's staging had a sweep and colour more characteristic of the Festival stage. But the banquets and processions were framed by a grim black surround, and the gorgeous characters seemed all too aware of how easily it might swallow them up. As in Phillips's *Measure for Measure*, the grand speeches were outnumbered by the frightened, conspiratorial whispers.

Elizabeth Shepherd, ideally cast, justified the epilogue's claim that the play is the portrait of a good woman but never pretended that she was a meek one: her Katharine of Aragon blazed with anger at her trial, and with charity at her death. William Hutt, who had sat the last four seasons out, returned to play a

## "Just talk as slowly as you can..."

### Lucy Peacock

I was playing a waiting woman in *Henry VIII* and understudying the role of Anne Bullen. In those days, Stratford didn't do understudy rehearsals until after opening week. I had sort of vaguely kept an ear out, knowing that in ten days or so I'd have to have it under my belt.

We went in for the rehearsal on the day of the opening. And at three o'clock, all of a sudden the director stood up and said, "We're going to have to stop that now because Lucy's going on tonight as Anne Bullen." The actress playing the part had gotten her foot caught in the hem of her gown, fallen on the stage, and broken her ankle.

My face got all red. I was just apoplectic about it. I had to get squished into the costume because Camille Mitchell was so much smaller than I was. Everybody was racing around. I remember just before I walked on stage, I thought, "I know the words. Just talk as slowly as you can."

And away I went. When you don't get your head in the way and it's just sort of free, then Shakespeare does all the work for you…. I got a very favourable review!

*(Above) Lucy Peacock as the Singing Gentlewoman stands behind Camille Mitchell as Anne Bullen in* Henry VIII *(1986).*

superbly impenetrable Wolsey, a consummate hypocrite and power broker whose sudden conversion after his downfall was powerfully disorienting; it seemed so real it could have been an act.

Between these polar opposites moved the great survivor, Henry himself, looking every inch the Holbein monarch and sounding as if one of the portraits had acquired a voice. Leon Pownall had played small-to-medium parts at Stratford from 1965 to 1971; he now returned as an actor of singular, subtle authority. Irving Wardle in the London *Times* labelled his Henry a "portrait of a tyrant as a small boy . . . an autocrat looking for someone to lean on." The play, with its announced theme of "how soon this mightiness meets misery," may be the first dramatic examination of the celebrity culture.

Neville himself, at the Avon, directed a straightforward *Hamlet*, in which Brent Carver played a nakedly young, quiveringly vulnerable prince with a marked gift for hysteria and an equal talent for taking it out on other people. This may not be all of Hamlet but it is a sizeable part of him. Carver's speech could be odd and gabbled, but it could also — as in the sudden meditation on "What a piece of work is a man" — take the audience's breath away.

Elizabeth Shepherd was again ideally cast, though in an entirely different role; her Gertrude was a warmly sensual woman destroyed by the collision of her two great loves, sexual and maternal. James Blendick's Claudius was a villain, and little more, but Richard Curnock, another returning veteran entering on a fine late period, made an unusual Polonius, a vain and imperious ex-officer; and Eric House, back from Stratford's earliest era with his comic flair intact, played a great

Gravedigger. Ophelia was Lucy Peacock, newly graduated from the Young Company, and like most Ophelias, she impressed especially in her mad scene. Neville contrived to let her see her father's body dragged off by her lover, which sent her most persuasively over the edge.

The 1986 season was intricately planned, with each of the Avon Shakespeares cross-referenced with a modern play. For *Hamlet*, it was Tom Stoppard's *Rosencrantz and Guildenstern Are Dead*.

Every production of *Rosencrantz* implies a production of *Hamlet* going on somewhere in the wings and periodically moving in and taking over. Most productions rightly make this implied *Hamlet* as conventional, and hence as immediately recognizable, as possible. However, when an actual *Hamlet* exists side by side in the repertoire, the rules change: that current production has to be the one invoked. The Stratford casting played rigorously fair: every actor in the Stoppard took the same role as in the Shakespeare except for Rosencrantz and Guildenstern themselves, played — excellently — by Keith Dinicol and William Dunlop. They reversed roles: fair enough considering that even they seem uncertain which of them is which.

John Wood's actual staging of the interpolated Shakespeare scenes did not so much echo Neville's production as parody it, with the cast having fun spoofing their own performances. Carver indulged, according to David Prosser, in "three times as many leers, postures, and wigglings of the buttocks" (and in about one-twentieth of the time), Peacock made a manic entrance with a teddy bear, and Shepherd piled on the sexiness. Wood was criticized for turning the pirate battle in the last act

into an *hommage* to the previous season's buccaneers from Penzance, but the play can take it — seems, indeed, to demand it. And, after all the word- and horseplay, the darkness that eventually overtakes Stoppard's hapless heroes powerfully descended.

*Henry VIII* was paired with *A Man for All Seasons* — less satisfyingly, since Robert Bolt's history play does not depend on its Shakespearean counterpart but merely happens to be set at much the same period and to involve a few of the same people. These include the king himself, and Leon Pownall, in his one scene, was able to repeat and vary his template performance to scintillating effect. Another is the Duke of Norfolk; David Schurmann gave him, in both plays, a bluff world-weariness that would stand him in excellent stead during numerous later seasons at the Shaw. A third was Thomas Cromwell, a Good Thing in Shakespeare and a Bad one in Bolt but, as played by Michael Fawkes, conceivably the same person.

A fourth was Cardinal Wolsey, and here the doubling scheme broke down. David Gardner played the Cardinal (another effective single-scene role); Hutt moved over to Sir Thomas More — mentioned but not presented by Shakespeare — and turned his Wolsey inside out. Instead of cynicism masquerading as piety, he offered true conviction cloaked in good fellowship. The wry, resounding voice made him as easy to love as to believe. Walter Learning directed.

There was symmetry even in the 1986 productions of the Young Company, which, under the one-season-only direction of Tom Kerr, offered a brace of plays about tyrants. One was a dispiriting *Macbeth*, a choice of play that proved hard on its inexperienced cast

In 1986, Hamlet *was paired with* Rosencrantz and Guildenstern Are Dead. *(Above) In a* Hamlet *rehearsal, John Neville (far right) gives directions to (from left to right) James Blendick, Scott Wentworth (foreground), Elizabeth Shepherd, Hazel Desbarats, Brent Carver (foreground), and Christopher Thomas. Sue LePage designed the Edwardian costumes for Elizabeth Shepherd and Brent Carver in* Hamlet *(right) and for Keith Dinicol and William Dunlop (below) in* Rosencrantz and Guildenstern.

and harder still on the audience. The other was *The Resistible Rise of Arturo Ui*, Bertolt Brecht's satire on Hitlerism, set in a mythical Chicago, with the Führer seen as Al Capone, and the Night of the Long Knives presented in terms of the St. Valentine's Day Massacre. This was far better, with Maurice Godin, whose Porter was the brightest damned spot in *Macbeth*, hitting the right blend of white-faced clowning and implacable menace as Arturo.

The 1987 season had less symmetry but more theme. Five of its thirteen shows were professedly about war, and a couple more might conceivably have qualified. The centrepiece was Neville's own production of a more substantial if less enjoyable Brecht, *Mother Courage*: a decent attempt that fell slightly flat, as this bitter chronicle of the Thirty Years' War invariably does in English. There may not have been a great Mother Courage, in any language, since Brecht's wife, Helene Weigel. Susan Wright, humorous and earthy, was a good one, and that some critics faulted her for being too sympathetic and others for not being sympathetic enough is probably a tribute to her. Her sister, Anne Wright, found great eloquence in Courage's mute and victimized daughter, as did Kim Horsman as a camp follower, swollen by prosperity into a state of blissful immobility.

Courage's cart retained its force as one of the great images of twentieth-century drama; the Festival balcony had to be removed to make way for it. Neville moved the action steadily forward in historical time: a reasonable, universalizing idea that he capped with a slide projection of an atomic explosion that seemed, if the expression can be pardoned, like overkill.

Shakespeare's contribution to the

*Susan Wright pulls Mother Courage's famous cart. Brent Carver, who played her son, recalls: "One of the great gifts at Stratford is that you are supported by artisans who know their craft and practise it. They built this extraordinary cart [full] of things [for Susan] to put in and take out."*

war effort was *Troilus and Cressida*, which David William directed as if the words "conservative" and "academic" had been hurled in his direction just once too often. This was one of the most determinedly outrageous productions in Stratford's history, and one of the most hated. "*Troilus and Cressida* lays an egg," ran a typical headline in the *Toronto Star*, referring specifically to the entrance of Helen of Troy (Goldie Semple) inside a giant Fabergé object, from which she emerged in strategically jewelled scanties. Actually, considering the legend of the lady's birth, this seems a not inappropriate image; nor does the spectacle of Ajax (James Blendick) forcing Thersites' head down a latrine appear that unlikely, judging by the way they talk to one another. Edward Atienza's scabrous and scabby Thersites was the outstanding performance of the production and his Stratford career. The trouble was, it was all like that; or it tried very hard to be. This was a production without a good word to say for anyone, least of all the hero and heroine.

It was set, as far as it was set anywhere, in the First World War with Achilles as Baron von Richthofen (though his Myrmidons were very nasty heavy-metallers); and 1914–18 — the junction-point at which old-style heroics met modern mass slaughter — has become the favoured matrix for depictions of war in the theatre. The trenches are a universally potent image, and plays are still written about them. The season included a production of a recent British piece, Stephen MacDonald's *Not About Heroes*, which *was* about the wartime poets Wilfred Owen and Siegfried Sassoon. Directed by Robert Beard (now a Festival staffer), it was affecting though it relied considerably on the power of the poems themselves as delivered by

Nicholas Pennell and newcomer Henry Czerny. (The production was repeated the following year.)

Two plays — the season's only Shakespeares on the Festival stage — were on the perimeter of the war zone: *Much Ado About Nothing*, most of whose male characters are soldiers back from campaigning, and *Othello*, which begins with a war, though one that is rather quickly abandoned. *Much Ado* was given a pleasant but superficial production by Peter Moss, handsomely set (by Christina Poddubiuk) among the Edwardians, and offering a brainy Beatrice with the soul of a suffragette. This was Tandy Cronyn, daughter of Stratford's favourite acting couple and named for both of them, and she radiated considerably more than did her Benedick, who was Richard Monette in blunt and stolid mood, his acting career now winding down in favour of other pursuits. A special treat was the sight (and sound) of William Hutt as Leonato and Edward Atienza as Don Pedro singing barbershop harmonies on the ballad "Sigh no more, ladies."

*Othello*, directed by Neville, was a bust, despite a frighteningly plausible Iago by Colm Feore and a flaring Emilia by Goldie Semple; for once they appeared a believable couple. For the first time, Stratford had a black actor to play the Moor, but in all other respects the American Howard Rollins was ill-prepared for the role, and was hardly helped by having a Desdemona (Wenna Shaw) who seemed not only more assured than he did, but older.

Two bedrock modern classics appeared at the Avon. *Nora* turned out to be a driven compression of Ibsen's *A Doll's House* (children vanished, servants dismissed, and all references to the heroine as her husband's "little

squirrel" sternly excised) prepared by Ingmar Bergman for his own production in Sweden and here restaged by Brian Rintoul. The production now seems most significant for marking the decisive emergence of Lucy Peacock as Stratford's new leading actress: the most durable, or so it was to prove, since Martha Henry. Peacock smoothed out the play's supposed inconsistencies by making Nora a woman of strength and resource who had been using her talents in the wrong way. Bergman's adaptation emphasized this point, but it was Ibsen who made it.

John Wood, who had been responsible for several fine Chekhov productions elsewhere in Canada, directed *The Cherry Orchard* in a manner that was briskly unsentimental without being crass. He used a determinedly demotic text by the English playwright Trevor Griffiths, author of *Comedians* ("Up yours, butterballs," said the reactionary old servant Firs to the pushy young servant Yasha, leaving the audience wondering if Chekhov really wrote something like that and, if so, why more timorous translators had been keeping it from them all these years). A set by the English designer Ultz extended the Doric architecture of the Avon auditorium on to the Avon stage; this made Madame Ranevskaya's house seem an unwelcoming place, but then, with its inhabitants always packing or unpacking and in constant fear of being evicted, it probably was.

The madam herself, in Pat Galloway's performance, rendered the temperature even chillier, but a stageful of other characters sprang to life. James Blendick, like Douglas Campbell before him, was both sensitive and aggressive as the peasant-millionaire Lopahin. Nicholas Pennell's Gaev and

*(Above) Sheila McCarthy played Lady Teazle opposite William Hutt's Sir Peter Teazle in* The School for Scandal. *(Below) One of Ann Curtis's costume sketches for Hutt.*

William Needles's Firs were predictably splendid; Joseph Ziegler's perpetual student Trofimov was a startling blend of virulent passion and corpulent absurdity; and Colm Feore's oily, unfeeling Yasha was the work of an actor caught at precisely the right moment: on the brink of stardom but still able to play a small part with detail, distinction, and not a hint of condescension. This fine production had a footnote: *Intimate Admiration*, a new play by Richard Epp, a Calgary dramatist, also directed by Wood, about Chekhov and his wife, the actress Olga Knipper (the original Madame Ranevskaya). Neville himself played Chekhov, but neither he nor Lucy Peacock was able to make it more than a grimly literary exercise.

Above all, though, 1987 will be remembered as possibly the greatest of the Robin Phillips years, especially remarkable considering that he was no longer running the place. He directed four shows, all of them phenomenal. The only one to occasion any doubts was *The School for Scandal*, which he directed on the Festival stage on an off-white set and with a blue-chip cast. William Hutt, it goes almost without saying, was immensely touching and witty in his handling of Sir Peter Teazle's passions and perplexities, and Sheila McCarthy, already a popular comedienne, delightful as his lady; at the end their May-December union looked, as it should, perilous but worth preserving.

The two designers, Michael Egan and Ann Curtis, worked from an elegant rather than joyous palette of creams and light greys. The production began with a group of voyeurs observing an apparently naked woman through a curtain; the effect was not so much titillating as cautionary. This play meant

business. It was rapturously applauded by all the critics, with two exceptions: both Ray Conlogue and David Prosser accused Phillips of having turned a frothy, exuberant comedy of manners into a glowering exposure of a corrupt society. Scott Wentworth played Charles, the supposed hero, not as a charming scapegrace but as a loutish debauchee, and the scene in which he puts up his ancestors' portraits for auction became, according to Conlogue, "a nightmarish dream sequence."

This, on any reasonable reading of the text, was perverse (and possibly easier than making the play funny). But *The School for Scandal* is a strange piece that keeps changing direction. It starts as the advertised satire on malicious gossips, then narrows its focus to become a comedy of ruptured marriages and attempted seductions, and in the end brings back its original cast of characters. It adds up to a pleasant play on an unpleasant theme. Phillips was at least able to bring the elements into a whole, and if he did this partly, for example, by having Wenna Shaw emphasize the viciousness of Lady Sneerwell, the headmistress of the scandalous school, he was taking his cue from the script which calls her "a fury." He won on points.

His other productions were knockouts. All three were for the Young Company, whose direction he had taken over after the preceding poor year. Though all the actors in this new group were unquestionably youthful, with none of the mentor figures of his or Langham's earlier Young Companies, they were a more experienced bunch than the one Tom Kerr had put together. Working with them, and in the intimate confines of the Third Stage, whose platform was reconfigured to his own specifications, obviously released something in Phillips: his productions had all their old authority and imagination pared down to a new simplicity, even innocence, that was profoundly moving.

*Romeo and Juliet* was especially breathtaking, its setting changed to a North American military academy populated by rival cliques of spoiled young men with weapons for the using. The twenty-three-year-old Albert Schultz was a headlong Romeo, one whom love took by storm and who coped just as full-bloodedly with his hysteria when banished as with his passion for Juliet. He was one of the few Romeos to seem worthy of his lady. Susan Coyne captured all the fervour of Juliet: a believably awakened teenager who could act through the verse as well as around it. The balcony scene was fine and unusual, played with humour as well as fire and tenderness, and staged from her viewpoint rather than his, in a kind of reverse-angle. The audience seemed to be inside Juliet's bedchamber, felt her stirrings as she rhapsodized over Romeo's name and her delighted joy when he appeared at her window, her dream made flesh. (The two actors, who met for the first time in this production, ended up getting married.) Peter Donaldson was a scarily tyrannical Capulet, and Nancy Palk a sultry big-sister of a Nurse, probably the closest ever to her spitfire equivalent in *West Side Story*.

Phillips located the vernal scenes of *As You Like It* in what appeared to be rural Ontario, a home-brewed community that seemed peacefully and purposefully to have cut itself off from the modern world. Into it, in a farmhand's overalls, strode Nancy Palk as the disguised Rosalind, a beguiling mixture of grace and gawkiness, to take

charge of the unsentimental education of Nigel Hamer's engaging Orlando. (Their greatest duet was played, magically, in an imaginary pool.) The play's riper cynicism was muted; Peter Donaldson's fine Jaques wore his misanthropy gently. Susan Coyne, however, brought unaccustomed sizzle to the pouting shepherdess Phebe, and Mervyn Blake (not quite *all* the company was young) repeated what was by now his regular old Adam. Phillips's main-stage production with Maggie Smith had been rich and sweet; he now distilled that mixture into an individual piquancy, soothing and astringent by turns.

The Young Company's third production tuned in to the season's war theme, with a production of R. C. Sherriff's *Journey's End*, the play that — at least until the appearance of *Oh, What a Lovely War!* — was the English theatre's classic depiction of the carnage of 1914–18. Phillips's cast did not explicitly turn the play's British officers (and a few men) confronting the near-certainty of death in their dugout into Canadians, but the actors kept their own accents, thereby universalizing the play in one sense, particularizing it in another, and — very helpfully — relaxing the stiffness of its upper lip. Beneath this veneer, the play remains very powerful: the characters' public-school bravado is partly a matter of verbal habit, but it's also the only kind of morale they have, their only shield against terror. This was brilliantly brought out by Albert Schultz as Stanhope, the company commander who has to steady his subordinates' nerves while his own hang in tatters. He was finely flanked by William Webster as an avuncular older officer, and John Ormerod, who was himself to die sadly young, as a hero-worshipping recruit.

## "There is divinity in odd numbers"

### The Winter's Tale

- Cost of Festival tickets in 1953: **$1** to **$6**
- Miles of rope and cable used to erect the tent: **10**
- Number of Stratford Festival productions that have involved William Hutt as an actor or director as of 2001: **102**
- Number of Shakespeare plays in which Mervyn ("Butch") Blake has appeared: **37 (out of 37)**
- Average number of spools of thread used each year by the wardrobe department: **3,647**
- Average number of pencils issued to the stage management office for the use of actors in rehearsal: **1,823**
- Average number of messages for actors left at stage management by agents: **316**
- Number of publicity pieces (posters, news releases, brochures) mailed by the Festival marketing and sales department in 2000: **1,014,500**
- Number of pairs of prescription eyeglasses lost in the Festival's theatres in 2000: **82**
- Number reclaimed by their owners: **20**
- Number of tickets sold in 2001: **614,226**
- Total number of tickets sold since 1953: **19,559,197**
- Total number of performances since 1953: **17,680**
- Current number of Festival employees: **875**
- Number of three-bedroom houses that could be lit for three hours by the energy required to light a single Festival performance: **360**
- Gallons of coffee consumed daily in the Festival Theatre green room: **25**

The effect, as the audience in its confined space watched them in theirs, was overpowering.

The same group, with a few additions, stayed together for the 1988 season, in which Phillips refined his vision of two more plays he had previously directed on the Festival stage. *Twelfth Night* had a hilarious duel scene but was

stilled it with his songs. Illyria in this production was a melting-pot: Peter Donaldson's Malvolio unbendingly Japanese, John Ormerod's Sir Andrew deliriously Scots, and William Webster's Toby blackguardedly English.

There is a brief scene in *King Lear* that shows the king about to travel from the house of one ungrateful daughter to

course in that small space. Hutt names it as his favourite of the three Lears he played at Stratford, perhaps because he was able to do so much, so subtly. He came on stage as a believable failing old man; like Ustinov, he made no attempt to out-roar the storm, the crucial difference being that had he chosen to, he could have. His unhinged insights were not rhetoric but the quiet arguing-out of new-found truths.

The Young Company's last offering was a double bill of Sophocles' *Oedipus* (in a new adaptation by John Murrell) and Sheridan's *The Critic*: two crazily dissimilar plays that have been yoked together ever since Olivier triumphantly combined them at the Old Vic just after the war. For him the incongruity (and the kick of playing a tragic and a farcical lead in one night) seems to have been the point. Phillips looked for links and found them: *Oedipus* a tragedy performed, *The Critic*, as per its subtitle, a "Tragedy Rehearsed." In *Oedipus*, Phillips blended ritual (the chorus embodied the plague that devastates Thebes) with humanity (Stuart Hughes's Oedipus began by cradling a victim in his arms).

*(Left to right) Vincent Dale, Johnny Lee Davenport, John Ormerod, William Hutt, Jeffrey Hutchinson, William Webster, Albert Schultz, Susan Coyne, Peter Donaldson, Kevin Gudahl, Marion Adler, and Doug Hughes appeared in* King Lear *(1988).*

otherwise a pensive production in which several performers further explored character types they had broached the year before. Nancy Palk's Viola was amused and bemused by the consequences of her own masquerade but never defeated by them. Susan Coyne's Olivia was another rich study of flirtatiousness, and of a woman toppled from what she had thought was a sure emotional perch. Schultz's crippled Feste, a great advance on his previous year's Touchstone, disturbed the house with his mockery and

that of the other. In Phillips's production, for which William Hutt came in to play Lear, the location was changed, to show Lear actually in his carriage, in transit. So his line "Are the horses ready?" ceased to be a purely functional inquiry and became the first sign that his mind was giving way, producing alarm in his attendants and giving frightening immediacy to his "Let me not be mad" in the same scene. It was one of a succession of searing moments, rendered all the sharper of

*The Critic* may have been the funniest production Phillips ever directed at Stratford. His strike-rate over these two seasons was extraordinary, in fact unparalleled. The actors might reasonably have expected to progress into the main company the following year but — for whatever reason — hardly any of them did. They did, however, have a collective future. In 1989 Albert Schultz announced that a nucleus of former Young Company actors was starting its own company. "Children and television series," in Schultz's later words, led them into other areas. But finally, in 1998, the Soulpepper Theatre Company began operations with two classical productions at the Harbourfront Centre in Toronto.

Of the twelve actors who created it, six had been in Phillips's Young Company: Schultz, Susan Coyne, Nancy Palk, Stuart Hughes, William Webster, and — the one actor to have survived from Tom Kerr's 1986 group into Phillips's — Michael Hanrahan. Three more — Diego Matamoros, Joseph Ziegler, and Ted Dykstra — had been in earlier Young Companies. Two — Martha Burns and Diana Leblanc — had other Stratford experience. The one founding member without Stratford connections was Robyn Stevan, unless you count the fact of her being Diego Matamoros's wife. (They were a very intermarrying group.) Phillips directed the first two shows and then, by prior agreement, bowed out. Soulpepper went on to become — had already become — a formidable force. Children of Stratford, they were also a healthy challenge to Stratford; for the first time a Toronto-based classical company confronted the Festival on its own level.

The most successful of the 1988 Festival productions had a more immediate effect on Stratford's future. Richard Monette made his directorial debut on the Festival stage with *The Taming of the Shrew*. Like previous Stratford *Shrews* it was exuberantly comic and — as far as Colm Feore's Petruchio and Goldie Semple's Katherina were concerned — unabashedly romantic. But it had one unaccustomed subtlety: the taming process put as much of a strain on Petruchio as it did on Kate. Monette had looked intelligently enough at the text to notice that, in keeping his bride awake, Petruchio had to go without sleep himself; in denying her food, he

denies it to himself. This may not make his actions any more palatable, but it gives the actors far more to play: a shared desperation to take them towards the wager at the end.

Other than this, the production was notable for its sheer energy and resourcefulness. As usual in this play, there was a contagious rash of lively

supporting performances. Geraint Wyn Davies's hopeful simpleton of a Hortensio was the most original, followed by Ron Hastings's Baptista, a hulking paterfamilias, and Scott Wentworth's sharp-suited Tranio. The Italy that Monette and his designer, Debra Hanson, depicted was that of the 1950s: a last outpost of chauvinism and cheesecake. Tanya Moiseiwitsch, who of course had designed Guthrie's production back in 1954, declared that this one was "full of splendid inventive bits.

Tony would have loved it."

This being the thirty-fifth Festival — presumably that was the reason — there were the ritual new productions of Stratford's first two plays. Both disappointed. *Richard III* featured, as it must, a dazzling solo performance. Unfortunately it was given not by Richard himself but by Scott

*Colm Feore and Goldie Semple starred in Richard Monette's directorial debut on the Festival stage. "On opening night of the Shrew," recalls Monette, "the first act got just one laugh — and the cast was brilliant, truly brilliant. Then, in the second act, they started to laugh and laugh. And it got a standing ovation. To this day, I don't understand why there's such a variety of response."*

Wentworth as Sir James Tyrrel, who is suborned to arrange the murder of the Princes in the Tower, and who has only two scenes. One of these is the soliloquy "The tyrannous and bloody deed is done," and Wentworth delivering it had the audience in thrall; the theatre's temperature changed. Colm Feore, having conquered nearly every villainous role in the Shakespearean range plus a few outside it, should have reached the summit in this one, but he remained obstinately lightweight. A painful truth

*Nicholas Pennell as Thomas Becket (above) stands in the middle of the crucifix-dominated set designed by Debra Hanson for the 1988 Avon production of* Murder in the Cathedral. *The following year, at the Festival Theatre, Brian Bedford played Shylock in Michael Langham's* Merchant of Venice. *Designed by Desmond Heeley, this production of an always controversial play raised critical eyebrows at the time by depicting Shylock as an exotically-costumed outsider in what was an otherwise conventionally Victorian world. There was also controversy over Langham's cutting of the text.*

was revealed: those other classic creeps work by insinuation; none is required to dominate his play. Richard is, and Feore lacked the vocal and temperamental heft. The director was Brian Rintoul, who after his Avon *Henry VIII* had looked like a natural for the Festival stage; what he delivered here, though, was routine.

Much the same was true of Peter Moss's Avon *All's Well That Ends Well*, set beautifully (by Christina Poddubiuk), but bafflingly during the American Civil War. Helena, a poor physician's daughter, is hardly the same kind of adventuress as the heiress Scarlett O'Hara, and Bertram is too wet to be Rhett. And if North versus South is the issue, then the play's other social distinctions hardly matter. Lucy Peacock drove things along as a surprisingly cheery Helena. As often in this play, the elders came off best: Susan Wright as the Countess, Joseph Shaw as the King, Richard Curnock as Lafew, and Allan Gray as Lavatch. To Moss's credit the details of the bed-trick, by which Helena takes another woman's place in her own husband's arms, have never been made so clear, and neither, by the same token, has the play's sad, accepting view of the power of sexual fantasy.

The 1988 season's remaining Shakespeare was *The Two Gentlemen of Verona*, bravely given a spin on the Avon stage but not really justifying the compliment. Robert Beard — working with one of Stratford's favourite designers, Brian Jackson — gave it, of all outrageously experimental things, a picture-book Elizabethan setting. It looked lovely. In most other respects it was somnolent, with the outstanding performance coming, by general consent, from Crab Apple, a dog, as Crab, the dog: a role he was obviously born to play.

Non-Shakespearean shows were

plain and fancy. The plain was T. S. Eliot's *Murder in the Cathedral*, which did unexpectedly well at the box office, thereby giving rise to three competing theories. One: people thought it was by Agatha Christie. Two: the title had educational recognition-appeal — the lure of the modern classic struck again. Three: there was an untapped hunger for plays on spiritual themes. Most people went for Two, though David William, the director, plumped not unnaturally for Three. One, alas, is untenable; no hordes of disillusioned thriller fans were observed furiously decanting themselves into Downie Street. Many people were bored, but they stayed respectfully put.

The struggles of Thomas Becket are too inward and too stripped of physical action to fascinate any but the devout. So at least it seemed at Stratford, where Nicholas Pennell was far too well cast as Becket. Having spent years expanding into ever fleshier roles, he was suddenly yanked back into the arms of sanctity, and the result was divine unction.

Pennell went to the opposite priestly extreme as Cardinal Richelieu in *The Three Musketeers*: the same Peter Raby adaptation that Hirsch had directed, now niftily restaged by Richard Ouzounian with things going on all over the Festival stage, many of them fights. Geraint Wyn Davies, perhaps more obvious casting than Douglas Rain had been, was a similarly brash and disarming D'Artagnan, Colm Feore proved the melancholy Athos the most actor-worthy of the musketeers, and a newcomer, Juan Chioran, made a sinister impact — the first of many — as Rochefort.

The highlight of 1989, Neville's last season, was the return of Brian Bedford, to play Shylock in *The Merchant of*

*Venice*, and of Michael Langham to direct it. The production, derived from one the two men had worked on together in Washington, was given a Victorian setting by Langham's old collaborator Desmond Heeley. Langham, now entering his seventies, retained his old mastery both of the Festival stage and the Shakespearean text. He dug into the words, but he also, more than almost any other director, probed the spaces between and around them. Thus his productions had both mystery and solidity. In *The Merchant* he aimed — as he had done as far back as his famous RSC production with Peter O'Toole — to reconcile the play's two opposing faces: its integrity as a romantic comedy and the disconcerting humanity of its villain, Shylock. Bedford, burying himself in heavy robes and a Yiddish accent, still had his flashing wit: he was a bitterly humorous man, hoarding injuries and determined to return them: with interest.

The production — or rather the announcement of the production — aroused more controversy about the play's alleged anti-Semitism than Stratford had known since the time of Frederick Valk. Langham's approach to the problem was ambiguous. At some points he met it head on. Taking a cue from the line "Why, all the boys in Venice follow him," he had Shylock, in his rage and distress over his absconded daughter, followed on stage and pelted by a gang of urchins. Goaded beyond endurance, he picked up one of them, held him, and delivered "Hath not a Jew eyes?" right into the boy's terrified face. It was an unforgettable image: Shylock's suffering and his ferocity fused together. However, what moderns regard as the defeated Shylock's ultimate degradation — the court's demand that he become

a Christian — Langham ducked altogether; he simply cut the lines.

His rationale was that to us the moment is so shocking that we lose the ability to respond to the rest of the comedy as the author intended. He may well be right: perhaps the most shocking thing about the forced conversion is that, to Shakespeare, it does not seem to have been an especially big deal; it doesn't even top the bill of Shylock's penalties. (That closing spot goes to the insistence that he make Lorenzo and Jessica his heirs.) Nor does Shylock himself have anything to say about it, though perhaps he is too stunned to comment. But: the lines are there, and we are not Elizabethans and never can be, and Langham had dealt so sensitively and inventively with the rest of the text that one wished he had faced up to this portion as well.

Way back in 1956, Langham had inaugurated his own Stratford regime with a more or less straightforward affirmative production of *Henry V*. It was still possible then. As if to point up how things had changed, John Wood's new production at the Avon cast as the Chorus the same actor, William Needles, who had played it thirty-three years before, and presented him as a spry but stiff-legged veteran from a local Legion hall. He laid poppies on a memorial to the dead of Agincourt and, in effect, called them back to life. The reference point, once again, was the First World War, and the vision was more blood and mud than hope and glory. Henry's responsibility for the killing of his prisoners was brought starkly home. But this was still a careful, nuanced interpretation. Geraint Wyn Davies's Henry adhered to what was by now the standard picture of the young man learning on the job. World War I also

inspired Richard Ouzounian's *A Midsummer Night's Dream*, maybe the only production in which Philostrate (Douglas Chamberlain) has carried off the acting honours.

Neville's commitment to the lesser plays was reaffirmed at length in a Festival Theatre double bill of *Titus Andronicus* and *The Comedy of Errors*. Jeannette Lambermont staged *Titus* in Kabuki style: an increasingly popular approach to plays that seem to require a rigid formality and one, as Ray Conlogue pointed out, that here resulted in Tamora's slaughtered sons being served up not as meat pies but as sushi. But the transplant failed to take, and anyway the play's dignity was fatally compromised by heavy cutting, so that it became merely one atrocity after another. Nor was Nicholas Pennell built to the scale either of Titus's suffering or of his madness.

Richard Monette's production of *The Comedy* had the inventiveness of his *Shrew* but not the soul. It was dominated by a large, cute clock: a reasonable device in a play that is full of jokes about Time, and whose plot is governed by a series of very strict deadlines. Each pair of twins was played by a single actor, which spoiled the fun by leaving the audience as confused as the other characters, and of course necessitated the bringing on of doubles in the final scene.

Monette did better with John Vanbrugh's *The Relapse*, which gave Brian Bedford the chance to play the most elaborate of all Restoration dandies, the newly created Lord Foppington (formerly Sir Novelty Fashion) who discourses at length on the glorious, exhausting daily round of a gentleman of leisure while still keeping a beady eye on the main chance: sexual or financial or (preferably) both. Piled high with perukes, powdered and befrocked — courtesy of Susan Benson — to within an inch of his life, Bedford still conveyed the shrewd arriviste beneath: he might consider himself irresistible to women but he was still prudent and unkind enough to keep his impecunious, and inconveniently personable, younger brother (sharply played by Geraint Wyn Davies) firmly at arm's length. His discomfiture when that same brother overreaches him, and steals his bride and her fortune, was very funny. The play's other, loosely related plot about marital fidelity and the alternatives, was played out by Nicholas Pennell (uncertainly reformed rake), Wenna Shaw (loving, beleaguered wife), Goldie Semple (determinedly merry widow), and Geordie Johnson (perversely gallant *gallant*). Stratford was doing fairly well, and fairly regularly, by Restoration comedy.

Its record with Shakespeare's contemporaries was far less commendable, so it was a matter for applause when the Festival Theatre actually presented an Elizabethan comedy that wasn't by Ben Jonson. David William, announced as Neville's successor, had directed Thomas Dekker's *The Shoemaker's Holiday* in London in 1964; it was possibly his most successful British production. He could not recapture the magic in Canada thirty years later, but he did fairly well: none of the critics questioned the point of doing the piece in the first place, which is progress. The play is an upbeat patriotic treatment of an upbeat patriotic story: the rise of Simon Eyre, from London master cobbler to the highest civic honours (he becomes Mayor Eyre), while alternately spoiling and bullying his apprentices and helping the course of true love to run smooth. It's a quintessential bourgeois fairy-tale, and

William respected its values.

James Blendick provided a vivacious outline of Eyre's irresistible rise, and Pat Galloway was properly proud and giddy as his wife, the Eyress. Simon's shoe-shop, with the quietly eloquent Brian Tree as its conscientious foreman, was conspicuously cheerful; the workers knew their place and liked it. There is no point in dragging this play out of its period, and Debra Hanson's sets and costumes were firmly and richly Elizabethan.

As for the year's modern classics, or possible classics: Robert Beard directed *Cat on a Hot Tin Roof*, which confirmed that Tennessee Williams's third most famous play was not the equal of *Menagerie* or *Streetcar* (already the Southern Gothic was being layered on too thick) but which did provide bravura opportunities for Goldie Semple as Maggie the Cat and James Blendick as a credibly shrinking Big Daddy, and a good showing for Geordie Johnson in the testing — because largely passive — role of Brick. Neville himself, an infrequent director, had a fine swan song with a *Three Sisters*, in Michael Frayn's translation, that was downbeat without being depressing. The sisters themselves — Wenna Shaw's strong Olga, Lucy Peacock's Masha, and Sally Cahill's Irina — made a scary triptych of hopes destroyed, leaving only the capacity to endure. Allan Gray probed all the attractive weaknesses of Vershinin, philosophizing and philandering; and Eric McCormack, then a small-part Stratford juvenile of four years' standing, had his first well-taken break as a funny-pathetic Baron Tusenbach. Bernard Hopkins hovered over the play in its funniest and most disturbing role: the elderly, drunken doctor in whom benevolent disillusion

has reached the end of the line.

Hopkins was also mentoring his juniors — one hopes, more cheerfully — in real life, since this season he had taken over direction of the Young Company. The results, unfortunately, were a regression to pre-Phillips days. Another *Love's Labour's Lost* demonstrated that though youth is a vital component of this play, it amounts to very little without personality and technique, two qualities that only Julia Smith (as the Princess) seemed able to supply. *The Changeling*, directed by Kelly Handerek, was more warmly received but was equally a travesty. It was good, in the season of *The Shoemaker's Holiday*, to see Stratford also essaying a great Jacobean tragedy (by Thomas Middleton and William Rowley) but this was a play that really needed experienced, or at least dynamically directed, performers. A subtle, driving study of two obsessed people — a headstrong young woman, a pockmarked, lust-driven man — came off as flesh-creeping, ineptly spoken melodrama: *Beauty and the Beast* robbed of its happy ending.

None of this four years of drama — good, bad, and indifferent — was responsible for putting Stratford back in the black. That was down to the musicals.

Neville had set his face against the previous regime's commitment to Gilbert and Sullivan at the Avon. He turned instead to old Broadway successes, and put them on in the larger Festival Theatre, on the principle that, if you have a cash cow, you may as well milk it to its greatest capacity. And he was up front about it. He opened each of his first two seasons with a musical.

He began in 1986 with the 1938 show *The Boys from Syracuse*: a logical choice as one of the few American musicals — indeed the first ever — to be based on a Shakespeare play. It was cooked up from *The Comedy of Errors* by Broadway's master farceur George Abbott (who attended the Stratford first night, aged ninety-eight and still working), retaining only two lines of the original text but including the introductory disclaimer "If it was good enough for Shakespeare, it's good enough for us." The show does stick closely to the Shakespearean plot-line — which sticks closely to a comedy by the ancient Roman master, Plautus — but it takes its style from good old American burlesque.

The show is crammed with jokes so bad they're great, but they do require skilled clowns, rather than mere actors, to put them across. That was one problem at Stratford. Another is that the script is definite proscenium-arch, lined up in front of the-audience material; a platform stage dissipates it. So Douglas Campbell's production lacked style. But nobody could say it wasn't fun. The score, by Richard Rodgers and Lorenz Hart, is golden, and it was well sung, if not to the highest musical standards. Neville was insistent that the musical company be fully integrated with the acting company, so audiences got to hear Colm Feore and Geraint Wyn Davies singing romantic ballads as the Antipholus twins (Feore was better at it). Alicia Jeffery, later an agent, played Adriana, with a real voice, and harmonized irresistibly with Marion Adler (Luciana) and Susan Wright (Luce) on the eleven-o'clock number "Sing for Your Supper." A more surprising trio consisted of Mervyn Blake, William Needles, and Bruce Swerdfager, a small-part player in the Festival's first four seasons — the ones under canvas — and its general manager until 1976. When these revered seniors went into a

sedate soft-shoe, the house could do nothing but roar.

*The Boys from Syracuse* was a success, but it may also have been a false start. At any rate, it remains an anomaly: the only Broadway-style musical presented at Stratford from the years before the Second World War. All subsequent choices have been from the line of brand-name shows that essentially began with *Oklahoma!* — shows, to put it bluntly, that everybody has heard of (and, in most cases, has seen the film of). So it was with the John Kander–Fred Ebb *Cabaret* (1987), which brought back Brian Macdonald (he had been offered *The Boys from Syracuse* but turned it down). *Cabaret* was a better candidate for the Festival stage, which prefers epic musicals and was here handed the birth of Nazi Germany, as reflected in the much-adapted Berlin stories of Christopher Isherwood. Macdonald relished the nightclub numbers, which provide a graphic and garish commentary on the increasingly terrifying times, and everybody had a good time being decadent. Sheila McCarthy, not a great singer but with the right quality of cigarette-ash in her throat, threw herself into Sally Bowles, and Brent Carver was a magnetically writhing and insinuating Master of Ceremonies.

The next year brought *My Fair Lady* and, sadly, the last Stratford production of Jean Gascon, who died shortly before the show opened. It was handsome and stately, much like the original; probably no major musical is less dependent on choreographic staging. None depends more on acting in the classical tradition or at least gives more opportunity for it, thanks to the substantial portions of Shaw's *Pygmalion* left

*Polly Scranton Bohdanetzky, who designed the costumes and set for* The Boys from Syracuse, *is best known as the Festival's long-time specialist in bijoux. Her skill is apparent in the sparkling costume and extravagant jewellery she created for Goldie Semple as the Courtesan (above). (Overleaf) One of Susan Benson's costume sketches for* Cabaret.

embedded in the dialogue. The Alan Jay Lerner–Frederick Loewe score, which is essentially operetta, makes other demands. Generally the male lead goes to an actor, and the female to a singer; here, both were actors. John Neville joined the line of graceful, insouciant Henry Higginses and had a rattling good time with the patter songs. Eliza Doolittle must be, for a North American performer, the most terrifying role in the musical-comedy repertoire: she has to act a Shavian heroine, assume two different English accents (and get them right, since they are what the story is about), and sing songs composed for the soaring soprano of the young Julie Andrews. Lucy Peacock fulfilled most reasonable expectations. Douglas Campbell exceeded them, bringing ripe music-hall humour, and a rich music-hall voice, to Alfred Doolittle; Richard Curnock was a sterling Colonel Pickering; and everybody loved hearing the songs again.

The Avon weighed in late in 1988 with *Irma La Douce*, for once not an American show but a French one that had achieved some success in New York in the fifties after enjoying a much bigger success in London. Susan Henley played the title character, the most popular prostitute in Montmartre, with plenty of charm and possibly insufficient guts, but then the piece is hardly a blistering documentary. Scott Wentworth distinguished himself, musically and comedically, as the shy law student who becomes her protector. (Neville had played the role in London.) There was a modesty (of scale, that is) about this musical that was rather refreshing: nobody seemed out to bust any blocks. Jeff Hyslop proved to be a clever and sympathetic director, and many people loved hearing the songs for the first time.

In 1989, the musical component of the Festival returned to its Shakespearean roots with *Kiss Me, Kate*. Donald Saddler, a veteran Broadway choreographer who had worked at Stratford on *My Fair Lady* and the long-forgotten *Happy New Year*, this time got to direct as well, and his work was colourful and platform-filling. All the same, the result had less musical snap than the average Festival production of *The Taming of the Shrew*. The Cole Porter score consists of one distinguished tune after another, and the lyrics could hardly be wittier, but it is surprisingly hard to make them count in the theatre, perhaps because the book, a complicated musical-within-a-musical, plods: it is good for its time (1948) but not for the ages, a matter not of attitude but of inspiration.

The Stratford principals failed to lift it. Jayne Lewis was to develop into a good musical actress, but she was not yet Kate or the prima donna who plays her, nor was Victor A. Young credible as Petruchio or as the ripe ham playing *him*. Their main qualification — neither performer was well known — seemed to be that they were husband and wife in real life. There was a certain fitness to this (Sam and Bella Spewack, also married, had based their script on the backstage squabblings of the Lunts), but it was not enough. The gangsters (Douglas Chamberlain and Dale Mieske) stopped the show, as always, with their dainty Bowery-waltzing injunction to "Brush Up Your Shakespeare." It seemed like advice worth heeding.

All these shows did well at the box office, usually better than anything else in the season. Musicals were at the Stratford Festival to stay. Everybody knew why. The outstanding questions were which and how.

## "My appendix blew up during the dress rehearsal..."

### John Neville

As everyone knows, *My Fair Lady* is a modern classic, and I felt we should put it on the main stage. I gave my acting a rest while I ran the Festival, but everyone felt that I should play Professor Higgins. And I was right for the role, I think.

During the rehearsal period, we had a calamity: Jean Gascon died, having done a brilliant production. A great actor and a fine director, he did a great job on that musical.

The next thing that happened was my appendix blew up during the dress rehearsal. I think I came back for the final preview, heavily strapped up, with people gasping as I ran up and down those stairs to the balcony. It was an eventful production.

*John Neville and Lucy Peacock in*
My Fair Lady *(1988)*

# Chapter Seven

# The William Years

All the musicals produced at Stratford during David William's regime were directed by Brian Macdonald. They started from strength, in 1990, with *Guys and Dolls*, the perfect blend of narrative integrity and musical-comedy fun: smart dramaturgy, smarter dialogue, and a Frank Loesser score of indescribable brilliance, all at the service of Damon Runyon's comic vision of a New York populated by orotund gangsters and gold-digging showgirls. Macdonald's staging, with gamblers shot out of sewer pipes like human cannon-balls to take their places for the crap-game ballet, was well up to his usual standard of choreographic inventiveness. This is also a musical for actors, and Stratford of course had them in spades. Scott Wentworth was by now inevitable casting for the high-rolling Sky Masterson, and the Festival could muster somebody as craggy and reliable as Peter Donaldson to play the minor but emblematic role of Harry the Horse — though Macdonald unwisely took the character's name as a cue to have him whinny at the end of every line. That kind of arch literalism is not what Runyon, or *Guys and Dolls*, is about, and in general Macdonald tried need-lessly hard to make the show funny.

John Neville, when Stratford first started presenting Broadway musicals, had pointed in justification to the British National Theatre's production of this show a few years earlier. A giant success, with less visual dazzle than Stratford's but more humanity, it had taken its place in the repertory as a masterpiece among masterpieces. (The previous show was *The Oresteia*.) But there are not many musicals in that league, and few of those offer as much to a classical acting troupe. Stratford,  now economically committed to a musical a year, rather quickly ran out of masterpieces.

At least Macdonald was around for the cream. In 1991 he directed *Carousel*, finest and darkest of the Richard Rodgers–Oscar Hammerstein shows, and once again electrified the Festival stage. The dancing was superb; the New England seaboard, which gives the piece so much of its flavour, was majestically represented; and the carousel itself was a life-size thing of wonder. There were good if not ideal lead performances by John Devorski and Allison Grant, and finely sung supporting ones by the established and operatic Marsha Bagwell and the up-and-coming

*David William, Stratford's seventh artistic director, recalls a school performance: "I remember seeing a mackintosh over somebody's head during the play and I thought, oh God, are they playing some kind of joke? At the end of the play, the raincoat came off the head, and it was a boy of about seventeen who'd been weeping: so moved had he been. Shakespeare had taken possession, and that of course is the best kind of tribute one could hope for."*

## *"The little tricks of the trade..."*

### Berthold Carrière

All the music of the Festival is tailor-made for the plays. I don't think there is another theatre in North America that does that.

Louis Applebaum was my mentor. The first week I arrived they were rehearsing *King John*, I think, and the director said, "Lou, I need something dramatic here," and Lou said, "Whoever's closest to a bass drum, hit it. You on the cymbal, roll it." And it made all the difference. Those are the little tricks of the trade I picked up from him.

When the musicals were moved from the Avon to the main stage, it was difficult at first because you're dealing with the loft upstairs. But it worked out. I find myself very comfortable up there now. We're casual. Nobody can see us and I've got a great orchestra of twenty-seven musicians. At the end of the show, I pop my head out from the loft. The first time I did it, people didn't know who I was. But I take my baton now so they know I'm the conductor.

*Berthold Carrière with members of the orchestra*

and musically comic Karen Wood.

Macdonald staged another great parade in 1993 in *Gypsy*, the story of the rise to fame of an unlikely stripper, under the eye and thumb of the mother of all theatrical mothers. Macdonald began the evening with the kind of vaudeville panorama that the show's Broadway director, Jerome Robbins, had intended the entire musical to be. Eventually, Robbins backed away from this concept, telling the authors — librettist Arthur Laurents, composer Jule Styne, lyricist Stephen Sondheim — "It's your show. It's a book show." He was right; it's one of the tightest and most story-driven of all musicals. This may not have made it ideal for Macdonald, but he came through with more than spectacle. Sandra O'Neill, a cabaret performer, lacked the lungs to carry off a string of powerhouse numbers conceived for Ethel Merman, but she managed Mama's dynamic self-absorption and was properly harrowing when going to pieces at the end. Monique Lund as the evolving Gypsy Rose Lee travelled tantalizingly from introvert to exhibitionist; Karen K. Edissi, the bronchially challenged Miss Adelaide of *Guys and Dolls*, led a trio of proud if jaded strippers ("Once I was a schlepper / Now I'm Miss Mazeppa"); and Peter Donaldson was Mama's lover and manager who, when asked why a powerful producer would take his advice, utters one of the great truths about the world's insecurest profession: "This is show business. Everybody listens to everybody."

They don't write them like that any more; but then they hardly ever did.

Already, in 1992, between *Carousel* and *Gypsy*, Macdonald had forsaken the Broadway canon in favour of the one popular Gilbert and Sullivan he had yet

to attempt. His *HMS Pinafore* was maybe the funniest of them all. It began with the crew tumbling out of their hammocks to sing the opening chorus in their underwear, continued with Douglas Chamberlain as the First Lord of the Admiralty paying his official call in a balloon, and peaked in a second-act trio whose participants evolved, come encore time, into an impromptu brass band. And in 1993 Macdonald's *Mikado* was brought back for an unprecedented fourth season. It lived up to its legend.

Stratford had no need to apologize for doing Gilbert and Sullivan, who are the biggest fact in the English-speaking theatre between Sheridan and Wilde (what else survives?). It didn't dare, though, to attempt their less familiar works. G&S were there to make money, and in fact *The Mikado* — which shared the season with *Gypsy* — turned out to be an insurance policy. *Gypsy* is one of the half-dozen finest musicals, but it is too hard-edged to make the general public's list of favourite shows, and it was never a popular film. It did badly at the Festival box-office and sent the programmers running back to those talismanic brand-name shows. The problem with Stratford's musical policy was not the effect it had on the Festival's choice of plays but the effect it had on its choice of musicals.

It was unfortunate, and somewhat unjust, that this should have become apparent on David William's watch. He was a compromise appointment (the board had hoped to get Phillips back and thought for a time that they had him) and a low-profile one; his Englishness was so apparent that few people realized that he had been a landed immigrant for years and lived in London, Ontario. His overall choice of repertoire was more enterprising than that of any Stratford director since Gascon, but he got equally little credit for it, though for opposite reasons. Gascon had trouble recruiting guest directors, but his own productions were among the strongest points of his regime; William's were among the weakest. He knew the Festival stage, having directed there for every one of his predecessors except Guthrie, but of this considerable body of work only *The Winter's Tale* and the long-ago *Volpone* awakened very warm memories. He knew the plays; he was a published Shakespeare scholar of conservative bent, and as a director too he had the reputation of being an academic. In practice he was not that rigorous a purist, and he could be good with isolated effects, but his more adventurous productions — *Troilus and Cressida* being the extreme example — often suggested that he was being carried away by forces beyond his control.

William directed three main-stage Shakespeares during his own term of office. His *Macbeth* (1990), co-directed with Robert Beard, began with a fierce battle, followed by the witches coming on to pluck the corpses. Shock-horror effects included the onstage rape and murder of a pregnant Lady Macduff and the ghostly appearance of Macbeth's victims to haunt him at his death as if he were Richard III. The shell, however, was empty. Brian Bedford brought intelligence and imagination to Macbeth but no real conviction. He was probably too civilized an actor to reach deeply inside this role; wonderful at cold villainy or creased neurosis, he could not encompass terror. Goldie Semple was an expectedly forceful Lady Macbeth with an expectedly effective sleepwalking

*Douglas Chamberlain, as Sir Joseph Porter, arrives on stage in 1992's HMS Pinafore. Painted to look perfectly spherical, the Styrofoam-and-fibreglass "balloon" was completely flat at the back and only slightly convex in front. The "ropes" were actually a metal frame that supported the whole structure.*

scene, but no more than that. Barbara Bryne, a character actress from the Gascon years now returned (she had been a rare female Puck in Hirsch's first *Dream*), came off best as the First Witch.

*Hamlet* (1991), in a by-now-conventional nineteenth-century setting, lacked even the surface excitements of *Macbeth*. Colm Feore was thoughtful but curiously bland in the lead; he seemed to have been cast because it was his turn. Leon Pownall managed an interesting king, a brilliant but guilt-ridden politician with great reserves of charm, who finds it all too easy to fall back on brutality. (The production showed him beating up an unco-operative prisoner.) Otherwise the star turn was Mervyn Blake, still hanging in there to great effect, as the Gravedigger.

William had long been associated with *The Tempest* (1992). Back in 1960 he had written a fine essay on it, a latter-day Granville-Barker *Preface,* in which he had described it as "the noblest of the revenge plays" and stipulated that Prospero should not be seen to control the opening storm; the audience should take it for the real thing and *then* find out who was responsible. Thirty years on, he seemed to have changed his mind; his Prospero appeared on the balcony and conjured up the tempest, which proceeded to rain down on the voyagers below. He was surely right the first time, especially as the storm that he and his technicians came up with looked absolutely genuine. It was created with lights, ropes, and swaying actors; and it reminded Geoff Chapman (in the *Toronto Star*) of Armageddon. Once it was over, however, the play with Alan Scarfe as Prospero merely plodded along.

William did better with some of his non-Shakespearean classics, though not with Congreve's sharp but mellow *Love*

*for Love* (1990), a late Restoration comedy that he methodically and moralistically drained of laughter. The subdued approach was more appropriate for *The Importance of Being Earnest* (1993), where the main joke is that everybody's passion is under wraps and that only snobbery is allowed free speech. Some of the subdued performances did not seem to have much to subdue. Lady Bracknell was Pat Galloway, who had been Gwendolen last time around but did not seem to have realized Jack Worthing's fear that she might grow up to be as formidable as her mother. (Admittedly *her* mother had been Bill Hutt whose standards in formidability were formidable.) Barbara Bryne as Miss Prism was happily incorrigible, however, and Colm Feore made an impeccably earnest Ernest, a *nice* hypocrite.

Feore went to the opposite temperamental extreme as Dionysus, god of all licence, in Euripides' *The Bacchae*, which William directed that same season at the Third Stage, now fittingly renamed the Tom Patterson in honour of the Festival's founder. In another way the contrast may not have been so great; Dionysus, who has an iron will that destroys all who come in its path, requires iron control in the actor, and this Feore supplied. The production, of an impossible but compulsively fascinating play, was one of William's most notable. Something in its unresolvable conflict between reason and ritual, intellect and instinct, may well have spoken to him, and — despite inevitable shortcomings — he made it speak to the audience as well.

Perhaps more obviously Dionysiac — certainly hectic, raunchy fun — was the same season's Festival stage production of *A Midsummer Night's Dream*. This had Feore as a velvet-voiced and

leather-codpieced Oberon matched with a slinky Titania from Lucy Peacock, Ted Dykstra playing Bottom as the ultimate amateur ham, Frank Zotter as a pelvically propulsive hip-hopping Puck, and Sheila McCarthy a hilarious Helena with a voice like Betty Boop. The director was Joe Dowling, who had previously staged a very similar production at his home base, the Abbey Theatre in Dublin. Pop references were promiscuously slung about, and it was almost ceaselessly funny. If the lovers sometimes seemed about to out-clown the mechanicals, the latter fought back ferociously: Brian Tree was Quince, a role for which this drily funny actor was born, and Barbara Bryne, more surprisingly cast, was Robin Starveling alias Moonshine. The play, which sometimes seems as if it has arrived in the theatre by default, this time took the stage as if it had a reason to be there.

This was the only Shakespeare of the period to be directed by an outsider. Of those working from within, Bernard Hopkins, a pillar of the acting company, mounted two main-stage Shakespeares — *The Merry Wives of Windsor* (1990) and an Avon *Twelfth Night* (1991) — but, apart from the fantastical Malvolio of the Quebec actor-director Albert Millaire, they are best forgotten. Hopkins fared better as an actor, in the role of Dull, the heart-warmingly uncomprehending constable of *Love's Labour's Lost* (1992). This was yet another enchanting revival — and yet another in Edwardian dress — of one of Stratford's favourite plays. It must certainly have been a favourite of Marti Maraden, who had first come to notice as an actress in it, and now directed it as her first production. She had an enviable cast, with Colm Feore's Berowne and Alison Sealy-Smith's

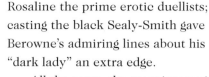

BACCHAE
CHORUS #6

(Left) A costume
designed by
Alan Barlow for
one of the chorus
in 1993's Bacchae.
(Inset) Under the
mask is Colm
Feore as Dionysus.

Rosaline the prime erotic duellists; casting the black Sealy-Smith gave Berowne's admiring lines about his "dark lady" an extra edge.

All the same, the most interesting Shakespeares came from past and future artistic directors. Michael Langham continued to display an unmatchable blend of freshness and authority in his 1991 staging of *Timon of Athens*, the play with which he had had a surprise success nearly thirty years before. He retained the modern setting and the Duke Ellington score. It was a sign of the times that so unpopular a play could no longer be risked on the Festival stage, but presenting it at the Tom Patterson had other obvious advantages of contact and immediacy. He took a new and less satiric view of Timon himself, possibly inspired by the perverse but visionary critic G. Wilson Knight, who had rated this play above all the others. The compulsively generous Timon of the first half here appeared as almost a Christ figure, radiant among his riches. Brian Bedford was ideally cast; dazzling in white suit and smile, he looked like one of his own favourite Noël Coward heroes. When the crash came — when the money ran out and the friends followed suit — he had a springboard into madness, and he found and focused

179

the passion that had eluded him as Macbeth. Nor did his comic skills go to waste; he found an ashen, apocalyptic wit in Timon's tirades.

In 1992 Langham gave Stratford its second great *Measure for Measure* (and much the funnier). Bedford, whose superbly twisted Angelo had been his calling card at Stratford, now moved over to the Duke and was allowed to take a comparatively benign view of him. He was charming, mischievous, self-important, but seriously concerned. Feore, completing his cycle of Shakespearean misfits, was a haggard, self-flagellating Angelo, and Elizabeth Marvel, an American actress and one of Langham's Juilliard graduates, had the right freshness and fervour for Isabella.

Robin Phillips returned in 1993 to perform a rescue operation on what had become the most hapless play in the canon, *King John*. Again, staging a problematic play in the Patterson meant great gains in clarity, as did the use of a First World War setting. Nicholas Pennell played John as what might be called a single-dyed villain: a skilful politician certainly, and moderately well-intentioned but weak-willed, fatally able to choose evil as the easy way out and plausibly royal enough to take others at least some of the way with him. The laconic scene in which he tempts Hubert (Scott Wentworth) to the murder of the boy Arthur was transfixing. He also

established John as the second most mother-fixated protagonist (after Coriolanus but ahead of Hamlet) in Shakespeare, continually looking at the dowager Queen Elinor (Janet Wright) for her approval, and silently falling apart after her death. This was a good production for mothers, with Goldie Semple remarkable as Constance in both her

*Victor A. Young (centre) played Duke Senior in Richard Monette's 1990* As You Like It. *Designed by Debra Hanson, the production featured canoes, Indians, and coureurs de bois.*

possessiveness and her bereavement; indeed it was a good production for women, with the helpless Blanch — married to one side, kin to the other — vividly portrayed (by Michelle Fisk) as the cynically manipulated pawn of both. As much as any Shakespeare, this play shows what politics can do to people; the Cardinal (Edward Atienza) and the Dauphin (Diego Matamoros) emerged here as breathtakingly cool operators even by the shameless standards of the histories, while Stephen Ouimette as the

Bastard commented honestly, humorously, and magnetically from the sidelines. It was (at least to date) Phillips's last Shakespeare production at Stratford — indeed his last production there of any kind — and it made a beautiful capstone.

The most prolific guest director was Richard Monette, who continued his line of comedies in 1990 with an

*As You Like It* set in New France just before the British invasion. William, extolling the play's themes of harmony and reconciliation, called it the company's Meech Lake production; to that extent it recalled Langham's initial *Henry V* with its celebration of what turned out to be a precarious sense of national unity. Frankly, it was difficult to see how the mildly political elements of *As You Like It* — one good duke, one bad — squared with Canadian history, though Berthold Carrière supplied some

180

lovely Québécois songs. Jamie Portman approvingly described the production's ambience as an "idyllic Never-Never Land"; true enough, just as *Peter Pan* juxtaposes pirate ships and mermaids' lagoons to create a timeless adventure playground, so Shakespeare's greenwood changes scene by scene from beast-infested jungle to village park. Monette's production was engagingly multicultural: on the one hand an Indian chief standing in for Hymen, god of marriage, and on the other a kilted Touchstone (William Dunlop) matched with a bumpkin Audrey (Susan Wright) who was hilariously broad where a broad should be broad. Two performances, though, dominated: Lucy Peacock as a witty and unshakeably confident Rosalind and — as a stylish and uncompromisingly bitter Jaques — David William showing himself a spectacularly authoritative actor.

Monette's *Much Ado About Nothing* (1991) took fewer liberties — or, if you will, fewer chances — but then it had little need of any. It was, in fact, an unusually well-balanced production that looked honestly at the lesser lovers, the trusting Hero and self-centred Claudio, and had them played (by Sidonie Boll and Paul Miller) precisely for those qualities, with only their youth to plead for them. Meanwhile Colm Feore and Goldie Semple — a soldierly Benedick and livewire Beatrice — were able to refine their earlier *Shrew* partnership for the same director.

Monette, who in his acting days had never been typecast, was now being labelled as a director of comedy: this despite the fact that during this period he directed three productions of the tragedies that were, at the least, interesting. His *Julius Caesar* (1990) was probably the closest to success

Stratford has ever come with this play, only letting itself down in the dangerous closing sections when the characters, after leading blameless Hollywood-historical existences in tunics and togas, cheapened themselves by putting on nasty yellow T-shirts, stencilled with slogans to show which side they were on. Some called this postmodern; others, a failure to trust the audience. Nobody thought it worked.

Earlier the production had great physical excitement. Brian Bedford was an ideal Brutus: the weary handsomeness of both his voice and his face conveyed all the character's high-minded sweet-reasonableness; his charm explained his friends' devotion; while his wit — the actor's, not the character's — functioned as a frame for the performance, highlighting the idealist's exasperating and finally fatal disconnection from reality, without ever condescending to it. Cassius was another of Colm Feore's feverish malcontents, and Scott Wentworth, his rhetorical skills hugely sharpened, was a thrilling Antony. Caesar himself was Nicholas Pennell, and so nice a man that it was unclear why anybody would want him assassinated.

The responses to Monette's 1920s-set *Romeo and Juliet* (1992) confirmed that reviewers usually see what they look for. Some thought that the lovers were too frivolous (but see "I have forgot why I did call thee back"); others that they were too doom-haunted from the start (but see "I have no joy of this compact tonight"). Everybody agreed that Feore's Mercutio dominated the play until his death: to that extent the production was traditional. The leads were Antoni Cimolino and Megan Follows, the daughter of old Stratford favourites Ted Follows and Dawn Greenhalgh. Both were authentically

## "A couple that made sense..."

### Antoni Cimolino

Richard Monette, who directed *Romeo and Juliet*, had to find a couple that made sense, and that wasn't easy. They auditioned a lot of people. It was cast quite late. I was in New York, in a rehearsal hall, when I got called out by the producer, Colleen Blake, to tell me they'd found a Juliet for me. It was Megan Follows. I had seen her on stage once and thought she was unbearably cute, but I hadn't seen her in *Anne of Green Gables*. She was terrific as Juliet.

Colm Feore as Mercutio was extremely generous during the process. He had played Romeo before and I was being directed by someone who had played Romeo, so there was no shortage of opinions about what to do at any given moment. I think there were some things I managed to succeed in and other things that I failed in. I felt very at home in the ball scene. There was a magic that came over the audience that worked.

181

young and seemed younger. Cimolino's Romeo was a believably shy and love-struck teenager, but he stuck in that groove when tragedy struck; it was Follows's Juliet who matured more deeply and convincingly — which admittedly is how Shakespeare, however he may have planned the roles, actually wrote them. (History suggests that playing Juliet is a treat while playing Romeo is a chore.)

Adding *Caesar* to *Romeo*, Rome to romance, Monette duly arrived at *Antony and Cleopatra* (1993). This was given a nineteenth-century look, the Roman army of occupation in Egypt kitted out like the British army of occupation in Egypt. This was a sardonic comparison that Bernard Shaw had made in his own *Caesar and Cleopatra*, or at least in its prologue, and putting Shakespeare's play into Shaw's own time gave it something of a Shavian tone. Stephen Ouimette's Octavius, in particular, was a very cool and collected modern politician, an incipient velvet-gloved dictator. The costume scheme certainly made it easy to tell Romans and Egyptians apart, but even traditional designs usually manage to make that much of a fashion statement. The play's built-in problem for a modern audience — that its protagonists are seldom on stage together and spend more time squabbling than smooching when they are — again proved a hurdle. Goldie Semple sparkled, raged, and teased as Cleopatra, to great effect. Antony, a role that usually goes to a mature matinee idol, was played by Leon Pownall, who in his youth had been nobody's first choice for Romeo or Orlando. He had all the passion and authority for Antony, but the phenomenon known as *optique du théâtre* comes into play here; he was, according to

common expectation, the wrong shape. Nor did he really suggest the free-spending generosity that inspires such loyalty in Antony's friends and breaks the hearts of those who desert him.

Reverting to laughter, Monette turned in a tight, comely production of Molière's *The School for Wives* (1991) with Brian Bedford as Arnolphe, the man who in going to neurotic lengths to avoid cuckoldry inevitably blunders right into it; the role is one long series of double takes, physical and mental, and Bedford's command of both was immaculate. Albert Millaire turned the cynical Chrysalde — not a great role in itself — into a firework display of authentic French style. Millaire himself directed Stratford's next Molière, *The Imaginary Invalid* (1993), passable fun which brought William Hutt back to the Festival after an absence of five years and back to the hypochondriac role after a break of twenty. Playing a character whose greatest happiness was to imagine himself at death's door, he seemed hardly a day older; his relish of symptoms and treatments and his resentment of doctors' bills and recalcitrant offspring were as rich as ever.

The Young Company had a fitful existence in William's time. Its members played minor roles in major productions, but the company itself staged only one show a year. In 1990, it was Francis Beaumont's Jacobean comedy *The Knight of the Burning Pestle* which, like that previous Young Company success *The Critic*, is a good play about the performance of a bad one. Bernard Hopkins and Pat Galloway directed a thoughtlessly anachronistic production that nevertheless proved popular enough to be revived the following year. In 1992 Marti Maraden took over, beginning operations with an endearing

production of that Young Company standby *The Two Gentlemen of Verona*. Once again, the minor role of the maid Lucetta served as a lively introduction to a major actress. On the previous occasion it had been Lucy Peacock; on this, it was Yanna McIntosh. She shone again, playing another maid but a far more prominent one, in *The Illusion* (1993). Newly fashionable after long neglect, this early play by the seventeenth-century French master Pierre Corneille is another multilevelled meta-theatrical piece, but one that only reveals its full complexity at the close. This makes it the more fascinating, and Maraden and her troupe did it well, using a translation by Ranjit Bolt that proved again how well English rhyming couplets can work in a comic context.

*The Illusion* is a comedy, but its author is better known as one of the two masters of French neo-classical tragedy — a genre that the English-speaking theatre has fearfully avoided. Stratford finally took the plunge in 1990 with *Phaedra*, the greatest play of Corneille's greater contemporary, Racine. The play is as fearsome an indictment of emotional repression as *The Bacchae*, and presents an even greater challenge, since its passions cannot be externalized in song, dance, or trendy ritual. Brian Bedford directed, using classical costume and a minimum of movement. Patricia Conolly, in the legend-encrusted title role of the queen driven to despair by raging desire for her unattainable stepson, reached for the grand manner and often grasped it. She was surrounded by some of Stratford's strongest. Leon Pownall was an imposing Theseus, though Colm Feore as the adored Hippolytus seemed uncomfortable, maybe because of the skimpy Greek tunic run up for him by

## "Our Lofty Scene"

Although the thrust stages of the Festival and Tom Patterson theatres allow plays to be performed with little or no scenery, individual elements — like the canopy above, from the 1990 Third Stage production of *The Knight of the Burning Pestle*, designed by Gary Thomas Thorne — can be used to spectacular effect. More elaborate sets are customary at the Avon Theatre, a traditional proscenium-arch venue. (Below, left) The statues of saints that decorated the stage in *Murder in the Cathedral* (1988), designed by Debra Hanson, were assembled from components carved out of Styrofoam. (Centre) Roy Brown, head of props for the Avon and Tom Patterson theatres, spray-paints a finished statue. (Right) Gary Thomas Thorne's set model for *Entertaining Mr. Sloane* (1992).

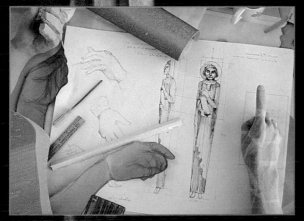

*(Above) Yanna McIntosh as Lyse, sitting atop Gerry Mackay as Adraste, shone in the 1993 Young Company production of* The Illusion; *the following year she played Maria in Richard Monette's production of* Twelfth Night *at the Festival Theatre. (Below) In* Entertaining Mr. Sloane *(1992), Ted Dykstra — who later went on to co-create the hit play* Two Pianos, Four Hands — *played the leather-clad young lodger who exerts his dubious charms on both his land-lady and her brother, Ed, played by Alan Scarfe.*

Desmond Heeley. Lucy Peacock contributed strength and humanity as Aricia, the third point in the triangle. Even the attendants were cast to strength: Shirley Douglas, Roberta Maxwell, and Nicholas Pennell as the show-stealing tragic messenger.

More recent and theoretically more malleable classics at the Patterson were actually less exciting. *Uncle Vanya* (1992), directed by Joe Dowling in a glum style at the furthest imaginable remove from his hyperactive *Dream*, was one of Stratford's rare failures with Chekhov, though Alan Scarfe lit up the title character's buffoonery and heartbreak and David William again showed himself a fine and fastidious actor by mercilessly delineating the play's perfectly horrible Professor. William Gaskill made his long-delayed Stratford debut by giving the festival its first taste of Pirandello, with whose plays he had recently had considerable success at the National Theatre. In *The Rules of the Game* (1991), the rules in question are the old Italian ones relating to honour, jealousy, and marriage; and the play shows a despised cuckold turning them to his advantage and eliminating his rival. It is a brilliant geometric exercise whose heartlessness is likely, in English, to register as bloodlessness; which was pretty much what befell it here.

Far more stirring was Martha Henry's 1991 Avon production of *An Enemy of the People*. Since quitting the Festival in 1980, Henry had turned increasingly to directing and was now artistic director of the Grand Theatre, London. The Ibsen play was Henry's first major assignment at Stratford. Ray Conlogue noted that the play "has various seductions for us today, not least the themes of industrial pollution and political cover-up": all this a decade

before Walkerton — worth mentioning since the pollution is that of a civic water supply, though the real and fictitious scenarios don't quite match up. David Fox played Dr. Stockmann, the medical officer who takes on not just a rotten town but a whole rotten society. Fox, with his unsettling capacity for switching from beamingly likeable to gloweringly uncomfortable, was accused of going over the top, but then the same charge has been levelled at the character, not least by Ibsen himself. Excessive behaviour does not stop a man from being right, any more than being right will protect him from his own excesses, and that rebounding paradox is at the heart of the play. Fox's mad expansiveness was complemented by Nicholas Pennell's whiplash meanness as his fraternal antagonist the Mayor; Phillip Silver designed a bold panelled set to exorcise the familiar spectre of horsehair-sofa Ibsen; and eagle eyes observed that the black-clad figure in the town-meeting crowd was David William.

Vivian Matalon returned to direct, impeccably, two prime cuts of hometown Americana: O'Neill's *Ah! Wilderness* (1990) and Thornton Wilder's *Our Town* (1991). O'Neill's wistful evocation of the childhood he wished he had had was an especial delight, with Andrew Dolha standing in for the young author, chafing at his own shyness, and Vickie Papavs for the girl next door, infuriatingly locked into hers. The older people, the play's main attraction, were a treasury, with Douglas Rain as the gently alcoholic uncle, Barbara Bryne, Susan Wright, and — a veteran of the earliest years of the Festival but largely absent since — Roland Hewgill, playing an enchanting father figure who could not have been less like James Tyrone.

*Our Town* featured several of the same actors, with Wright again playing a mother and Dolha sharing with Ann Baggley the unspoken-proposal scene, at once heartwarming and heart-rending, in the archetypal corner drugstore. Rain, as the druggist, helped greatly in this episode, though he came close to upstaging everybody with his mimed mixing of an ice cream soda — done, in accordance with the play's aesthetic, entirely without props. This of course was part of his consummately played role as the narrating Stage Manager, who conjures up the town of Grover's Corners from the resources of a bare stage. Wilder's vociferous rejection of naturalism and his belief in simple theatre magic had made him the favourite modern playwright of Tyrone Guthrie, so it was fitting that his flagship play should eventually turn up at Stratford, though not on the platform stage he would have favoured.

Nostalgic even in the 1930s when they were new, these two twentieth-century classics were doubly nostalgic now. A much later American piece proved more easily sentimental than either. This was *Love Letters* (1991), part of the playwright A. R. Gurney's continuing dramatic campaign to prove that WASPs are people too. A pair of thoroughly civilized New Englanders reconstruct a past relationship by reading their correspondence on stage. Since the play has minimal staging requirements, needing only a couple of seasoned actors who don't even have to learn their lines, it has proved an extremely popular regional-theatre piece. Douglas Rain and Pat Galloway did the honours at Stratford, with William directing.

William programmed more new —

or at least recent — plays in his four years than had any of his predecessors. The results were not invariably golden. Stratford's choices among contemporary British plays have often seemed arbitrary (no Osborne, no Pinter, no Stoppard, apart from the special-case *Rosencrantz*) and William's were no exception. David Storey's *Home* (1990) is a tenuous mood-piece. Marti Maraden's production gave it dignity, with Nicholas Pennell and James Blendick perfectly in tune as the two old gentlemen who find themselves in a mental home, and Barbara Bryne and Pat Galloway as the two rude ladies who interrupt their reveries. William himself directed *Entertaining Mr. Sloane* (1992). Joe Orton's later plays — *Loot* and his masterpiece, *What the Butler Saw* — are both more chilling and more hilarious; *Sloane* now risks seeming as chintzy as the suburban living room it purports to subvert. Barbara Bryne was right on the beam as the landlady who lusts after the young intruder of the title; Alan Scarfe was right off it as her similarly motivated brother; and somewhere in between were Ted Dykstra as the object of their attentions and Edward Atienza as the old man whom he cheerfully bludgeons to death while murmuring, "You brought this on yourself."

Willy Russell's monologue *Shirley Valentine* (1992), directed by Richard Monette, seemed a very modest piece even for Stratford's smallest stage. Janet Wright as Shirley hugged the back wall of the Tom Patterson for the first half of the play when she was still the suppressed Lancashire housewife, and advanced boldly on to the platform when finding liberation on an Aegean holiday. Wright's accent did not convince many people, but her warmth

did. The role had actually been intended at Stratford for Susan Wright, Janet's sister, who had died in a fire before the season started: a cruelly premature end to the career of one of the Festival's — and the country's — most vital actresses.

A few other uncategorizable solo shows appeared at the Patterson. One, already tried out under the previous regime, was a triumph: *The Lunatic, the Lover, and the Poet* (1990), a one-man Shakespeare recital by Brian Bedford. Bedford was able to reprise some of his greatest roles, and to offer a tantalizing taste of at least one, Lear, that he has yet to play.

Brand-new Canadian plays had rarely been seen at Stratford since Robin Phillips's time. They now began to reappear. Admittedly, the playwright most heavily promoted was Stratford's own dramaturge, Elliott Hayes, whose job it was to do the choosing. However, accusations of insider-trading were defused when Hayes's play *Homeward Bound* (1991) proved to be a family comedy of commendable toughness, mixed up with a drama about euthanasia. Marti Maraden directed a top-notch cast, with Barbara Bryne outstanding as a wife and mother whose sick husband (Douglas Rain) is slipping away from her and who takes refuge in endless erudite chatter.

In the same season, Hayes did less well when, as Stratford's first major venture into what is dispiritingly known as "family entertainment," he adapted *Treasure Island.* David William's production showed, as would his *Tempest* the following season, that he could stage an exciting storm. Shakespeare's play, of course, demands a storm; Stevenson's novel makes no mention of one, and its presence here was a spectacular irrelevance, taking up time that might have been better devoted to exploring the book's almost embarrassingly rich reserves of narrative, character, and dialogue. A more successful Hayes adaptation — certainly a more full-bloodedly theatrical one — was his version of Robertson Davies' *World of Wonders* (1992), one of the few world premieres to be mounted at the Avon, though it was probably Davies's name rather than the scale of the piece that prompted the promotion. Richard Rose, of Toronto's Necessary Angel company and an important figure in Stratford's future, organized Davies's parade of freaks, charlatans, and other artists into something between a carnival and a black mass. It was, however, more spectacle than play: a whole trilogy of novels had to be boiled down into a two-and-a-half-hour play, with an inevitable loss in style and focus, and the piece's windier philosophizing sounded unpersuasive when coming out of flesh-and-blood people.

Sharon Pollock, whose *Walsh* had been at least a partial success back in 1974, had another historical play premiered in 1993. This was *Fair Liberty's Call*, set in New Brunswick in 1785 and dealing with the embittered response of a family of United Empire Loyalists to Britain's loss of its American colonies: abandoned by the old order and detesting the new. It was an impressive play, if localized in its appeal; Canadian critics were more enthusiastic about it than the Americans, who found it pedagogic. Guy Sprung directed, and the cast, as usual with new plays at Stratford, was excellent. Once again there was a dominating role for a grieving mother, played by Janet Wright, and her daughters were strongly played by Kristina Nicoll and Philippa Domville.

Already, in 1990, the Festival had revived a ten-year-old play of Pollock's, on an overtly contemporary theme. *One Tiger to a Hill* was a grimmer and more confining piece than *Fair Liberty's Call*: literally so, since it was set in a maximum-security prison whose inmates had rebelled and taken hostages. John Wood, Pollock's collaborator on *Walsh*, gave it a semi-environmental production in which some members of the audience sat hemmed in, on the Patterson stage. Roger Honeywell (much later the only Canadian actor ever to reinvent himself as an opera singer) grabbed some lightning as a retarded prisoner, and James Blendick gave a powerful performance of a warden who had willed himself into becoming a hard man. The play had clearly not aged into a masterpiece. Ray Conlogue, its strongest advocate, admitted its grinding quality but predicted that its proven dramatic situation — the jailbreak stand-off — would make it "a crowd-pleaser": an inaccurate prophecy and, given the Festival's attendance record with Canadian plays, a remarkably optimistic one.

What *was* hopeful about this production was that it gave a new airing, at the highest level, to an existing Canadian play, offering hope that there might be some potential, or even actual, Canadian classics. This policy was followed through, with some gratifying results. John Murrell finally got a play of his own on the Festival boards in 1990, when *Memoir*, his haunting and witty piece about the declining days of Sarah Bernhardt, was revived under the fittingly French direction of Albert Millaire. Even more appropriately, the play turned up in the same season as *Phaedra*, one of Bernhardt's greatest vehicles. Pat Galloway played the

wooden-legged tragedienne and Douglas Chamberlain the faithful, fretful secretary, dragooned into impersonating figures from her past life so that she may dictate her autobiography.

*The Wingfield Trilogy* (1992) truly belongs in the same old-new category; this sly, sharp, and hugely successful set of one-man plays details the adventures and misadventures of a stockbroker-turned-farmer, in the supposed form of a series of letters to a local newspaper. Widely seen elsewhere, it had family reasons for arriving in Stratford: the author was Dan Needles, son of William Needles, and Walt Wingfield was played by a younger old Stratford hand, Rod Beattie. (Beattie's brother Douglas reinforced the family atmosphere by directing.) It also had cultural resonance; how many occasions did this theatre in rural Ontario have to pay tribute to rural Ontario? And there was artistic justification, lots of it; the infinite sly variations that Beattie could ring on his invariable sign-off — "Yours, Walt" — were a treat in themselves.

However, it was not Ontario but Quebec that loomed largest in Stratford's exploration of the Canadian repertoire. The Festival's productions of three Michel Tremblay plays in as many years amounted to the most important body of work, other than the Langham Shakespeares, staged under the William imprimatur. The first was *Forever Yours, Marie-Lou* (1990). Lorne Kennedy, a former company actor, here made his Stratford directorial debut, and the women in his cast were especially fine; Susan Wright, in the title role as a wife locked in the bitterest of marital unions, filled the theatre with uncorked fury, and Marti Maraden as one of her daughters, in almost her last acting appearance at Stratford, switched brilliantly between aghast girl-hood and a religious quietude bred of desperation rather than belief. The play's power was universally saluted, though some found the static convention — four reminiscing characters at a table — oppressive and the exposure of a dysfunctional family unconscionably stark. (But are there any good plays about functional families?)

Easier to take was 1991's *Les Belles-Soeurs*, Tremblay's first and still most popular play, as uncompromising as *Marie-Lou* in its depiction of the lives of working-class women in a Montreal slum, but more emphatically comic and, in both its scenic plan and the size of its all-female cast, considerably more spacious. This time Maraden directed, with casting so rich that, in Conlogue's words, "it feature[d] Kate Reid in a *small* role." All three Wright sisters — Anne had made her Festival debut in *The Resistible Rise of Arturo Ui* in 1986 — were involved, not to mention such Festival favourites as Pat Galloway, Barbara Bryne, Mary Hitch Blendick (James's wife), Patricia Collins, and Goldie Semple, plus comparative ingenues Julie Winder, Shannon Lawson, Ann Baggley, and Sidonie Boll, and a highly-rated Toronto recruit, Nancy Beatty. They made magic. For all its abrasiveness (the Avon theatre had never heard such language), the production ranked with *Ah! Wilderness* as one of the most-loved shows of the period.

*Les Belles-Soeurs* also softened people up for Tremblay's own favourite among his plays, *Bonjour, là, Bonjour* (1992), which, as a piece that considers incest and decides it to be on the whole not such a bad idea, was tactfully housed at the Patterson. Albert Millaire's production was the final panel in a memorable triptych, with Marc

Ruel and Barbara Fulton as Serge and Nicole, brother and sister, who find in one another the best refuge from another fearful Tremblay family, though one more compassionately seen than most. Douglas Rain was the father who,

for once, comes to accept his son, and Kate Reid and Janet Wright fizzed as the young hero's disapproving aunts. (This was Reid's last role at Stratford; she died at the beginning of 1993.)

All three Tremblay plays were presented at Stratford in spruced-up English versions by their original translators John Van Burek and Bill Glassco, and all three were uncommon in their

spirit and intensity. Panorama or chamber piece, they were the right size for Stratford. Like the work of Robert Lepage, they had style and audacity on a classic scale; a scale that anglophone Canadian drama rarely approaches. The

*With its stellar all-female cast, Marti Maraden's 1991 production of* Les Belles-Soeurs, *by Michel Tremblay, was one of the biggest hits of the David William era. Susan Wright, whose sisters Janet and Anne were also in the cast, played Germaine Lauzon (left). Tragically, it was her last Festival role: she died with her parents in a house fire in December of the same year.*

Canadian theatre is lucky to have this modified French tradition within its own national borders, and it has fertilized Stratford ever since Langham's bicultural *Henry V.* It is evident in the Festival's constant returns to Molière. It is noteworthy, too, that both of Stratford's two Canadian-born artistic directors have been Québécois. The second of them was the next incumbent.

## Before the Performance

All performers must sign in no later than "the half" — actually thirty-five minutes — before a performance, though some arrive as much as two hours beforehand. Pre-show tasks include checking stage management notes for corrections or changes, as Gabrielle Jones (left, top) does before a performance of *Camelot* in 1997. For dancers like Michael McLennan (left, bottom) stretching exercises are essential, but most performers do vocal and physical warm-ups, including mandatory fight rehearsals for anyone involved in stage combat. On opening night, dressing rooms are crammed with cards and gifts, like those received by Yanna McIntosh (inset) as Maria in 1994's *Twelfth Night*. (Right) This unusual view of the Festival stage, shot from one of the two tunnels or "voms" that lead from the stage to under the auditorium seating, shows Tom McCamus making an entrance as Arthur in *Camelot*. Already on stage is Cynthia Dale as Guinevere.

# Chapter Eight

# The Monette Years

The Canadian theatre — more than the American, and far more than the British — has smiled on the actor-director. Most of Stratford's artistic directors have been established professional actors. The exceptions are Langham, Hirsch, and maybe Guthrie, who acted as a way of getting into the theatre and gave it up when he began to be recognized for his real talent. None of them, though, had quite the same thespian credentials of Richard Monette.

Monette is the only Stratford chief to have worked his way steadily up within the organization. Between 1965 and 1987 he had acted in fifteen different seasons, progressing from walk-ons to leads. He had won additional fame, or notoriety, at the tempestuous general meeting that followed the dismissal of the Gang of Four in 1979; as the chairman of the board of governors wound up the proceedings, leaving many questions still unanswered, Monette had screamed at him: "You pig! We have spent our life in this theatre. We have given our time, and we care about art, not about money

all the time. You have no morals. I don't know how you can sleep."

For all the nerve that he had demonstrated, on and off stage, Monette gradually developed a crippling stage fright that turned him from acting to directing; and after his first Stratford success with the 1988 *Taming of the Shrew*, he became the Festival's most frequent and reliable guest director. Obviously, he was being groomed for the top position. As was by now the custom, Monette spent the 1993 season shadowing and working with the outgoing director, David William, but in truth he had been serving a thirty-year apprenticeship.

Monette once drew up a list of the two types of director who have, by and large, alternated at Stratford: the showmen (Guthrie, Gascon, Phillips, Neville) and the intellectuals (Langham, Hirsch, William). The distinction is not exactly watertight, but most people, including himself, would agree in putting Monette in the first category; he directs with an actor's sensibility and an actor's sense

*"Variety is the essence of a festival," says Richard Monette, who opened the 1997 season with the musical* Camelot, *shown in rehearsal at left. The season also included a revival of Tyrone Guthrie's 1954* Oedipus Rex, *which was directed by Douglas Campbell.*

of fun. This — plus the fact that, unlike any of his predecessors, he had never run a theatre before — led to his appointment being greeted with a mixture of enthusiasm and wary condescension.

The enthusiasts had it in 1994. Monette's first season included two of the best productions in the Festival's history. Michael Langham returned (for the last time to date) to direct *Husbands and Cuckolds*, a double bill of two lesser-known pieces by Molière, given as if presented by a wandering troupe from the author's own time. This was unusually venturesome programming for the main Festival stage, but it did have Brian Bedford as insurance.

In *The Imaginary Cuckold*, Bedford appeared with "sparse, flyaway red hair and a great potato of a nose" (H. J. Kirchhoff in the *Globe and Mail*) as Sganarelle, the name invariably bestowed by Molière on the crafty or credulous buffoons who were his own specialties as an actor. In *The School for Husbands* Bedford was another Sganarelle, a more serious self-tormentor who, like his counterpart in the later and more familiar *School for Wives*, loses his bride by trying too hard to keep her. Langham's direction was beautifully precise, mellow, and inventive; while Bedford, both as lank farceur and suave tragicomedian, was consummate, a twice-crowned king of the double-take. The production was more sadly notable for the last appearance of Nicholas Pennell, who died, still comparatively young, before the start of the next season.

If *Husbands and Cuckolds* was a triumph, *Long Day's Journey Into Night*, directed by Diana Leblanc at the Tom Patterson and revived and filmed the following year, was an instant legend.

Simply, the actors and the director had realized that the Tyrones, thinly disguised surrogates for O'Neill's own family, love one another: this is what lies behind the obsessive guilt-raking and grievance-hugging that drives them toward the drugged and drunken oblivion of their shared midnight. A drama that can sometimes induce only a gloomy awe here yielded heartbreak.

As played by William Hutt, James Tyrone's plea to his wife as she renewed her enslavement to morphine — "Mary, can't you stop now?" — seemed drawn, heart-stoppingly and spontaneously, from the core of his being. (Laurence Olivier, intent in a celebrated London performance on making this a Great Moment, had been nothing like as believable, and hence nothing like as moving.) Peter Donaldson, surliness peppered with generosity, gave uncommon weight to the bitterly perceptive Jamie, and Edmund was newcomer

Tom McCamus, with a smile half cynical and half disarming. The only possible flaw was that as Mary, the one civilian in this nest of burned-out actors and incubating playwrights, Martha Henry gave the most theatrical performance: her descent into hell seemed calculated. When she reached bottom, however, in her tranced recollection of her convent girlhood, she was sublime. Leblanc's orchestration of five extraordinary performances (since Martha Burns also had unprecedented presence as the maid) was perfection.

A third production almost matched these. *Cyrano de Bergerac*, unattempted at Stratford since the Langham-Plummer-Colicos cavalcade, had been slated for Robin Phillips. He cancelled and was hastily replaced by Derek Goldby, who had already staged the play to acclaim at the Shaw Festival. He brought much of that luscious staging with him and raised the

stakes with an inferno of a battle. As Cyrano, Colm Feore fenced rhapsodically with sword and tongue and drenched every eye in the house in his farewell scene with Martha Burns's Roxanne. It was a glorious finale to thirteen all-but consecutive Stratford seasons in which Feore had emerged as Stratford's biggest home-grown star since Plummer.

Monette's own contributions to the 1994 season were a brace of Shakespeares: the paradigm tragedy, *Hamlet*, and the paradigm comedy, *Twelfth Night*. The first was a clipped and sober production mounted (unusually for this director) at the Patterson, and it repaired a gap in Stratford history by starring Stephen Ouimette, who had been pencilled in for the role by the Gang of Four thirteen years before but who still seemed young. His was a fanged, unromantic, and sardonically eloquent performance: heavy-lidded and dagger-voiced.

Continuity was further honoured in Monette's *Twelfth Night* at the Festival Theatre. David William stayed on as an actor to play a fine, purse-lipped Malvolio, while Brian Bedford shifted into a commandingly melancholy Feste. Once again the season's Hamlet doubled divinely as its Sir Andrew Aguecheek; Ouimette as the sweet, cowardly knight wore a large Napoleonic hat and was accompanied by a Yorkshire terrier wearing a scene-stealingly small Napoleonic hat. Yanna McIntosh was one of the strongest Marias Stratford has known, and Lucy Peacock a piquantly cheerful Viola. Some thought the production too emphatically dark: an interesting divergence from what was fast becoming the facile received opinion on Monette's talents as a director.

Ever since his initial success with the *Shrew* he had been typed by critics as a farceur, with the implication that he would do anything for a laugh. Some of his later productions admittedly supported this. A Victorian *Merry Wives of Windsor* (co-directed with Antoni Cimolino in 1995) was energetically boisterous, though it had William Hutt's richly deflated Falstaff to give it a human face as well as a ruefully human voice. It was Hutt's second try at the role, and much the happier.

Monette's *A Midsummer Night's Dream* (1999) also had at its centre a great Stratford actor remembering, with advantages, a role he had played before. This was Brian Bedford as Bottom, marvellously easygoing in his vainglory, and especially beguiling when stepping out of character in the last scene to lecture Theseus on one of the finer interpretive points of *Pyramus and Thisbe*; delivered in his friendliest, firmest Yorkshire

*Diana Leblanc's* Long Day's Journey Into Night *(opposite, with Martha Henry, Peter Donaldson, William Hutt, and Tom McCamus) was the unexpected hit of 1994. The same year, Colm Feore played poet-swordsman Cyrano de Bergerac (left), and in 1995 Stephen Ouimette (right, with Barbara Bryne) did some fancy fencing of his own as Dr. Caius in* The Merry Wives of Windsor.

Much Ado About Nothing, *with Martha Henry, Brian Bedford, and William Hutt, transferred to New York with* The Miser *in 1998.*

accent, this became one of those great moments in which the natural rhythms of actor and character magically fuse. Magic was otherwise in short supply, with Juan Chioran's Oberon chanting rather than speaking his lines. In one respect the production was quite recklessly experimental: its ancient Greek characters were costumed as ancient Greeks.

Perhaps the richest of Monette's pure comedy productions was *Much Ado About Nothing* (1998). This too had some loved performers revisiting former triumphs. Brian Bedford and Martha Henry, who had previously

played Benedick and Beatrice opposite other partners, now squared off together. They were of course older than the average B&B, but the text does — to some extent — support the idea that these two have been around the track several times before, or have spent a long time sitting acerbically on the sidelines. Guido Tondino designed a 1920s palazzo that Cole Porter might have been pleased to rent; the men were recently and wearily returned from (again) the First World War, and the women had grown spiky waiting for them. Bedford and Henry presented a

wedding of wits rather than hearts, each of them too intelligent for the company they were generally required to keep, and smarting at it; and of course it was a pleasure merely to hear them time the lines. There were two other golden reprises: William Hutt's Leonato, getting delicately drunk on dry Martinis, and Brian Tree's Verges, an especially ripe second banana.

Monette's finest Shakespeare productions were the two that he built around William Hutt, whose King Lear and Prospero — he was playing each for the third time at Stratford — were the most momentous re-encounters of this period. *King Lear* was staged in 1996 when Hutt was seventy-six. This made him chronologically young for the role ("fourscore and upward, not an hour more or less") but theatrically old: Olivier played the part on television when he was in his seventies and Gielgud on radio when he was ninety, but genuinely old actors seldom have the stamina to do it live. So what was amazing about Hutt's performance was its sheer voltage. His rages may have been carefully husbanded, but that made them more frightening when they actually came. He strode on to the stage (apparently into a Victorian Christmas party) with mischief in his eye and walk, a man confident in his own outrageousness, and far too used to being a king to be able to take on a new career as a subject. He was, surprisingly, less effective in the quiet bits: in the stupendous scene at Dover, and in the reconciliation with Cordelia. The best was at the last: Lear's confrontation with Cordelia's hanging — and in Monette's staging, her corpse truly looked as if it had just been cut down from the gallows. His vocal powers were at their fullest stretch here, and his technique — as the king's mind wandered again, sure of nothing but the fact of that dead body — was like quicksilver. Here was the tragic experience: to despair of humanity and to marvel at it, simultaneously. Hutt was still inventing on the last night. ("He's never done heart attacks before," said his director during the interval.) Jordan Pettle was an excellent young Fool (he and Hutt seemed to be moving in and out of one another's heads), and Geordie Johnson played an original seeming-virtuous Edmund, cheekily got up as a candidate for the priesthood.

# *The Player King*

For William Hutt, then a struggling actor in his early thirties, the advent of the Stratford Festival was a godsend. Half a century later, having participated in all but a handful of Festival seasons, he is widely acclaimed as one of the greatest classical actors of our time — many would argue *the* greatest. "People say, 'Why didn't you spend more time on Broadway? Why didn't you make movies?' And my first answer is: neither of those is going to make me a better actor. I'm not going to be a better actor because I do eighteen months in one show on Broadway. I'm not going to be a better actor because I do one film, or two films, or three films. Maybe some people regret that I haven't the international reputation that they think I should have. Had I wanted that, the only way to get it would have been to go to Hollywood and do a lot of films. But I never wanted a film career. I like making films, but I didn't want a career of it. And to be associated with one of the greatest theatrical minds in the English-speaking world, meaning William Shakespeare: what more can you ask?"

*(Right) Hutt in the title role of* King Lear *(1996). (Above) This Stratford Festival commemorative stamp, part of Canada Post's Millennium Collection, featured Hutt as Prospero in the 1999* Tempest.

*The 1997 season's Shakespearean productions included an exciting* Richard III *at the Tom Patterson Theatre, with Stephen Ouimette (above) in the title role, and, at the Festival Theatre, an updated* Taming of the Shrew *with (below) John Gilbert as Baptista, Cynthia Dale as Bianca, and Lucy Peacock as Katherina.*

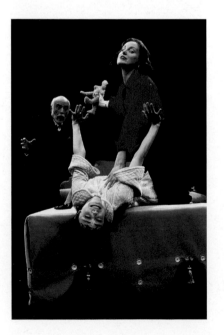

Hutt's performance in *The Tempest* (1999) confirmed him the finest verse-actor on the English-speaking stage. The taut, flexible viola voice, the sustained and witty phrasing, the architectural prowess that built each speech into an ongoing wave of sense and sound, the fusing of these to create a character: all were thrillingly in play. Hutt presented Prospero as a troubled, benevolent, and uniquely powerful intelligence facing the limits of its own achievement. Before taking the tough but inevitable decision to forgive, he held a pause of extraordinary length while the audience held its breath; the acceptance energized him for the great speech summarizing and renouncing his magic powers, in which he was magnificent. There was a rumour going around — false as it turned out — that this would be Hutt's last season, so there was a special if temporary resonance to his appearance in this greatest of valedictory roles; when he bade farewell to "this bare island," he might also have been quitting the bare Festival stage. This was Stratford's best-balanced account of a notoriously treacherous play; even the courtiers' scenes worked.

Between 1996 and 2000 only three non-actors directed Shakespeare productions at Stratford. One was the still-undervalued John Wood, responsible for an exciting *Richard III* (1997, at the Patterson) in which Stephen Ouimette played a misfit usurper with a lacerating sense of humour. A second was Jeannette Lambermont, whose *As You Like It* (2000) seemed to have been inspired by Rosalind's remark that "there's no clock in the forest." The play was set within a giant timepiece, which set off savage alarms at the usurper's court but went beatifically

quiet after the characters took to the woods; at the end Hymen appeared bearing a smaller clock, as if to signal that holiday was over and that the newly married couples must now return to the real world. It was clever, but looked brutal. Lucy Peacock reprised her witty and accomplished Rosalind, and Juan Chioran found his ideal Shakespearean role as a deeply plangent Jaques.

Last of the trio, and the most prolific guest director of this regime, was Richard Rose, whose background in Toronto experimental theatre was far removed from Monette's own but some of whose productions were surprisingly similar. His comedies were as frenetically knockabout as Monette's, perhaps even more outrageously inventive, but not in the end as funny. "This," Rose's more farcical productions seemed earnestly to be telling the audience, "is *clowning*; aren't you impressed?" This was especially the case with a mechanistically misanthropic *Comedy of Errors* (1994, revived 1995) for the Young Company in which not even Tom McCamus and Stephen Ouimette, playing the Dromios, managed to assert their personalities over some futuristic police-state trimmings. Relaxation took hold in Rose's production of *As You Like It* (1996). Kristina Nicoll and Jane Spidell alternated as Rosalind and gave winningly energetic performances. So did Tamara Bernier and Caroline Gillis, their respective Celias, with David Jansen as Jaques lending a dark finish to the prevailing brightness.

Rose graduated to the main stage and the main company with *The Taming of the Shrew* (1997), a production that trumped Monette's 1950s-Italian version of a decade before by shifting the scene to 1960s New York, with characters continually referring to

"New Padua," a rewriting that the sensitive greeted with a shudder. Characters drove around the stage in toy cars, and the piece yielded its usual quota of enthusiastically cartooned supporting performances, notably from heavy-father John Gilbert and new light-heavyweight Robert Persichini. Cynthia Dale was a brilliantly sugary Bianca. The play was indeed sweetened rather than illuminated, though it was a clever touch to have Petruchio tame his bride by taking her back to the Old Country, as far from feminism as from New World comforts. In the main roles, Peter Donaldson and Lucy Peacock worked out their own love-comedy: he a sympathetic buccaneer turning up for his wedding in cowboy gear, she a witty termagant with an ironic spin on her concluding declaration of dependence.

Rose ended his voyage through the early comedies with *The Two Gentlemen of Verona* (1998), the weakest play given the strongest production. In a 1900-or-thereabouts setting, the dubious duo were seen as recent graduates of a North American high school. Valentine (Graham Abbey) was the confident hockey-team hero, and Proteus (David Jansen) the studious outsider, compensating for his unpopularity with a feverish devotion to poetry and his girlfriend. Rose also, and perhaps more characteristically, directed hard-edged productions at the Patterson of two of the Roman tragedies. His *Coriolanus*

*Graham Abbey (front row, centre) led the team as Valentine in* The Two Gentlemen of Verona *(1998).*

(1997) was slanted against everybody, especially the hero. There was nothing likeably gauche or imposingly Herculean about Tom McCamus's performance; he was pure thin-lipped, war-loving, crowd-despising psychotic. Martha Henry's Volumnia was similarly powerful and had a similarly ambiguous impact. Jamie Portman found "no evidence of her psychological authority over Coriolanus"; Kate Taylor in the *Globe and Mail* thought they had a "spectacularly detailed relationship" that climaxed when, having persuaded her son to spare Rome and thus doom himself, she left the stage "shaking like an old crone."

It must be some kind of portent that Stratford has now staged *Titus Andronicus* as often as *Coriolanus*;

Rose's *Titus* (2000) summoned the play's public world exceptionally well in a between-wars Italian setting. Frock-coated senators ineffectually debated, while black-shirted storm troops besieged the Capitol and generals in desert fatigues addressed the public ostensibly for its own good. Gripping, though not moving, it featured James Blendick as an honest and believable Titus who lacked the character's terrible logical insanity.

*Julius Caesar*, currently less fashionable than *Titus*, received an unhappy, stylistically muddled production in 1998 from Douglas Campbell, Stratford's veteran of acting veterans. Brian Bedford, still a neophyte by comparison, mounted a more complexly unfortunate *Othello* (1994), another production

*(Above) James Blendick played the title role in Richard Rose's gripping production of the notoriously violent* Titus Andronicus *(2000). (Below) Seana McKenna and Scott Wentworth were paired in* Macbeth *(1995), a much more popular but hardly less difficult study in horror. "I am appalled by evil," commented the production's director, Marti Maraden, "but like most of us I'm fascinated by it."*

inherited from an absent Robin Phillips. It was set in and around Washington circa 1945, considerably sharpening the play's military and racial contexts: Brabantio (Lewis Gordon) was able to state the case for prejudice with the confident authority of an influential senator from the South. Iago (Scott Wentworth, in a role originally earmarked for Bedford himself) was good at being bad, and the splendidly named (certainly in this context) Dixie Seatle was a telling chain-smoking Emilia. Once again, though, the tragedy foundered on an inadequate Moor (Ron O'Neal).

Much finer was Bedford's production of *The Winter's Tale* (1998) at the Patterson (given a beautiful white design by Ming Cho Lee in one of his less grandiose moods). Leontes, once one of Bedford's own great Stratford roles, was now played by Wayne Best with hysterical intensity but without the same sense of thwarted nobility. Kate Trotter's Hermione and especially Diane D'Aquila's Paulina brought great assurance to the Sicilian scenes. The always tricky Bohemian sheep-shearing became a 1960s hippie carnival, nostalgically inspired perhaps by the line "They have made themselves men of Hair." Geordie Johnson presided over it as a very merry Autolycus.

Joseph Ziegler, a Stratford acting ornament of the eighties now increasingly active as a director, made his debut with a handsome, straightforward *Hamlet* (2000). The same might have been said for his leading actor, Paul Gross, riding high on his success in the television series *Due South*. There was nothing intrinsically wrong with bringing in a TV star, especially one who proved well able to make both literal and rhythmic sense of the text. What was disturbing was that there was not a young actor in the regular company, current or recent, who seemed an obvious contender. (Tom McCamus came nearest, and he had already played the part in Toronto.) Gross's Hamlet was a diffident, unchallenging young man who was at his best in the "rogue and peasant slave" speech, ruefully mocking his own pretensions to passion as compared to those so richly acted out by Juan Chioran's First Player. This was part of a fine triptych performance by Chioran that also encompassed the Ghost and a sardonic First Gravedigger: three signposts along Hamlet's — and the King's — way to the tomb.

Actress-directors did especially well under Monette, though Marti Maraden failed to break the Festival Theatre jinx on *Macbeth* (1995); it started promisingly but by its closing scenes had resolved into the usual diagonal parade of anonymous warriors clad in plaid. The play came briefly and suddenly to life only when Bernard Hopkins as the Porter took command of both the stage and his one big speech, just as Scott Wentworth had once done as Tyrrel in *Richard III*. Wentworth was now playing Macbeth, but neither he nor Seana McKenna as his lady were able to make the central roles their own. Maraden fully redeemed herself, however, with an Avon *Merchant of Venice* (1996) set in pre-Fascist Italy, with Shylock making a last doomed stand for justice. Douglas Rain, in one of the finest of all his Stratford performances, gave him the caution and the dignity of a Rothschild, but with a destructive rage simmering underneath. He had to lose his case, but the forced conversion can seldom have seemed uglier, or the final scene more haunted. This was one of the most exciting of Avon Shakespeares; they usually start at a disadvantage

compared to those at the Festival Theatre, whose stage, whatever else, confers automatic authority.

Martha Henry, at the Patterson, directed a highly intelligent *Richard II* (1999) that made brilliant use, both practical and metaphorical, of the play's key images: the mirror that Richard smashes at his abdication; the prophetically labelled "gay apparel" in which he bedecks himself and his favourites; the game of bowls that distracts the queen before she learns of her husband's downfall; the ground of England on which he famously sits to lament the death of kings and to foretell his own. Geordie Johnson's fair-haired Richard, though lacking in anger and irony, was fluent and excitingly fast, accepting his defeat and enjoying it. In white singlet and shiny silver pants (everyone else was unobtrusively medieval), he stood in pointed contrast to John Dolan's grey, balding Bolingbroke.

Diana Leblanc, on a roll with modern plays, expanded into main-stage Shakespeare with a *Romeo and Juliet* (1997) that for once seemed more interested in making love than war; the fights took second place to the lyricism. Jonathan Crombie and Marion Day were a personable pair of lovers. The setting was nineteenth-century Caribbean, with an especially notable black Capulet from Roy Lewis. Leblanc's real triumph, however, came in 1999 when she presented Stratford with, at last, a good *Macbeth*. She received small thanks for it in the press and

## "What makes Hamlet so amazing..."

### Paul Gross

I started to look at the soliloquies as a progression in the interior state of Hamlet. He gradually becomes much more organized. The interior thoughts become more structured, till you finally get to the last one — "How all occasions do inform against me" — which is practically one sentence, with sub-clauses, and it's perfectly put together. The first one — "O that this too too solid flesh would melt" — is extraordinarily broken up: he can't quite complete sentences.

This started to make sense to me from a dramatic writer's point of view. With the first soliloquy I thought, yeah, he wants to start Hamlet off as wrecked. Ordinarily that kind of emotion would be the deepest, a climax of something. But what makes *Hamlet* so amazing is that, no, we're going to start there and then we're going to go down and it's going to get weirder and broader and stranger and more frightening. Shakespeare's saying, "That's where we begin. Now we're going to go down to the real depths." Then it seemed to make sense to me.

(Above, from left) Diane D'Aquila as the Nurse, Marion Day as Juliet, Chick Reid as Lady Capulet, and Roy Lewis as Capulet in Diana Leblanc's 1997 production of Romeo and Juliet. (Below) Michelle Fisk as Alithea, Stephen Ouimette as Sparkish, and Benedict Campbell as Harcourt in The Country Wife (1995). "They're all hypocrites," said director Douglas Campbell of the obsessively lecherous characters in the play, "and performers too: they sort of act themselves out."

admittedly there were oddities. Presumably in the interests of universality, the Scottish play was shorn of all references to Scotland, though not, surprisingly, to specific Scottish towns. Rod Beattie's mastery of Walt Wingfield's soliloquies did not, it turned out, equip him for Macbeth's; he had, to put it rudely, trouble with the big words. But he also had moments of remarkable immediacy, moments in which the audience was made free of Macbeth's mind (which is what the play is about), and the slippery ease with which he briefed Banquo's murderers can hardly have been bettered.

Martha Henry (Beattie's real-life wife) was an insouciantly seductive Lady Macbeth, pushing her husband up the corporate ladder. Then, after he had outgrown her, she collapsed into an unbeatable sleep-walking scene, reactivating every disjointed line ("The Thane of Fife had a wife — where is *she* now?") with superbly unexpected naturalness. The play's other married couple — who never meet on stage — were also finely played: Sarah Dodd's vexed anxiety in Lady Macduff's one scene of fearful domesticity made the subsequent massacre even more horrible than usual, and that was matched by Peter Hutt's poleaxed anguish when he received the news. Sound effects, in the blessed confines of the Patterson, were superb, every thunderclap, owl-shriek, and knocking at the door precisely calibrated. Scene after scene, character after character, rose freshly from the text. Critics who had been bemoaning a lack of good acting at Stratford failed to recognize a production that was loaded with it.

Greek tragedy, with which Stratford has a sparse but respectable record, received two radically contrasting productions. The famous Guthrie *Oedipus Rex* returned to the Festival stage in 1997 under the direction of Douglas Campbell, one of its original actors, and with three more of its founding players in the cast: William Needles was again the Old Shepherd, Roland Hewgill now played Creon, and Douglas Rain made a fearsomely bodeful Tiresias. The production was less a restaging than a tribute, above all to Tanya Moiseiwitsch's costumes and masks. The ritualistic trappings again made terrifying demands on the leading actor. Benedict Campbell — less sonorous than his father but more so than James Mason — was valiant and sometimes moving. One major departure was the addition of a farcical satyr-play — not after the tragedy, as the Greeks would have had it, but before, to bring a modern audience up to speed on the myth. There was something inevitably self-defeating about this freeze-dried Sophocles, but it was worth doing once.

At the opposite extreme was Euripides' *Medea* (2000), directed at the Patterson by Miles Potter. This began with masks (and a smattering of Greek) but then, having paid its respects, settled down to full-blooded realism. The text, a fifty-year-old adaptation by the American poet Robinson Jeffers, sometimes trivialized ("Medea, you shouldn't . . . " said Jason, on receiving her fatal wedding gifts), but also helped. Seana McKenna was sulphurous and coruscating as the heroine, both a believable sorceress and a very modern wronged woman. When she swapped marital recriminations with Scott Wentworth's Jason, their joint mastery of the blame-game was bruisingly recognizable. Wentworth failed, as any actor might, to encompass the bereaved Jason's despair, but the production rescued him: there was a thunderclap, the lights went down and came up to reveal him masked once more, locked forever into his desolation. Past and present, ritual and reality, joined hands. This was a stunning evening.

Moving down the millennia, Douglas Campbell directed a nonsensical production of *The Alchemist* (1999). Most stagings of this marvellous booby-trapped play end up either pedestrian or raucous; this one was both. It was all the more lamentable because, in 1995, Campbell had directed a superb *Country Wife*, Stratford's third and best. Apart from being lubriciously and cruelly funny, with a gorgeously decadent design, it realized one fundamental truth about Restoration comedy. The plays are constructed like vaudevilles: each character in turn gets to stand up and glory in his own obsession. The Festival stage, for those who can tame it, is the ideal springboard. Three actors took both text and platform by the scruff of their respective necks while holding the audience in the palms of their hands, which is some trick: Scott Wentworth's Pinchwife rushing enraged into cuckoldom, Tom McCamus's Horner coolly and exultantly accepting the proceeds, and Stephen Ouimette's Sparkish preening in an ecstasy of unawareness.

Richard Monette directed a bevy of classic comedies. His *A Fitting Confusion* (1996), an early Feydeau, was generally damned but was actually very fast and funny, with Stephen Ouimette absolutely in his element as the hero-schemer-victim. *The Miser* (1998) was as comprehensively slammed for being vulgar: perhaps with more justification, though much of the vulgarity was Molière's own. The play, with William Hutt inevitably in the lead, was taken to New York at the end of the

*In 1997, Tyrone Guthrie's legendary 1954 production of* Oedipus Rex *was remounted on the Festival stage. Douglas Campbell, who had taken over the title role from James Mason in the 1955 revival, directed his son, Benedict, as Oedipus (above, with Douglas Rain as Tiresias). John Colm Leberg re-created Tanya Moiseiwitsch's original designs for the tragedy.*

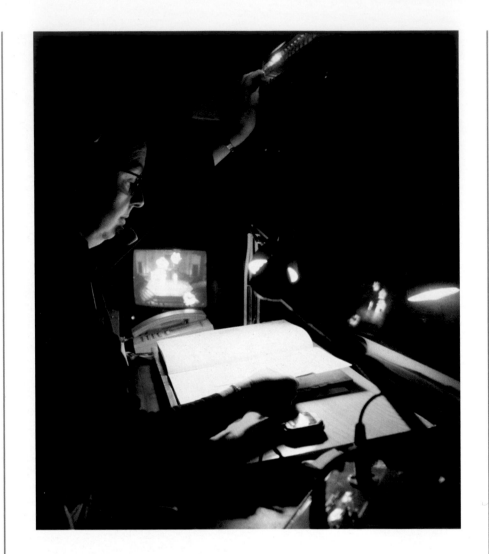

## *"Part One Beginners: Places, Please"*

Though never seen by the audience, the stage manager plays as crucial a role in a theatrical performance as does the conductor of a symphony. From a glassed-in booth overlooking the stage, a stage manager like Ann Stuart (above) runs the show from her "bible," a copy of the script that has been taken apart and remounted on large blank pages on which are noted every actor's movements and every technical cue. Using a stopwatch (left) and communicating with the performers and crew via a headset and a panel of switches that turn on backstage "cue lights," the stage manager ensures that every performance unfolds as it should, from the summoning of the actors to their places for the beginning of the show to the last fade of the lights on the curtain call.

season in tandem with Monette's *Much Ado*, and the American reviewers reversed the Canadians' verdict by preferring the Molière to the Shakespeare. (In truth, they were not wild about either.) Monette later came up with a perfectly straight *Tartuffe* (2000) which, with the Festival in an increasingly retrospective mood, restored two glories of the Hirsch production: Brian Bedford's "hang-up-my-hairshirt" hypocrite and Tanya Moiseiwitsch's design.

Monette's production of *The School for Scandal* (1999) also had Bedford at his best, as Sir Peter Teazle. Critical reaction was strangely muted, as if Brian Bedford being impeccable, especially in comedy, could somehow be taken for granted, but this was a superb performance in which literally every line the actor spoke was both hilarious and emotionally truthful. Seana McKenna's Lady Sneerwell was both wounded and wounding; Steven Sutcliffe, new to Stratford though known outside as one of Canada's best, was a most accomplished Joseph Surface; and two company discoveries, Michelle Giroux and Donald Carrier, made pleasant impressions as Lady Teazle and Charles.

In 2000 Monette reached *The Importance of Being Earnest* and went back to the original four-act script that Wilde's original producer had cut to three. The familiar version is undoubtedly the better, but the ur-text naturally has its own fascination, and it is a relief to go to *The Importance* and hear some new jokes. (Also some new names, though Patricia Collins's Lady Bracknell seemed somehow less imposing for being called Lady Brancaster.) The play came up fresh, with the extended action centring it more firmly than usual on the escapades of the two young men: Donald

Carrier's Jack a permanent outsider (the mark of the handbag on him for life) and Graham Abbey a tellingly immature and increasingly charming Algy.

The production was part of a Wilde mini-festival at Stratford. The season also included a staged reading of Gilbert and Sullivan's *Patience*, which features a lampoon of Wilde in his heavy aesthetic phase; Bruce Dow impaled him like a sulky butterfly. And there was a revival of *Oscar Remembered*, a one-man show whose author, Maxim Mazumdar, had performed it at Stratford in 1975 under William Hutt's direction. Hutt directed it again, with Michael Therriault as Lord Alfred Douglas, an overbred puppy-dog with a grievance. Oscar still had all the best lines, and the evening was mainly devoted to recycling them.

*The Cherry Orchard* has been a lucky charm for Stratford. Diana Leblanc's 1998 production was one of the best, though its centre was blurred by Martha Henry's Ranevskaya, so restlessly the grande dame that she never came into focus. The others, radiating out from her, were meticulously detailed. The emotional peak was the failed proposal scene between James Blendick's Lopahin and Sarah Dodd's poignantly uncompromising Varya: two lives wasted in full view. As a sensitive reading of a theatrical score, this rivalled Leblanc's *Long Day's Journey*, and visually, within the confines of the Patterson, it was far bolder.

Leblanc's triumph with O'Neill led her to other American classics. In *Death of a Salesman* (Avon, 1997), her handling of Miller's family dynamics — more immediately recognizable than O'Neill's and hence more easily moving — was equally acute. Willy Loman is a role in which conventionally unheroic actors — sitcom players and even stand-up comics — have traditionally found themselves as tragedians. They know about the salesman as glad-hand artist; and Al Waxman, television's King of Kensington returning to the stage after an absence of thirty years, was Willy to the sagging, crumpled, heart-rendingly cheerful life. Martha Henry was a heroic Linda whose grief was devastating.

Leblanc had less success with *Sweet Bird of Youth* (at the Patterson in 1996), but so would anyone. Kenneth Tynan described this Tennessee Williams play at its 1959 première as "antique melodrama pepped up with fashionable details," and though everybody would like to like it (it's Williams after all) few have seriously disputed Tynan's verdict. Most of Leblanc's Tyrone household were reassembled: Martha Henry as the fading movie star, Martha Burns as the girl infected to sterility by her first sexual experience, Tom McCamus as a Southern bossman's rodent son, Peter Donaldson as someone comparatively agreeable. They were reinforced by Lewis Gordon, David Jansen, Chick Reid, and — remarkably convincing in Paul Newman's role of the gigolo who courts castration — Geordie Johnson.

Johnson also appeared, acting up a tropical storm, as a defrocked priest (and current tourist guide) in a slightly later Williams play, *The Night of the Iguana* (Patterson, 1998), directed by Antoni Cimolino. Here the hothouse exoticism seems more honestly come by, the compassion less flamboyantly sentimental. It also offers a great role to an actress who can deliver a massive monologue with quiet but hypnotic intensity. Seana McKenna certainly could. She played the itinerant painter-daughter of "the world's oldest living

(Above) Al Waxman as Willy Loman in Death of a Salesman (1997). Waxman, who had never before acted at Stratford, was to have returned in 2001 as Shylock in The Merchant of Venice *but died shortly before the start of rehearsals.* (Below) Geordie Johnson as the Reverend Shannon in Antoni Cimolino's 1998 production of The Night of the Iguana.

and practising poet," a role in which William Needles gave the evening's other outstanding performance.

The extended Hubbard family of Lillian Hellman's *The Little Foxes* (1996) make Williams's characters look like anchorites. It is not a good play and, acted without fireworks, it can be intolerably dull. Acted with them, as in Richard Monette's Festival Theatre production, it can be melodramatically compelling and even acquire a certain depth. It had another of those Stratford catalogue casts: Bedford, Henry, *and* Hutt (by now a planetary combination), Peter Donaldson, Tim MacDonald, and — in a welcome return to acting — Diana Leblanc, whose nervous Birdie was the outstanding performance.

Monette himself came back to the boards in Eduardo De Filippo's *Filumena* (1997). The great Neapolitan actor-playwright had been neglected in English until the National Theatre staged his *Saturday, Sunday, Monday* in 1973. The West End followed suit with *Filumena* a few years later, but the plays have never caught on in the U.S. Canada at least knows that farce does not have to be knockabout, that family

emotion does not have to be sticky, and that the two can combine. Antoni Cimolino directed. (He had turned from acting to direction and administration after his 1992 *Romeo*, and is currently the Festival's second-in-command as executive director). Monette gave a charmingly guileful performance as a man puzzled by the sudden materialization of his long-time mistress's three grown sons. Lally Cadeau gave a monumental one as the lady herself.

In the same season — her first at Stratford — Cadeau blew the audience away as another archetypal mother in Sean O'Casey's *Juno and the Paycock*. James Blendick partnered her as a ripe and potentially brutal Captain Boyle, and Brian Tree was a superb, shuffling Joxer. Janet Wright directed a production as unselfconsciously funny and moving as the play itself.

*Waiting for Godot* received its third and best Stratford production from Brian Bedford in 1996 (revived in 1998). An ancient record played, and through the curtain came the now-familiar duo of McCamus and Ouimette, going through their routines with desperate skill to stave off time and, in the play's most res-

onant line, "to give ourselves the impression we exist." James Blendick had now expanded fully into the role of Pozzo, and Tim MacDonald was a scarifying Lucky. This was a great production.

The record of new plays — all of them done, inevitably, at the Patterson — was sparse but not undistinguished. The first was the worst: *In the Ring* (1994) by Montreal playwright Jean Marc Dalpé. Only his second play, it was an interesting enough portrait of the shadier boxing scene, damagingly intercut with symbolic dream-sequences. Richard Rose directed, and he also staged the more rewarding *Glenn* (1999), David Young's fragmented fantasia on the life and quirks of Glenn Gould. Rose, whose work was beautiful, had previously directed this stylishly self-indulgent piece in Toronto. His Stratford actors — Paul Dunn, Duncan Ollerenshaw, Rod Beattie, and especially Richard McMillan — were superbly intrepid as a chamber quartet of Goulds, overlapping and interweaving.

Timothy Findley, Stratford actor of 1953, made his long-awaited return as a playwright with *The Stillborn Lover* (1995). Based on the real-life

*(Left) In 1997 Richard Monette returned to the stage for the first time in a decade to play Domenico Soriano opposite Lally Cadeau in* Filumena, *directed by Antoni Cimolino. (Right) James Blendick as Pozzo, Tim MacDonald as Lucky, Stephen Ouimette as Estragon, and Tom McCamus as Vladimir in Brian Bedford's 1996 production of* Waiting for Godot, *designed by Ming Cho Lee.*

# A Moment of Magic

"On an April evening in 1962," recalls Martha Henry, "I found myself in the green room with a number of extraordinary actors I had only ever seen from the audience. One of these was Peter Donat, who was to be playing Ferdinand in *The Tempest*. 'Have you been in the theatre?' he asked me. 'Of course — I've seen lots of things.' 'But when it's empty?' 'No,' I allowed. 'Come on.' He took me through what seemed to be a secret passage and we found ourselves in the auditorium. We sat there and watched Tanya Moiseiwitsch's stage. After several minutes I realized the floor — the wood — was alive, was pulsating. We were watching it breathe." (Right) Henry as Frosine in *The Miser* (1998). (Insets, clockwise from top) As Marian Raymond, with William Hutt as Harry Raymond, in *The Stillborn Lover* (1995); as Mary Tyrone in *Long Day's Journey Into Night* (1994); as Princess Kosmonopolis, with Geordie Johnson as Chance Wayne, in *Sweet Bird of Youth* (1996).

case of a gay diplomat hounded to his death by the RCMP, it gracefully explored issues of loyalty, political and social, without bringing them to full dramatic life. Peter Moss's production featured an explosive performance by Martha Henry and a dignified one by William Hutt.

It was eclipsed, like much else, by Findley's second Stratford play, *Elizabeth Rex* (2000), the most spellbinding Stratford opening since *Long Day's Journey*. It is hard here to separate substance from occasion. The play concerns an imaginary encounter between Shakespeare's own company of actors and Queen Elizabeth I, who is seeking diversion on the night preceding the execution of her disgraced favourite, the Earl of Essex. It takes place in the royal barn. Seeing a band of modern Shakespeareans impersonating their ancestors in a converted hall on the banks of a River Avon was a thrill in itself. The play's ideas gripped less than its atmosphere and architecture. Brent Carver as the dying Ned, an actor of women's roles, added stricken anger and aching tenderness to his customary amazing grace, and Diane D'Aquila rose finely to Elizabeth's loneliness. Shakespeare himself was portrayed by Peter Hutt as watchful, secretive, and universally mistrusted. Allan Wilbee's set managed to be both spare and cluttered, Louise Guinand's lighting was smokily exquisite, and Martha Henry's direction was wonderful. Of all the new plays produced at Stratford, this one seems the likeliest to last.

It is quite a roll-call. Nevertheless Monette's regime appeared to attract as much hostility as admiration. Much

of the criticism took the form of self-fulfilling prophecy; Monette was cast as a lightweight and then treated as one. As a director, certainly of Shakespeare, he fell short of the style and vision of Langham, Phillips, or Hirsch. But he was good; and, unlike his immediate predecessors, he was able to put his own stamp on the theatre. Paradoxically he was most heavily attacked for the crime of balancing the theatre's budget — even, in some years, achieving a surplus.

The charge was that he had done this by adulterating the repertoire. In particular he programmed, usually at the Avon, the kind of safe, audience-pleasing material that John Neville had once described — and decried — as "boulevard theatre." (This was a year after Neville appeared at Stratford in *Separate Tables*.) What counts as "safe" is of course a matter of debate; *Waiting for Godot* is nowadays hardly a box-office risk. Then again, Stratford's boulevard choices (i.e., plays of recent date with a commercial track-record) vary greatly in quality. Jay Presson Allen's *The Prime of Miss Jean Brodie* (1998) is an excellent play — better than Muriel Spark's original novel — though Janet Wright's production and Lally Cadeau's central performance were lacklustre. Part of *Brodie*'s distinction is that it leaves the spectator in two minds about its spikily fascinating protagonist. Most popular theatre invites the audience to identify with the central character, and to bask at the close in an unearned moral glow.

This is true, at the high end, of *A Man for All Seasons*, which had its second Stratford outing in a 1998 Marti Maraden production (this time at the

Festival Theatre) with Douglas Rain unsurprisingly admirable as More and Brad Rudy effective but muted in what used to be regarded as the show-stealing role of the Common Man. It is certainly true of *The Miracle Worker* (also 1998), William Gibson's dramatization of the education of the child Helen Keller. The audience, having witnessed the feisty Irish teacher's ferocious and successful attempts to teach her unruly charge to speak, are left with the pleasantly exhausted sensation that somehow *they* have done it. A standing ovation is practically guaranteed. The Stratford recipients, in Jeannette Lambermont's production, were Cynthia Dale, whose Annie Sullivan displayed a toughness that nobody had thought she had in her, and the nineteen-year old Trish Lindstrom.

*The Diary of Anne Frank* (2000) was turned by its Broadway adaptors, Frances Goodrich and Albert Hackett, into a domestic drama with a death-sentence hanging over it. In Al Waxman's exemplary Stratford production, the actors playing the eight fugitive Jews stayed on stage even during the interval, to give us some faint idea (it could only be that) of the tedium and frustration of their two years hiding from the Nazis in an Amsterdam attic. The performances were excellent, with Diane D'Aquila, usually cast in loud regal roles, giving a beautifully modulated account of the permanently anguished Mrs. Frank. Waxman broke with tradition by bringing the SS on stage at the end; usually the audience only hears them on the stairs. Everything was done to make the action real. But reality is never as smooth and well-

*(Opposite) Of all Stratford's new plays, perhaps Timothy Findley's* Elizabeth Rex *(2000) most stirred its audiences' imagination. As Elizabeth I, Diane D'Aquila rose royally to the occasion.*

## The Practical Magician

Since first coming to Stratford in 1957, Desmond Heeley has designed thirty-four Festival productions. Wary of abstract notions of design "concept," he begins every production with a scale model of the stage and a list of essential objects. "You have to go to the needs of the play," he says. "It's terribly important that you establish the geography of the place: Who comes on and from where? Who goes off where? Who brings what on; who takes it off? Design is problem-solving. There's no magic; it's all mechanics. It's making things practical, that's all: inventing a little machine that can make the play happen."

A hands-on designer who works with the artisans to realize his highly impressionistic design sketches, Heeley is renowned for his ability to create the most opulent-looking effects from the humblest of materials. He has a strong affection for the craft of theatrical artifice and the illusions it makes possible.

Heeley and cutter Cynthia MacLennan add the finishing touches to a costume worn by Jennifer Gould as Katherina Cavalieri in the 1995 production of Amadeus. (Inset) Heeley's original design sketch for Cavalieri.

orchestrated as this production; and with this subject, that matters. Doubtless the only way to dramatize the Holocaust at all is to seize like this on a tiny fragment of it, but the fact remains: the audience, having shared vicariously in someone else's historical agony, left the theatre feeling drained, certainly, but also spuriously noble.

Peter Shaffer's two most celebrated plays, *Amadeus* (1995, revived 1996) and *Equus* (1997), may not count as commercial pieces: both were originally produced by Britain's National Theatre before going on to huge success in the international marketplace. In Stratford both starred Brian Bedford, self-lacerating as the psychiatrist in *Equus*, self-mocking as Salieri in *Amadeus*. But *Amadeus* in particular is a deeply suspect play. As a study of artistic jealousy it is compelling, rising to a fine first-act climax in the pious Salieri's challenge to God for having bestowed mediocrity on him and genius on the foul-mouthed Mozart. God, unfortunately, doesn't answer; so the conflict is over and we are left with schools-broadcast biography and a tour of Mozart's greatest hits. Monette gave it a suitably operatic production, with Stephen Ouimette capering to great effect as Wolfgang and Megan Follows and Colombe Demers playing the long-suffering Mrs. Mozart in admirable succession. But the underlying assumption that big names, big ideas, classical music, and fancy dress add up to great drama made the play's appearance at Stratford troubling and its reappearance downright depressing.

The earlier *Equus*, with all its imperfections on its hoof (its minor characters are ciphers, and the boy at its centre seems to have grown up in a social vacuum), is far more interesting.

The playwright has imagined amazing scenes, and they propel a debate on faith and feeling that is prosaically expressed but registers as passionately felt. Bedford himself directed, in admitted imitation of John Dexter's great original staging. So Stratford got a Dexter production after all: not just a stunning spectacle but a precision instrument for the generation of tension.

In an allied vein were two shows frankly mounted as vehicles for visiting stars. One of them was a *revisiting* star: Christopher Plummer, no less and at last, in and as *Barrymore* (1996). A Broadway-bound co-production with Garth Drabinsky's Livent Inc., and directed by Broadway's Gene Saks, William Luce's portrait of the great American actor in his turbulent, alcoholic decline was less a play than a richly taken opportunity for Plummer to jest, swagger, and declaim for a couple of enjoyable hours. His talents, unlike Barrymore's, had plainly not rusted, but they both deserved better material. The play, a duet for the hero and a faithful unseen prompter, was the latest in a surprisingly fertile line of actor-and-amanuensis double acts: a line that stretches back through *The Dresser* and *Memoir* to Chekhov's *Swan Song*, which had turned up at Stratford in 1990, under Jeannette Lambermont's direction and double-billed with a bit of Dostoyevsky.

More substantial was the arrival of Uta Hagen, the eighty-one-year-old doyenne of New York acting, in Donald Margulies's *Collected Stories* (2000), directed by William Carden. This was an author-and-amanuensis play. Hagen played a Manhattan writer and teacher, warmed and challenged by a young student and protégée (Lorca Simons, admirable). Scribbling and frowning,

Hagen established the essence of her character before saying a word, and then proceeded to expand on it, with a mixture of comic gusto, resentful frailty, and a capacity for meanness whose uncontrollability shocked even the woman herself. This was seamlessly great acting: one of Stratford's reasons for being.

For the family there were stage versions of four famous novels with child-friendly credentials. *Alice Through the Looking Glass* (1994; revived 1996) was a huge hit. It was certainly spectacular, in the sense of having eye-filling sets and costumes (by John Pennoyer), and Sarah Polley, in her stage debut, was as convincing an Alice as the Canadian stage is likely to see or hear. But James Reaney's adaptation and Marti Maraden's production were ploddingly unimaginative, and only Douglas Rain's Humpty-Dumpty was equal to Carroll's wit.

Maraden was on firmer ground with *Little Women* (1997), adapted by Marisha Chamberlain. Louisa Alcott's tartness proved easier to realize on stage than Jane Austen's a couple of seasons later. *Pride and Prejudice* (1997) was presented in a version by Christina Calvit that kept nearly all the plot but let most of the tart flavour slip through its fingers. Jeannette Lambermont's production was pretty in a Masterpiece Theatre way.

*The Three Musketeers* (a boy's book for a change) stormed the Festival stage yet again in a whirlwind production by Monette, superbly drilled and mounted and superficial in the very best way. There was a massed sword-fight even before the story started, and a cast of forty rushed round in an infinity of hats and cloaks, looking like thousands. The familiar Peter Raby

*(Top) Keith Dinicol as Tweedledee, Sarah Polley as Alice, Bernard Hopkins as Tweedledum, and Mervyn Blake as the Red King in* Alice Through the Looking Glass *(1994). (Above) Graham Abbey as D'Artagnan and Kate Trotter as Milady de Winter in* The Three Musketeers *(2000). (Below) Christopher Plummer in* Barrymore *(1996), for which he later won a Tony Award on Broadway.*

## "No finer place to stand and perform..."

### Cynthia Dale

I have never in my professional life been happier than I was on that stage. There is no finer place to stand and perform. It's a mix of the architecture of the theatre — the audience so much around you and so close to you — and also the ghosts, and the history, and the magic that has been left there by every single performer.

We opened the 1997 season with *Camelot*, and somebody had said to me, "Don't go to the theatre and watch any of the other shows until you've got your openings out of the way." I knew what they meant after I'd sat in the audience. There's so much energy on that stage, especially on the opening nights, that as an actor you sit there and think, "Oh my God, I will never be able to match up. I will never be able to live up to what is expected of me."

adaptation was enhanced by the restoration of Dumas's own bittersweet ending. There was even some acting: Graham Abbey actually managed to suggest a development in D'Artagnan, from callow bumpkin via ardently predatory lover to military hero. Benedict Campbell's Athos was excellent in its hard-bitten hauteur and Kate Trotter gleamed maliciously as Milady. The show was more dashing than some Stratford musicals.

These, for the first three years, remained in the care of Brian Macdonald, who was now going through the Gilbert and Sullivan canon for the second time. *The Pirates of Penzance* (1994), lovelessly burlesqued, suggested that he was getting bored. *The Gondoliers* (1995) was sometimes painful, sometimes brilliant; Lee MacDougall's hysterical Grand Inquisitor was both. A later English show, *The Boy Friend* (1995), Sandy Wilson's perfect spoof of a 1920s musical, had choreographic verve but no feeling.

Macdonald came through with his last show. Meredith Willson's *The Music Man* (1996) for all its Main Street setting and mainstream fame, is a maverick musical, one of a kind. Macdonald brought its old-time small-town Iowa to iridescent life, all over the Festival stage. Its only lack was a vital one: a proper leading man. Dirk Lumbard, formerly the super-hoofer of *Kiss Me, Kate*, had neither the voice nor the personality to run this show.

The first post-Macdonald musical was Lerner and Loewe's *Camelot* (1997), a show with a very moving ending. Getting there has never been much fun, and Monette's production was stodgy. Tom McCamus was a pleasantly boyish Arthur and Cynthia Dale sang sweetly as Guinevere; but the potentially tragic conflict remained inert. By contrast, *Man of La Mancha* (1998) was a first-rate production of an insultingly stupid show. Susan H. Schulman, a Broadway pro, gave it both a sense of confinement and an epic sweep (the windmill-tilting was first-rate); Juan Chioran was a wistful and melodious Don Quixote; and Cynthia Dale as the whore Aldonza tried hard to sound tough but revealed a heart of mush, rather like the show.

The 1999 season included two musicals, one of them — for the first time — new and Canadian, though the praiseworthiness of this initiative was somewhat dampened by the show itself. *Dracula* was a chamber-sized *Phantom of the Opera* with a turgid score by Marek Norman. Author-director Richard Ouzounian's staging was efficient and Douglas Paraschuk's sets spare and evocative, but Juan Chioran in the title role had regrettably little to sink his fangs into. However, this season also brought *West Side Story* and the next *Fiddler on the Roof*: two classic shows that at Stratford behaved like classics. *West Side*, directed by Kelly Robinson, took the stage with amazing freshness. For once, the Tony-Maria love duets were as compelling as the rumbles; even more uncommonly, in either play or musical, the updated Romeo (Tyley Ross) had the edge on his Juliet (Ma-Anne Dionisio). It was also a pleasant only-in-Stratford touch that Doc, Friar Laurence reborn as a

drugstore proprietor, should be an actor (Lewis Gordon) who had once played the Friar himself. Sergio Trujillo's choreography cleaved closely, but not slavishly, to the revered Jerome Robbins original.

Michael Lichtefeld did the same with the dances in *Fiddler*. Indeed some heretics felt that one scene — the challenge-dance "To Life" between Jews and Cossacks in the local tavern — actually worked better here than it had originally. (It invariably brought down the house.) Susan Schulman's production, played on a revolving floor backed by a Chagallian line of tumbledown houses, was peppered with fine performances from regular company members: Michael Therriault, for example, as the timid tailor Motel Kamzoil and Jonathan Goad as the Gentile who, in winning one of Tevye's daughters,

breaks her father's heart. Above all there was Brent Carver as Tevye.

Since last appearing in Stratford, Carver had established himself (in *Kiss of the Spider Woman* and *Parade*) as one of the best actor-singers in the world: maybe *the* best. He was also possibly the best in the world at conveying vulnerability and emotional need. Wrong for Tevye in some ways — not physically imposing or vaudevillean enough — he was wonderfully right in more important other ways: in warmth and pride and irony and pathos. Especially fine was his handling of the successive recitatives (or quasi-Hebraic chants) in which he confronts the loss of his daughters to progressively less eligible suitors.

Doing nothing but Shakespeare at Stratford is now an economic impossibility. (It may not be artistically desirable

*(Above) Raymond Rodriguez (foreground, left) as Bernardo with Daniel Murphy as A-rab in* West Side Story *(1999). (Below) In* Fiddler on the Roof *(2000) Brent Carver radically redefined the role of Tevye.*

*Stratford premièred four new plays in 2001. (Above) Richard McMillan as Hector Mackilwraith and Michelle Giroux as Griselda Webster in Richard Rose's adaptation of Robertson Davies's* Tempest-Tost. *(Below) Rod Beattie portrayed Walt Wingfield — and a host of other characters — in Dan Needles's* Wingfield on Ice.

either.) The audience for the plays will no longer support the size of the operation. But Stratford cannot realistically retrench. The Festival Theatre positively demands size, and size entails expense. And without the Festival stage, the Festival would have no reason to be.

Stratford is now very strong in acting. Stars apart, there is more colour and personality on its stages than was the case ten, twenty, or twenty-five years ago. Leading roles are still shared among too small a group of people, but there are signs of a breakthrough. Monette abolished the Young Company but he has instituted the Conservatory, a training programme for young actors of varying levels of experience who study (and are paid) in the months before a season and then proceed into the Festival company. It seems to be paying off. Some, like Michael Therriault and Michelle Giroux, are already prominent; and the 2001 season was studded with good performances from recent graduates.

It was altogether a remarkable season, a last chance perhaps for visitors to hold the history of the Festival in their hands. The company included octogenarian veterans of 1953, some of them still deservedly playing leads; a clutch of younger but mature favourites, pillars of the Festival over the previous twenty, thirty, or forty years; and a solid, lively corps of juveniles. They were spread over fourteen shows, of which only two were duds. One of these was *The Sound of Music*, Rodgers and Hammerstein's worst, in a production by Kelly Robinson even more anodyne than the material. The other, unhappily, was *The Seagull*, directed by Diana Leblanc and a sad successor to her *Cherry*

*Orchard*. It was drably set in what seemed to be a timeless void. Shakespeare can take this — he wrote anachronistically — but most moderns cannot. Martha Henry, despite some witty lady-of-the-manor moments, floundered as Arkadina, but Brian Bedford was definitive as the rapidly aging Sorin. His affectionate relationship with his nephew Konstantin (Michael Therriault) was the most palpable in the play. But little else jelled.

The year's twentieth-century classics were *Private Lives* and *Who's Afraid of Virginia Woolf?*, complementary studies of ill-matched couples, both hugely well done. Brian Bedford directed the Coward, and also repeated his performance of Elyot with the confidence of long experience and the freshness of perpetual discovery. His Amanda was Seana McKenna, and they quarrelled perfectly: she the edgier, he oddly protective even in violence.

Edward Albee's three-and-a-half-hour Walpurgisnacht (his description) was directed by William Carden with Peter Donaldson as George and Martha Henry as Martha. He gave a performance of consummate technical authority, the very soul and image of a cankered academic. She was rather forced in her swaggering, sashaying mode, but the pain in her eyes when she sat silent on the floor, her mouth working compulsively, haunted the mind. The younger couple who wander into their den were perfectly played by Sean Arbuckle and Claire Jullien. The quartet played together with awe-inspiring precision and flexibility; the play, as always happens in great ensemble performances, grew stronger by the moment, though not necessarily better; its last-act revelations are always hard to take, as are its philosophic pretensions.

The boulevard choice was *Inherit the Wind*, the trial for blasphemy of a Tennessee evolutionist, dramatized by the Broadway firm of Jerome Lawrence and Robert E. Lee. Monette gave it a populous, atmospheric production. William Hutt, fastidious and still electric, and James Blendick, bulky and booming, squared off to highly enjoyable effect as opposing counsel, that being the point of the exercise.

No fewer than four new plays were presented. The richest was *Tempest-Tost*, adapted and directed by Richard Rose from Robertson Davies's early novel. (This was a Davies celebration year.) It offered Richard McMillan an especially fine opportunity as a virginal schoolteacher driven to play Gonzalo (very badly) in an open-air production of *The Tempest*, all for the love of an unheeding eighteen-year-old girl. He started as a cartoon, with a shiny suit and a stiff, jerky walk, and finished — after the character had weathered both Shakespeare's storm and his own — with a chastened grace that was beyond praise. Not all the performances were that delicate, but Brian Tree was perfect as a pompous professor cast as Prospero, and Tara Rosling wonderful as his shy daughter, cast as his daughter. Rod Beattie came back as Walt in *Wingfield on Ice*, fifth instalment of the saga. (The fourth, *Wingfield Unbound*, had appeared in 1997.) The new one, a bit more thematically ambitious than the others, had the same writing and directing team and was just as attractive.

Some twenty years earlier, Timothy Findley had promised Stratford a play on Ezra Pound, poet, American traitor, and virulent anti-Semite. It finally arrived, having first been a radio script, as *The Trials of Ezra Pound*, a semi-documentary that kept posing the question "How can a great writer believe and propagate such filth?" without ever getting to dramatic grips with it. Pound himself, saved by being judged mad against his will, emerged as beamingly, brutally opaque. In Dennis Garnhum's production he was consummately played as such by David Fox, direct from his Toronto triumph in *The Drawer Boy*, and bringing his excellent colleagues, Jerry Franken and Tom Barnett, with him.

Newest of the new quartet was *Good Mother*, by a young member of the company, Damien Atkins. In the first scene a woman has a stroke; the rest of the play shows how she and her family come to terms with the irredeemably different person she now is. Directed by Miles Potter and movingly played by Seana McKenna, it was a conventional small-theatre piece, a species with which the Stratford Festival has been little acquainted but which it may get to know better, since its venues now include a small studio theatre adjacent to the Avon.

Most important, the 2001 season was golden for Shakespeare. Richard Monette, who had once refused to direct *The Merchant of Venice* because it was anti-Semitic, now staged it as a play *about* anti-Semitism. Shylock, though a confident financier, lived in a ghetto behind grated gates. Antonio (Peter Hutt), up against Shylock at the trial, witheringly measured out the words "his — Jewish — heart." After the decree of forcible conversion, Gratiano (in a gesture similar to one Monette must have remembered from when he played Antonio) pulled the covering from the Jew's head.

The two central performances drove the play. Lucy Peacock was a critical, self-possessed Portia. Shylock had been intended for Al Waxman, who dearly wanted to play it but who died before rehearsals started. He was replaced by Paul Soles, another Jewish actor who had done little Shakespeare. There were peaks of comedy and savagery that he left unattempted, but he spoke the part with uncanny conversational ease. His Shylock was pure businessman, intent and driven, and with a narrow but powerful cast of mind. Stratford's roster of Shylocks has been extraordinary: Valk, Davis, Cronyn, Neville, Bedford, Rain, Soles. The only other character to have elicited so many outstanding performances may be Sir Andrew Aguecheek.

He turned up again this season in the person of Michael Therriault, entering Illyria in cap and goggles — had he driven or flown? — and swinging metronomically between assertion and subservience. Caught wearing yellow, Olivia's least favourite colour, he stripped off the offending garments as if in some ceremony of self-flagellation, but could do nothing about his hair, which remained obstinately flaxen. He shared honours in Antoni Cimolino's production of *Twelfth Night* with two other conservatory graduates: Michelle Giroux, a coltish Olivia, and Tara Rosling, whose lucid, graceful Viola may have been Stratford Shakespeare's most accomplished female debut since Martha Henry's Miranda. (Which wasn't, strictly speaking, a debut: Henry had played Lady Macduff two nights earlier.) This was an unusually well-balanced production, barring some intrusive bouzouki music, with every part well played: superbly in the cases of Domini Blythe, an economically bossy Maria, and William Hutt — again — who even got laughs with Feste's jokes.

But for creating a company, nothing

beats the histories. In 1999 Stratford had launched a loose chronological cycle with *Richard II*. This year they picked up the story with both parts of *Henry IV* (Part Two again renamed *Falstaff*) and with *Henry V*. They were presented with different directors and at different theatres, but casting was continuous. Here one appropriately historic circle was completed. Douglas Campbell, a star (as Parolles in *All's Well*) of the first season, had played, repeatedly, the Falstaffs of *The Merry Wives* and of *Henry IV, Part One*. He had never played the Falstaff of Part Two; now, finally, he had the chance.

He was understandably less confident in the second play than in the first and this mattered, since vocal assurance was the core of what he had to offer. It made him — a surprisingly rare quality in Falstaffs — very funny. The tavern scene of Part One was

magnificent, both in its uproar and in the frost that fell upon it. Campbell's timing made his riposte to Prince Hal — "By the lord, I knew ye as well as he that made ye" — an authentic Great Shakespearean Comic Moment.

His son, Benedict Campbell, played the king, whom he presented as an embittered politician with an unfailing knack for saying the wrong thing. This left Graham Abbey as Hal caught in effect between a tactless, alienating father and a charismatic, dangerous grandfather. Costuming pointed this up. Falstaff was out of Merrie England, the king came from the First World War, and Hal was in neutral, modern black leather. Scott Wentworth, another actor making his directorial debut, delivered a strikingly lucid and intelligent account of the double play.

*Henry IV* was at the Patterson. Jeannette Lambermont directed *Henry V*

at the Avon, and her more elaborate staging also split periods. This was one war and every war. The English again fought as if it were 1914–18; the French were still living in the Middle Ages. Ceaseless video footage of marching, mud-soaked troops backed the action; meanwhile the Boy (Paul Dunn) camcorded the events on stage. This was an exciting production that found tension in unexpected places, with Sara Topham, an enchanting Katharine, giving Henry a harder time than most, and heralds, archbishops, and waiting-women coming to vigorous life. Graham Abbey is a hearteningly straightforward and unmannered actor, but as Hal this very openness allowed him to play the deep opportunist, all things to all men: a nimble comic artist with Falstaff, an honourable foe to Hotspur, a resentful but dutiful son to his father. He only froze up in soliloquy. As Henry — a

## *The Pioneers*

*Douglas Rain*          *William Needles*          *Douglas Campbell*          *Timothy Findley*

Besides William Hutt (left, as Prospero in the 1999 *Tempest*), there are three members of the original 1953 company who still regularly appear on Stratford's stages — and one, playwright and novelist Timothy Findley, whose work is presented there. Douglas Rain, shown above as Shylock in the 1996 *Merchant of Venice*, last appeared at the Festival in 1998. William Needles, shown here as the Bishop of Carlisle in the 1999 *Richard II*, marks his forty-third season in 2002. Douglas Campbell, shown here as Falstaff in 2001, remarks, "There are so many things to be said about these fifty years, that the space allotted seems totally inadequate. However, here are names that should be brought before you: Tyrone Guthrie, Tanya Moiseiwitsch, Cecil Clarke — the leader, the designer, the organizer. I am proud to have been part of this internationally known Festival and wish it well."

still young man easing himself consummately into a role, but at a cost — he learned to talk to himself. This was the education of a king. It was also the emergence of a star.

So the fiftieth season, 2002, had an auspicious act to follow. Inevitably, it was planned as both a retrospective and a progression. Christopher Plummer, most wished for, as King Lear with Barry MacGregor as his Fool and Domini Blythe and Lucy Peacock as his daughters. Graham Abbey and Claire Jullien, paired twice before as

Shakespearean lovers, arriving logically at Romeo and Juliet. Brian Bedford reprising *The Lunatic, the Lover, and the Poet*. The first Stratford production of *The Two Noble Kinsmen*, Shakespeare's last play, written in collaboration with John Fletcher and only recently granted scholarly admission to the canon. Stephen Ouimette directing his old partner Tom McCamus in *The Threepenny Opera*. *My Fair Lady* with Cynthia Dale as Eliza and three Higginses in succession: Colm Feore, Geraint Wyn Davies, and Monette him-

self. The opening of the Studio Theatre with seven new plays, including one by Timothy Findley. The conclusion of the histories with *Henry VI* (three parts redivided into two) leading on to *Richard III*, the latter directed by Martha Henry, whose *Richard II* inaugurated the cycle. The now-traditional commemorative revivals of Stratford's first two plays: *Richard III* joined by *All's Well That Ends Well*, directed by Monette, with William Hutt repeating his King of France. The continuity continues.

The *Oxford Companion to Shakespeare* (2001) has no separate entry on the Stratford Festival. It does, however, contain an essay on Canada, contributed from the University of Ottawa; and here Stratford rates a paragraph, no less. This acknowledges the influence of the Festival stage on subsequent theatrical architecture. It mentions just one production: Michael Langham's *Henry V*, praised for its use of French-Canadian actors in French roles, suggesting the possibility of "a unique Canadian Shakespeare." Since then, apparently, it has all been downhill, with the Festival's "British roots" leading to a dependence upon "'hired hands' — British and American directors and actors" and a forsaking of experiment for "an increasingly Hollywood-like emphasis on costumes, props and gimmicks."

A "unique Canadian Shakespeare" doesn't, and probably shouldn't, exist; anyway it can hardly depend on the few plays that happen to have both English and French characters. One wonders how many Stratford productions the author of this piece has actually seen. It reeks of received ideas, and not just from the academy; there is a similarly patronizing journalistic tradition dating back to Nathan Cohen's *ad hominem* attacks on Guthrie and Langham for daring to express a vision of the theatre different from his own. Just who are these American directors and actors who have apparently been infesting the place? How can people, wherever they were born, who have devoted years of their lives to Stratford be described as "hired hands"? One person's experiment is another's gimmick. (Cohen thought the French casting in *Henry V* gimmicky.) Shakespeare's own players were attacked by the Puritans of their day for

their rich costumes; what's so bad about looking good?

That *Henry V* was staged in 1956. The *Oxford Companion* (which misdates it by a year) implicitly — well, no, explicitly — dismisses all of Langham's subsequent work, all of Gascon and Phillips and Hirsch and Neville and William and Monette. The sustained acting achievements of Christopher Plummer, William Hutt, Douglas Campbell, Douglas Rain, Martha Henry, Brian Bedford, and countless others are presumably not worth mentioning. *Fifty Seasons at Stratford* was mostly written before the *Companion* appeared, but the essay's tone is symptomatic and this book is in part an attempt to redress the balance.

Tom Patterson wanted to help his home town. Tyrone Guthrie wanted to explore his ideas about staging Shakespeare. They both got more than they had ever expected, and recognized it. The Stratford Festival, literally since its inception, has been the second most important Shakespearean theatre in the world. It also has an impressive record of non-Shakespearean work. It created the professional English-speaking theatre in Canada. It has inspired great loyalty and also virulent opposition; but even that opposition has taken shape within the theatrical world that Stratford built. John Hirsch, a rebel and a loyalist at once, said in 1981, "It took thirty years to build this place. It could take a minute to die. It could take maybe 150 or 200 years to build it up again." It remains what it always was: a priceless resource. For what it has achieved, for what it has engendered, and for what it has provoked, the Stratford Festival is the best thing ever to have happened to the Canadian theatre.

# *Productions*

## 1953 – 2002

### TYRONE GUTHRIE

#### 1953

- Richard III
- All's Well That Ends Well

#### 1954

- Measure for Measure
- The Taming of the Shrew
- Oedipus Rex

#### 1955

- Julius Caesar
- Oedipus Rex
- The Merchant of Venice
- A Soldier's Tale

### MICHAEL LANGHAM

#### 1956

- Henry V
- The Merry Wives of Windsor
- The Rape of Lucretia
- Tamburlaine the Great (tour only)
- Oedipus Rex (tour only)

#### 1957

- Hamlet
- Twelfth Night

#### 1958

- Henry IV, Part I
- Much Ado About Nothing
- The Winter's Tale
- The Beggar's Opera
- The Broken Jug (tour only)
- The Two Gentlemen of Verona (tour only)

#### 1959

- As You Like It
- Othello
- Orpheus in the Underworld

#### 1960

- King John
- A Midsummer Night's Dream
- Romeo and Juliet
- HMS Pinafore
- Blind Man's Buff
- The Teacher

#### 1961

- Coriolanus
- Henry VIII
- Love's Labour's Lost
- The Canvas Barricade
- The Pirates of Penzance

#### 1962

- Macbeth
- The Taming of the Shrew
- The Tempest
- Cyrano de Bergerac
- The Gondoliers
- Two Programmes of Shakespearean Comedy (tour only)

#### 1963

- Troilus and Cressida
- Cyrano de Bergerac
- The Comedy of Errors
- Timon of Athens
- The Mikado

#### 1964

- Richard II
- Le Bourgeois Gentilhomme
- King Lear
- The Country Wife
- The Yeomen of the Guard
- The Marriage of Figaro
- Love's Labour's Lost (tour only)
- Timon of Athens (tour only)

#### 1965

- Henry IV, Part I
- Falstaff (Henry IV, Part 2)
- Julius Caesar
- The Cherry Orchard
- The Rise and Fall of the City of Mahagonny
- The Marriage of Figaro

#### 1966

- Henry V
- Henry VI
- Twelfth Night
- The Last of the Tsars
- The Dance of Death
- Don Giovanni

#### 1967

- Richard III
- The Government Inspector
- The Merry Wives of Windsor
- Colours in the Dark
- Antony and Cleopatra
- Così Fan Tutte
- Albert Herring
- Twelfth Night (tour only)

### JEAN GASCON

#### 1968

- A Midsummer Night's Dream
- Romeo and Juliet
- Tartuffe
- The Three Musketeers
- The Seagull
- Waiting for Godot
- Cinderella

#### 1969

- Hamlet
- The Alchemist
- Measure for Measure
- Tartuffe
- Hadrian VII
- The Satyricon
- Sauerkringle (tour only)
- Bust Out (tour only)
- Four Plays by Jean-Claude van Itallie (tour only)

#### 1970

- The Merchant of Venice
- The School for Scandal
- Hedda Gabler
- The Sun Never Sets
- The Architect and the Emperor of Assyria
- Cymbeline
- The Friends
- Vatzlav
- The Hostage (tour only)
- The Empire Builders (tour only)
- As You Like It (tour only)
- Three Plays by Mrozek (tour only)
- Tartuffe (tour only)

#### 1971

- Much Ado About Nothing
- The Duchess of Malfi
- Macbeth
- An Italian Straw Hat
- The Red Convertible
- Volpone
- There's One in Every Marriage

#### 1972

- As You Like It
- Lorenzaccio
- King Lear
- The Threepenny Opera
- Orpheus
- Mark
- She Stoops to Conquer
- Pinocchio
- Patria II: Requiems for the Party Girl
- There's One in Every Marriage (tour only)

#### 1973

- The Taming of the Shrew
- She Stoops to Conquer
- Othello
- A Month in the Country
- The Collected Works of Billy the Kid
- Pericles
- Inook and the Sun
- The Marriage Brokers
- Exiles
- King Lear (tour only)

#### 1974

- The Imaginary Invalid
- Pericles
- Love's Labour's Lost
- La Vie Parisienne
- The Summoning of Everyman
- The Medium
- King John
- Walsh
- Ready Steady Go

### ROBIN PHILLIPS

#### 1975

- Saint Joan
- The Comedy of Errors
- Twelfth Night
- Measure for Measure
- The Two Gentlemen of Verona
- The Crucible
- Trumpets and Drums
- The Fool
- Le Magicien
- Ariadne auf Naxos
- Fellowship
- Oscar Remembered
- Kennedy's Children
- The Importance of Being Earnest

#### 1976

- Hamlet
- The Way of the World
- The Merchant of Venice
- The Tempest
- Antony and Cleopatra
- The Importance of Being Earnest
- Measure for Measure
- Eve
- A Midsummer Night's Dream
- Three Sisters

#### 1977

- A Midsummer Night's Dream
- Romeo and Juliet
- All's Well That Ends Well
- Ghosts
- Miss Julie
- Richard III
- The Guardsman
- Much Ado About Nothing
- As You Like It
- Hay Fever

#### 1978

- The Merry Wives of Windsor
- The Devils
- Macbeth
- Uncle Vanya
- Candide
- The Winter's Tale
- As You Like It
- Judgement
- Heloise and Abelard: Love Letters from the Middle Ages
- Ned and Jack
- Medea
- Private Lives
- Julius Caesar
- Four Plays by Samuel Beckett
- Stargazing
- Titus Andronicus

#### 1979

- Love's Labour's Lost
- Ned and Jack
- Henry IV, Part I
- Richard II
- The Importance of Being Earnest
- Henry IV, Part 2
- Happy New Year
- The Taming of the Shrew
- The Woman
- Othello
- Victoria
- Barren/Yerma
- King Lear

#### 1980

- The Beggar's Opera
- Twelfth Night
- Henry V
- Virginia
- The Servant of Two Masters
- Titus Andronicus
- The Gin Game
- Much Ado About Nothing
- Bosoms and Neglect
- Brief Lives
- Foxfire
- The Seagull
- Henry VI
- King Lear
- Long Day's Journey into Night

## JOHN HIRSCH

### 1981

- The Misanthrope
- HMS Pinafore
- Coriolanus
- The Taming of the Shrew
- The Rivals
- The Comedy of Errors
- The Visit
- Wild Oats
- Virginia (tour only)

### 1982

- Julius Caesar
- The Mikado
- The Merry Wives of Windsor
- The Tempest
- Letters of Love and Affection
- A Midsummer Night's Dream
- All's Well That Ends Well
- Translations
- Damien
- Arms and the Man
- Mary Stuart
- A Variable Passion
- Blithe Spirit

### 1983

- Macbeth
- The Gondoliers
- As You Like It
- Richard II
- Blake
- Damien
- The Mikado
- When That I Was
- The Country Wife
- Tartuffe
- Love's Labour's Lost
- Much Ado About Nothing
- Death of a Salesman
- Translations (tour only)
- A Variable Passion (tour only)

### 1984

- A Midsummer Night's Dream
- Iolanthe
- Romeo and Juliet
- Love's Labour's Lost
- The Gondoliers
- Waiting for Godot
- The Two Gentlemen of Verona
- The Mikado
- Tartuffe
- Henry IV, Part 1
- The Merchant of Venice
- A Streetcar Named Desire
- Separate Tables

### 1985

- King Lear
- The Pirates of Penzance
- Twelfth Night
- Measure for Measure
- Antigone
- The Beaux' Stratagem
- She Stoops to Conquer
- The Government Inspector
- The Glass Menagerie

## JOHN NEVILLE

### 1986

- The Boys from Syracuse
- Hamlet
- The Winter's Tale
- Rosencrantz and Guildenstern are Dead
- Pericles
- Henry VIII
- The Resistible Rise of Arturo Ui
- Macbeth
- A Man for All Seasons
- Cymbeline

### 1987

- Cabaret
- Nora
- Mother Courage
- As You Like It
- Troilus and Cressida
- The School for Scandal
- The Cherry Orchard
- Romeo and Juliet
- Not About Heroes
- Intimate Admiration
- Journey's End
- Othello
- Much Ado About Nothing

### 1988

- Richard III
- All's Well That Ends Well
- The Taming of the Shrew
- Twelfth Night
- Murder in the Cathedral
- My Fair Lady
- King Lear
- The Two Gentlemen of Verona
- Not About Heroes
- The Three Musketeers
- Irma La Douce
- Oedipus/The Critic

### 1989

- Titus Andronicus/The Comedy of Errors
- A Midsummer Night's Dream
- The Merchant of Venice
- Three Sisters
- Kiss Me, Kate
- Henry V
- Love's Labour's Lost
- The Changeling
- The Shoemakers' Holiday
- The Relapse
- The Proposal
- Cat on a Hot Tin Roof
- Guthrie on Guthrie
- The Lunatic, the Lover, and the Poet

## DAVID WILLIAM

### 1990

- Macbeth
- The Merry Wives of Windsor
- As You Like It
- Home
- Guys and Dolls
- Love for Love
- Memoir
- Forever Yours, Marie-Lou
- Phaedra
- Julius Caesar
- The Knight of the Burning Pestle
- Ah, Wilderness!
- The Lunatic, the Lover, and the Poet
- The Grand Inquisitor/Swan Song
- One Tiger to a Hill

### 1991

- Hamlet
- Our Town
- Much Ado About Nothing
- Twelfth Night
- Carousel
- Les Belles-Soeurs
- Timon of Athens
- Homeward Bound
- The Rules of the Game
- Treasure Island
- The Knight of the Burning Pestle
- The School for Wives
- Love Letters
- An Enemy of the People

### 1992

- The Tempest
- Romeo and Juliet
- Love's Labour's Lost
- Measure for Measure
- World of Wonders
- HMS Pinafore
- Entertaining Mr. Sloane
- The Wingfield Trilogy
- Uncle Vanya
- Bonjour, là, Bonjour
- Shirley Valentine
- The Two Gentlemen of Verona

### 1993

- Antony and Cleopatra
- King John
- A Midsummer Night's Dream
- Gypsy
- The Wingfield Trilogy
- Bacchae
- The Mikado
- Fair Liberty's Call
- The Importance of Being Earnest
- The Imaginary Invalid
- The Illusion

## RICHARD MONETTE

### 1994

- Twelfth Night
- Long Day's Journey Into Night
- The Pirates of Penzance
- Hamlet
- Cyrano de Bergerac
- In the Ring
- Othello
- Alice Through the Looking Glass
- The Comedy of Errors
- Husbands and Cuckolds

### 1995

- The Merry Wives of Windsor
- The Boy Friend
- Macbeth
- The Gondoliers
- The Country Wife
- Long Day's Journey Into Night
- The Comedy of Errors
- Amadeus
- The Stillborn Lover

### 1996

- King Lear
- The Music Man
- Amadeus
- The Little Foxes
- A Fitting Confusion
- The Merchant of Venice
- Alice Through the Looking Glass
- Barrymore
- As You Like It
- Sweet Bird of Youth
- Waiting for Godot

### 1997

- Camelot
- The Taming of the Shrew
- Romeo and Juliet
- Oedipus Rex
- Death of a Salesman
- Little Women
- Filumena
- Equus
- Richard III
- Juno and the Paycock
- Coriolanus
- Wingfield Unbound

### 1998

- Julius Caesar
- Man of La Mancha
- A Man for All Seasons
- The Two Gentlemen of Verona
- The Prime of Miss Jean Brodie
- Much Ado About Nothing
- The Miracle Worker
- The Miser
- The Winter's Tale
- The Cherry Orchard
- The Night of the Iguana
- Waiting for Godot

### 1999

- The Tempest
- A Midsummer Night's Dream
- Pride and Prejudice
- The Alchemist
- The School for Scandal
- West Side Story
- Dracula
- Richard II
- Macbeth
- Glenn

### 2000

- Hamlet
- The Three Musketeers
- Fiddler on the Roof
- Tartuffe
- As You Like It
- The Diary of Anne Frank
- The Importance of Being Earnest
- Patience
- Titus Andronicus
- Medea
- Elizabeth Rex
- Collected Stories
- Oscar Remembered

### 2001

- The Merchant of Venice
- The Sound of Music
- Twelfth Night
- Inherit the Wind
- Private Lives
- Henry V
- Who's Afraid of Virginia Woolf?
- The Seagull
- Wingfield on Ice
- Henry IV, Part 1
- Falstaff (Henry IV, Part 2)
- Tempest-Tost
- The Trials of Ezra Pound
- Good Mother

### 2002

- All's Well That Ends Well
- Romeo and Juliet
- My Fair Lady
- King Lear
- The Threepenny Opera
- The Scarlet Pimpernel
- Richard III: Reign of Terror
- Henry VI: Revenge in France
- Henry VI: Revolt in England
- The Two Noble Kinsmen
- The Lunatic, the Lover, and the Poet
- High-Gravel-Blind
- Eternal Hydra
- Bereav'd of Light
- The Fellini Radio Plays
- Walk Right Up
- Shadows
- The Swanne: George III (The Death of Cupid)

# *Index*

# *Acknowledgements*

My first thanks must go to Richard Monette and Antoni Cimolino who, along with Don Woodley, chair of the Stratford Festival board of governors, commissioned this book and have cheered me with their faith and encouragement while it was being written, as have their Festival colleagues Anita Gaffney, Andrey Tarasiuk, and Pat Quigley. Above all I thank David Prosser, Stratford's director of literary services, who has overseen the book, who read it as it tortuously evolved, chapter by chapter, and who supplied welcome suggestions and corrections and even more welcome enthusiasm. He also took responsibility for the sidebars and captions, in association with Laurie Coulter, my editor at Madison Press. She, in turn, was endlessly acute and sympathetic in face of an overlong (not to say overdue) text and initiated cuts so tactful that sometimes even I failed to spot them. She was also very accommodating when I did notice and made counter-suggestions. The book took longer to write than any of us had anticipated: to all the above — and, also and especially, to Hugh Brewster at Madison — my gratitude and appreciation for their understanding and good humour under what must have been extreme provocation. To Gord Sibley, who designed the book, my dazzled appreciation. William Hutt submitted — kindly, warmly, and informatively — to an extended interview. Otherwise, my principal sources have been culled from the dauntingly comprehensive Stratford Festival archives. Jane Edmonds, the Festival's archivist and researcher; Ellen Charendoff, her archive assistant; and

their team of volunteers performed the Herculean task of supplying me with a comprehensive set of reviews and associated articles; Jane, who has an eagle eye, also corrected several of my omissions and mistakes. As will be obvious, I owe an enormous debt to all the critics, journalists and historians (and not just those cited by name) who have covered the Festival's previous forty-nine years in newspapers and magazines. Also in books: apart from the Davies-Guthrie-Macdonald trilogy mentioned in the Preface (*Renown at Stratford*, *Twice Have the Trumpets Sounded*, *Thrice the Brinded Cat Hath Mew'd*) I have profited especially from *The Stratford Festival, 1953-1957*, introduction by Herbert Whittaker (Clarke, Irwin); *A Stratford Tempest*, by Martin Knelman (McClelland & Stewart); *Stratford: The First Thirty Years* by John Pettigrew and Jamie Portman (two volumes, Macmillan); and *The Stratford Festival Story* by J. Alan B. Somerset (Greenwood Press). Without the last two, in particular, the job would have been impossible. Thanks also to the editors and arts editors of those publications for whom I myself have written about Stratford: the *National Post*, the *Globe and Mail*, and *Saturday Night*. My agent, Leslie Gardner, has been superhumanly supportive, not to mention terrifyingly practical. My final and most personal thanks go to Chloe, Anthony, and Mitchell for being here (and for providing, on occasion, humblingly expert technical support); and to my wife, Arlene Gould, without whom I would never have been able to write about the Stratford Festival in the first place.

*Robert Cushman*

The Stratford Festival of Canada wishes to thank all the actors, designers and photographers who so generously gave permission for their images to be used in this book. Special thanks are also due to Canadian Actors' Equity Association, and to Kevin Bell, Susan Benson, Canada Post Corporation, Lesley Fairfield, Alan Gough, Desmond Heeley, Don Lewis, Lois Mountain, the National Archives of Canada, the National Film Board, the Stratford-Perth Archives, Jennifer Surridge, Michael J. Whitfield, and Robin Wilhelm and Scott Wishart of the Stratford *Beacon Herald*. Central roles in assembling the book's visual material were played by Festival staff members

Jane Edmonds, Ellen Charendoff, Andy Foster and Ivan Habel.

Most of the celebrity anecdotes in this book were drawn from interviews conducted for television by Richard Ouzounian, and the Festival is indebted to him and to Kim Murton of the CBC for providing the transcripts. Special thanks also to Douglas Campbell and Martha Henry for providing written recollections.

The following Friends of the Festival volunteers spent countless unpaid hours assisting with archival research: Eric Adams, Dona Atkinson, Joyce Banks, Pam and Peter Brierley, Gwen Carleton, Cathy Clarke, Jeanne

Damery, Gerri Flint, Hazel Hewitt, Jill Hurst, Amelia Lenz, Rachel Massey, Betty and Walt McGibbon, Kathy Minor, Kathi Rasanen, and Jake Sheepers. Our warmest thanks to all.

*Fifty Seasons at Stratford* was initially conceived by the Stratford Festival's 50th Season Print Materials Committee, chaired by Ted McGee and comprising volunteers Molly Copus Christie and Alan Somerset, and Festival staff members Martine Becu, Jane Edmonds, Andy Foster, Anita Gaffney and David Prosser. Staff members Ted Glaszewski, Maureen McLaughlin, Jason Miller, and Ron Nichol also lent valuable assistance to the project.

# *Photo Credits*

Every effort has been made to correctly attribute all material reproduced in this book. If any errors have unwittingly occurred, we will be happy to correct them in future editions.

Richard Bain, 26 bottom, 176

Alan Barlow, 179 left

The Bell Family Collection, 13 bottom left

Susan Benson, 90 left; 148 middle, bottom; 150 bottom; 151 far left bottom, right; 153 top; 172

Ed Bermingham, 88 top

Polly Bohdanetzky, 171 bottom

Tessa Buchan/Susan Benson Collection, 148 top left, 148-149

Canada Post Corporation © 1999, reproduced with permission, 195 left

Canadian Conservation Institute — "Sanders portrait," reproduced with the permission of the Minister of Public Works and Government Services, © 2001, all rights reserved, 4

Patrick Clark, 156 left

David Cooper/Stratford Festival Archives, back cover top, third from right; 90 right; 138 bottom; 140 top right; 142; 143 left, right; 147; 151 left middle; 177; 180; 181

Michael Cooper, back cover bottom, 8-9, 155, 162, 164 top, 166, 167, 168 top, 173, 211 bottom, 214 second from right

Walter Curtin/Walter Curtin Collection/National Archives of Canada/, 14 bottom left (PA-129866), 16 middle (PA 160982), 18 middle (PA 160999), 18 bottom right (PA-160991)

Ann Curtis, 164 bottom

Daphne Dare, 94 right; 99 middle left, bottom left, right; 109; 116 left

Zoë Dominic, back cover top, third from left; 66 main; 94 left; 100; 105; 112; 118 bottom

Jane Edmonds, 37; 129 right top, right middle; 141; 183 bottom left, bottom middle, bottom right

Jane Edmonds/Susan Benson Collection, 67 top, 90 top, 106 bottom, 119 top left

Jane Edmonds/Stratford Festival Archives, front cover, 154

The Fairfield Family Collection, 36 middle

Robert Fairfield, 36 top

Robert Fairfield (Fairfield & Dubois), 14 top left

Famous Players Collection/National Archives/ PA-119581, 52 top right

Elisabeth Feryn, 208 top, 214 far right

Ted Glaszewski/Stratford Festival Archives, 202 bottom

Ronald H. Gough Collection, 18 bottom left

Fred Hampton/Stratford Festival Archives, 38 both

V. Tony Hauser, 92, 207, 214 middle

Desmond Heeley, 71 top, 138 top, 208 bottom, 144 right

Leslie Hurry, 45 top

Brian Jackson, 57 left, 63 bottom, 91 top right

Rod Jones/Stratford Festival Archives, 30 both

Murray Laufer, 80 bottom

Don Lewis, back cover top, far left; 49; 88 right

Grant Macdonald, 6; 23 bottom both; 24 top left, bottom left; 40 left

Terry Manzo/Stratford Festival Archives, 2-3, 42, 104 bottom

Donald McKague, 11, 26 middle, 29 bottom, 35 left, 139

Tanya Moiseiwitsch, 21, 34 bottom, 35 right

National Film Board of Canada, from the NFB production, "The Stratford Adventure" (1953), 10, 21 middle, 22 bottom

Herb Nott & Co. Ltd./Stratford Festival Archives, 15 bottom, 47 middle, 111

Robin Fraser Paye, 102 bottom

V. Beverly Payne/Stratford Festival Archives Collection, 17

Robert Prévost, 74 left

Robert C. Ragsdale, F.R.P.S./Stratford Festival Archives, front cover; 56 bottom right; 69; 72 both; 73; 77 right; 79; 81; 82 top; 87; 89 top; 97 both; 99 top left; 101; 102 top; 104 top; 107; 108; 113; 115; 116 right; 118 top; 121, 122 both; 123; 125 top, bottom; 126; 127; 131; 133 all; 134, 135 both; 137 inset; 144 left; 150-151; 151 top left; 153 bottom; 156 top right, bottom right; 157; 158; 159; 161 all; 168 bottom; 171 top; 174

Tom Skudra/Stratford Festival Archives, 128 bottom, 183 top, 187

Peter Smith & Co./Stratford Festival Archives, endpapers, 12; 13 bottom right; 14 top right; 15 top, middle; 16 top; 19 top right; 20; 21 top; 23 top; 24; 25; 27; 28; 29 top; 40 right; 43; 45 bottom; 46 both; 47 top right; 48 right; 50 both; 51; 53 bottom; 54 top; 55 all; 56 top; 57 middle, right; 58 both; 61; 63 top; 64 both; 65; 66 bottom left; 67 bottom right; 85 all; 129 bottom left, bottom right

Jeff Speed, 66 top left; 91 top left, bottom left; 106 top; 110 all; 119 bottom; 128 top; 129 bottom right; 140 left, bottom right; 188 all; 189; 202 top

Douglas Spillane/Stratford Festival Archives, 32-33, 53 top, 60, 68, 70, 71 left both, 74 right, 75 both, 77 left, 78, 80 top, 84

Peter Stackpole/TimePix, 31

STAR TRIBUNE/Minneapolis-St.Paul © 2002, 14 bottom right

Bruce Stotesbury, 212 bottom

Stratford Beacon Herald, 18 top

Stratford Festival Archives Collection, 13 top, middle; 16 bottom left, bottom right; 17 inset; 19 left, middle, bottom right; 22 top; 34 top; 36 bottom left, bottom right; 44 all; 47 top left, 47 bottom; 48 left; 52 middle all, bottom; 54 bottom all; 59 all; 82 bottom; 88 left; 89 bottom; 98 top; 125 middle; 152

Courtesy of Stratford-Perth Archives, 52 top left

David Street/Stratford Festival Archives, 91 middle, 136

The Record, 19 right middle

John Timbers/Stratford Festival Archives, 39

Cylla von Tiedemann, back flap; back cover top, second from left, second from right, far right; 5; 56 bottom left; 137; 175; 179 right; 184 top; 184 bottom; 190-191; 192; 193 both; 194; 195 right; 196 both; 197; 198 all; 199; 200 both; 201; 203 both; 204 both; 205 all; 209 all; 210; 211 top; 212 top; 214 second from left; 214 far left

Robin Wilhelm/Stratford Beacon Herald, 119 top right

Scott Wishart, 67 bottom left

| | |
|---|---|
| *Editorial Director:* | Hugh Brewster |
| *Art Director:* | Gordon Sibley |
| *Project Editor:* | Laurie Coulter |
| *Editorial Assistance:* | Susan Aihoshi, Sarah Jones |
| *Production Director:* | Susan Barrable |
| *Production Manager:* | Sandra L. Hall |
| *Colour Separation:* | Colour Technologies |
| *Printing and Binding:* | Friesens Corporation |

FIFTY SEASONS AT STRATFORD
*was produced by*
Madison Press Books, which is under the direction of Albert E. Cummings